D1322174

Riding Hood for All Ages

WITHDRAWN FROM
THE LIBRARY

UNIVERSITY OF
WINCHESTER

KA 0399950 5

 SERIES IN FAIRY-TALE STUDIES

General Editor
Donald Haase, Wayne State University

Advisory Editors
Cristina Bacchilega, University of Hawai'i, Mānoa
Ruth B. Bottigheimer, State University of New York, Stony Brook
Nancy L. Canepa, Dartmouth College
Isabel Cardigos, University of Algarve
Anne E. Duggan, Wayne State University
Janet Langlois, Wayne State University
Ulrich Marzolph, University of Göttingen
Carolina Fernández Rodríguez, University of Oviedo
John Stephens, Macquarie University
Maria Tatar, Harvard University
Holly Tucker, Vanderbilt University
Jack Zipes, University of Minnesota

A complete listing of the books in this series can be found online at wsupress.wayne.edu

Red Riding Hood

FOR ALL AGES

A Fairy-Tale Icon in Cross-Cultural Contexts

Sandra L. Beckett

WAYNE STATE UNIVERSITY PRESS · W · DETROIT

UNIVERSITY OF WINCHESTER

398.2
BEC   03959505

© 2008 by Wayne State University Press,
Detroit, Michigan 48201.

All rights reserved.
No part of this book may be reproduced without formal permission.
Manufactured in the United States of America.

Library of Congress Cataloging-in-Publication Data

Beckett, Sandra L., 1953–
Red riding hood for all ages : a fairy-tale icon in cross-cultural contexts /
Sandra L. Beckett.
    p. cm. — (Series in fairy-tale studies)
Includes bibliographical references and index.
ISBN 978-0-8143-3306-8 (pbk. : alk. paper)
  1. Little Red Riding Hood (Tale)—History and criticism. I. Title.

GR75.L56B43 2008
398.20943'02—dc22   2008009600

∞

Published with the assistance of a fund established by Thelma Gray James
of Wayne State University for the publication of folklore and English studies.

Designed by Lisa Tremaine
Typeset by The Composing Room of Michigan, Inc.
Composed in Fournier

To my mother and grandmother

UNIVERSITY OF WINCHESTER
LIBRARY

Contents

Acknowledgments

This journey with Little Red Riding Hood would not have been possible without the valuable assistance of a great number of people.

I am particularly indebted to the many authors and illustrators who graciously discussed their work with me and to those illustrators and publishers who generously granted permission for illustrations to be reproduced in this book.

I would like to express my gratitude to the following friends and colleagues for their assistance with the translation of a number of the texts: Irene Blayer, Signe Mari Wiland, André Muniz de Moura, Bill Vanlenthe, and Anne de Vries. I should further like to express my thanks to many other friends and colleagues who have contributed in some way to this project, in particular Denis Dyack, Corrado Federici, Marisa Fernandez Lopez, Yukiko Fukumoto, Ludek Janda, Lena Kåreland, Anne Kristin Lande, Claire Malarte-Feldman, J. Antonio Martos, John Mitterer, Jean Perrot, Graciela Risotto, Rolf Romören, Cristina Santos, Karin Beate Vold, and Jack Zipes. My deep gratitude goes to the staff at the International Youth Library in Munich and the International Institute for Children's Literature, Osaka, notably Jochen Weber and Yasuko Doi. I wish to acknowledge the generous financial support of the Social Sciences and Humanities Research Council of Canada, Brock University Chancellor's Chair for Research Excellence, the Humanities Research Institute at Brock University, and Brock University Experience Works Program.

Very special thanks go to my research assistants, Vladia Juskova, Christine McGovern, Lindsay Clark, and Carlene Thomas, who have tirelessly and enthusiastically accompanied me on this long journey with Little Red Riding Hood. Finally, I thank my husband, Paul, who shares all my journeys.

Les Contes de Perrault by Charles Perrault, illustrated by Gustave Doré, Pierre-Jules Hetzel, 1861.

Red Riding Hood for All Ages

Introduction

Sweet little myth of the nursery story—

. . .

Thou are so dear to me, Red Riding-Hood!

—JAMES WHITCOMB RILEY, "Red Riding-Hood"

The story of Little Red Riding Hood, probably the world's most popular and certainly its most retold tale, captures the imagination of readers of all ages. Little Red Riding Hood constitutes a universal icon, and the revisioning of her story is an international phenomenon in literature for all age groups. While *Recycling Red Riding Hood,* which I published in 2002, was devoted to contemporary retellings of the tale for children, *Red Riding Hood for All Ages* examines the recycling of the universally popular literary icon in contemporary fiction for readers of all ages. Around the world, authors and illustrators are recasting the story of the little girl and the wolf in works that speak to children, adolescents, and adults. Many of the international re-versions examined in the present study are crossover works, that is, they cross from child and/or young adult to adult audiences or vice versa. From its origins in the oral tradition the tale has had crossover appeal, and authors have been retelling it for audiences of all ages ever since its literary debut in France in the seventeenth century.

The first literary version of the tale, Charles Perrault's *Le Petit Chaperon Rouge,* is a crossover text. It can be appreciated on one level by very young children, but the author winks at adults in his ironic comments throughout the tale and especially in the moral at the end. Although the tale was told among upper-class adults at the end of the seventeenth century, the author also includes children in his intended audience. A comment written in the margin next to the climactic dialogue instructs the storyteller to say the wolf's words in such a manner that "the child" will be frightened. Perrault's collection of tales was attributed to his youngest son, Pierre Perrault d'Armancour, who was seventeen at the time of their writing and refers to himself as "a Child" in the preface dedicated to "Mademoiselle," Louis XIV's nineteen-year-old niece Elisabeth Charlotte d'Orléans.[1]

Some critics and authors, such as Zohar Shavit and Angela Carter, even consider children to be the "official" audience of Perrault's *Contes*. Shavit claims that the reading of fairy tales by a cultured audience in the seventeenth century was based on a silent pact between them and the author concerning "two implied readers—the child and the highbrow adult." In *Le Petit Chaperon Rouge*, Perrault seems to have maintained a perfect balance between the two audiences. "The ambiguous nature of the text was primarily intended to satisfy both its official and unofficial readers," writes Shavit. In her view, Perrault made clever use of the special status of fairy tales (as texts for children), "addressing them officially to children as the main consumers," while at the same time appealing to adults by means of the irony and satire of a sophisticated text.[2] Contemporary authors like Roald Dahl and Pierre Gripari, who retell *Little Red Riding Hood* in rhymed verse, use irony and satire in a somewhat similar manner. However, these literary techniques are no longer games reserved for adult readers; they have been commonly adopted in children's literature. Some critics feel the witty, ironical, sometimes even derisive tone that characterizes versions such as Dahl's may still address adults more than children, but that does not change the fact that these works are highly popular with children.

When Jacob and Wilhelm Grimm published *Rotkäppchen* (*Little Red Cap*) in 1812, they eliminated Perrault's sexual innuendos and added a happy ending. Their collection of fairy tales, *Kinder-und Hausmärchen* (*Children's and Household Tales*), was meant to appeal to all Germans, young and old alike. Jacob Grimm said he never intended it for children, though it made him happy to find out that they were, in fact, reading it.[3] Although subsequent editions were modified in light of this young readership, the preface to the second edition warned that some parents might still find certain parts unsuitable for children. Thus the Grimm brothers' collection of tales was not meant to constitute a children's book. For a time, however, *Little Red Riding Hood* was relegated, along with other fairy tales, to the children's library. An opinion poll conducted in Germany in the early 1970s indicated that Germans "absorbed" the Grimms' tales in childhood and never reread what had become a much-reduced volume of "tales for small children."[4] When the popular children's author Janosch published his parodic reworking of the Grimms' tales in 1972, his intention seems to have been to restore the tales to their original dual audience of children and adults. His well-known collection *Janosch erzählt Grimms' Märchen* (Janosch tells Grimms' fairy tales, 1972), which was translated into English as *Not Quite as Grimm* in 1974, is regularly reedited and has become a German classic appreciated by young and old alike.

Today the tale of *Little Red Riding Hood* is generally considered appropriate for all age groups. Writers and illustrators around the world have recognized the crossover appeal of the popular story of the little girl and the wolf. The tale presents a child protagonist who confronts problems of a grown-up nature, notably sexuality, violence, and death. These universal issues are presented in the form of a fairy tale, a genre that has traditionally addressed both adults and children. It is not surprising, therefore, that modern re-versions of the tale, like their classic pretexts by Perrault and the Brothers Grimm or their earlier hypotexts in the oral tradition, can appeal to audiences of all ages.[5] Little Red Riding Hood's well-known tale is undoubtedly the most effective of all literary intertexts. Intertextuality can be problematic for young readers whose literary competency is limited, but even young children are capable of decoding rather sophisticated allusions to such a familiar text.[6] The fact that intertextual play with this favorite childhood story can be recognized by young readers, while at the same time evoking a nostalgic pleasure in adults, explains much of the tale's appeal with crossover authors.

The story of Little Red Riding Hood allows authors and illustrators to explore somewhat difficult topics in books for all ages. "Adult" subjects that are often taboo in children's literature; for example, sexuality and violence may be more acceptable to adult mediators in retellings of a classic fairy tale.[7] One could cite Claude Clément and Isabelle Forestier's successful picture book *Un petit chaperon rouge* (A Little Red Riding Hood), which deals very tactfully with the subject of sexual abuse. The multilayered meanings of the short tale make it a perfect subject for multiple readerships. Critics have often lamented the fact that modern retellings have lost the depth of their classic model,[8] but that is certainly not the case for most of the retellings examined in this study. Precisely because of their depth and multifaceted dimension, many of these versions appeal to adults as well as young readers. Literary critics and experts from other fields have continually pointed to the fact that fairy tales offer multiple layers of meaning for readers of all ages. In his best-selling psychological study of fairy tales, *The Uses of Enchantment*, Bruno Bettelheim writes: "All good fairy tales have meaning on many levels; only the child can know which meanings are of significance to him at the moment. As he grows up, the child discovers new aspects of these well-known tales."[9] The cherished childhood tale provides adults with fresh meanings, many of which are of a sexual nature.

In a highly parodic reworking, the French author-illustrator Pef juxtaposes child and adult perspectives on the tale. When the narrator offers a number of rather absurd hypotheses concerning the heroine's red color, including one that would bring dishonor on the little girl, the validity of such perverted "adult" theories is immediately questioned by the indignant child protagonist. A homely Little Red Riding Hood voices her vexation at the depravity that has millions of children swallowing "this idiotic story that generations of adults are incapable of forgetting" (393).[10] A parenthetical note on the title page, which indicates that this tale is a "settling of scores," is a clever play on words since *compte* in the French term "règlement de compte" is a homonym for *conte*, the word for "fairy tale" (391). Although the text is targeted chiefly at adults, Little Red Riding Hood appears to be settling the score with adult readers on behalf of child readers everywhere.

There is at least one truth in Pef's nonsensical story: adults do, indeed, seem unable to forget the tale. *Little Red Riding Hood* has a special place in the hearts as well as the memories of many adults worldwide. When the Allensbach pollsters asked German adults which fairy tales they still remembered, *Rotkäppchen* topped the list. Adults have a very complex relationship with fairy tales like *Little Red Riding Hood,* which shape our imaginations early in life and descend deep into our psyches. Many authors and illustrators, including Charles Dickens, have admitted the powerful and lasting impression left by the tale. In the preface to an award-winning collection that reworks Perrault's *Contes,* the French author Pierrette Fleutiaux explains how, at a difficult time in her adult life, she returned to the tales of her childhood, the only literature she was psychologically able to assimilate at that point in her life. Marked by her reading of Bettelheim's book, the author insists that familiar fairy-tale characters like Little Red Riding Hood are there "to console and guide us in the strange encounters that each of us makes with life" (10). They fulfill that function, she believes, for adults as well as children. Her rereading of *Le Petit Chaperon Rouge* as an adult resulted in a sophisticated, feminist version of the tale that was published for adults. The Swedish-language Finnish author Märta Tikkanen deals with both her childhood and her adult life as a woman writer in an autobiographical novel titled *Rödluvan* (Little Red Riding Hood, 1986), which also appeared for adults.

Many authors have retold *Little Red Riding Hood* for an adult audience. Among the English-speaking writers that immediately come to mind are Olga Broumas, Angela Carter, Anne Sexton, Gwen Strauss, and James Thurber. One critic claims that in comparison with English literatures in particular, late twentieth-century French and Francophone literatures have produced strikingly "few literary fairy tales written primarily for adults."[11] *Red Riding Hood for All Ages* nonetheless mentions quite a number of versions published for adults, including those by Jean Ache, Pierrette Fleutiaux, Pierre Gripari, Warja Lavater, and Pierre Léon. One could also cite the rather risqué remake of *Le Petit Chaperon Rouge* by the Quebecois author Jacques Ferron, which appeared in his collection *Contes* (1968), and was later published in English in *Tales from the Uncertain Country* (1972). Adult re-versions of *Little Red Riding Hood* in other parts of the world range from Märta Tikkanen's *Rödluvan* and Annie Riis's "Ulven og Rødhette" (The Wolf and Little Red Riding Hood) in the Nordic countries to Manlio Argueta's *Caperucita en la zona roja* (*Little Red Riding Hood in the Red Light District*)[12] and Luisa Valenzuela's "Si esto es la vida, yo soy Caperucita roja" ("If this is life, I'm Red Riding Hood") in Latin America.

Contemporary recastings of *Little Red Riding Hood* for all ages may be playful and witty, intent upon subverting or even perverting the traditional tale. Such retellings deliberately demythologize or demystify the hypotext. Often, however, the classic tale is rewritten in a more serious, sometimes even a minor mode, especially in crossover versions or those that address adults or young adults. These re-versions can still challenge and subvert the traditional tale, but they do so in a more subtle and significant manner. The traditional characters, motifs, and images are used to address important psychological and metaphysical issues, such as solitude, fear, freedom, love, compassion, and death. The mythic content of the age-old tale is made meaningful for today's readers. In her article "Real 'Wolves in Those Bushes': Readers Take Dangerous Journeys with *Little Red Riding Hood*," Cornelia Hoogland insists on the importance of enhancing "children's ability to carry on an imaginative dialogue with the tale."[13] That dialogue is made possible for readers of all ages in many of these international versions, which offer philosophical, psychological, or spiritual journeys with Little Red Riding Hood.

Contemporary authors rewrite the classic tale with a modern, if not postmodern aesthetic, for adult, adolescent, and child readers. The postmodern trends of adult literature have pervaded children's literature. As was demonstrated in *Recycling Red Riding Hood*, many retellings for children use rather complex narrative structures and techniques. This trend facilitates the crossover of many retellings from adults to children or young adults and vice versa. The re-versions of *Little Red Riding Hood* examined in this study, regardless of the target audience, tend to be quite sophisticated and challenging. Many use inventive wordplay, subtle intertextual allusions, and clever metafictive discourse. They may explore aspects of the tale that have been forgotten or neglected. An increasing number of authors appropriate the motifs, patterns, and archaisms of less familiar oral versions. Illustrators as well as authors frequently engage in a sophisticated dialogue with the inherited forms and contents, both folkloric and literary, of the age-old tale. The result is often a complex layering of narrative versions that needs to be read in the context of the lengthy *Little Red Riding Hood* tradition. Open texts that can be read on different levels and interpreted in multiple ways oblige readers of all ages to engage in their own dialogue with both the retelling and the traditional tale.

Authors and illustrators use exciting, innovative aesthetic experimentation in order to renew the classic tale. The hybridization of genres is a widespread trend in contemporary re-versions. Originally an oral tale and then a literary tale, *Little Red Riding Hood* has been hybridized with almost every other literary genre as well as all the new media technologies. The famous fairy tale has been told following the conventions and codes of poetry, short fiction, theater, novella, novel, western, horror, picture book, and comic book. It has been adapted to cartoons, posters, advertisements, musicals, films, animated films, video games, television, and the Internet. In contemporary culture, *Little Red Riding Hood* has become almost as protean as the heroine herself.

The visual interpretations in the international retellings examined in this study are as multilayered, sophisticated, and complex as the textual recastings. They challenge adults as well as children. In his foreword to Molly Bang's 1991 book *Picture This*, which uses an illustration of Little Red Riding Hood as the working example, the art theorist Rudolf Arnheim writes: "It seems that the differences in the ways grown-ups and children look and behave and in what they like and dislike have become less important in our time than they have ever been." He sees Bang as a pioneer because her *Picture This* constitutes "an eye-opener for adults" as well as "a unique gift for children" (ix). The picture books and other illustrated works included in *Red Riding Hood for All Ages* demonstrate that Bang is far from being the only illustrator to have reached a dual audience of children and adults with her visual interpretation of *Little Red Riding Hood*. The tale has inspired artists for generations, and some of the best-known illustrations have appealed to a crossover audience, notably the unforgettable works of Gustave Doré, Walter Crane, and Arthur Rackham.

Denis-Luc Panthin, curator of the *Figures futur* international illustration exhibition devoted to *Little Red Riding Hood* in 2004, reminds us, however, that many of the visual interpretations of the tale have been far less memorable. He may simplify the situation somewhat, but he rightly points out: "Basically, there have always been two ways of illustrating it: watered-down versions created exclusively for children . . . and the visual interpretations of artists who do not hesitate . . . to propose demanding images. These images are the ones in which the child has the most chance of finding herself/himself when she/he grows up." Panthin feels that good illustrations, even those as terrifying as Susanne Janssen's or Sarah Moon's, are always good for the child (plate 1).[14] The illustrations discussed and reproduced in this book are of the second type described by Panthin, that is, those that can be appreciated by both children and adults. The visual interpretation of these illustrators enriches the text, adding further narrative layers and levels of meaning. An exciting international collaboration resulted in an entire volume of retellings, *Érase veintiuna veces Caperucita Roja* (Once upon . . . twenty-one times, Little Red Riding Hood), which was published in 2006 by the innovative Spanish publisher Media Vaca. The highly original book was the outcome of a workshop the Spanish publisher organized in Tokyo in 2003 for Japanese illustrators. Although the starting point was Perrault's version of the tale, Media Vaca encouraged the illustrators not to limit themselves to the classic version, but to feel free to change it as they saw fit. The book opens with Perrault's tale, illustrated by Kaori Tsukuda, but it is followed by twenty other versions that not only offer remarkable visual retellings but also rework the original text (plate 2). *Érase veintiuna veces Caperucita Roja* appeared in Media Vaca's series Libros para niños (Books for Children), but, as the back cover explicitly and emphatically states, the series is "NOT ONLY for children!"

Red Riding Hood for All Ages contains more than fifty illustrations, which, for the most part, have been taken from works that will be unfamiliar to the majority of English-speaking readers. In addition to the black-and-white illustrations throughout the body of the text, there are several pages of color plates. It is hardly necessary to point out the importance of color in a study devoted to a fairy-tale heroine whose identifying trademark is the color red. These illustrations provide a sample of the many outstanding visual interpretations of the tale available for all readers. Representative of a variety of mediums and cultures, they include works by illustrators and artists from Belgium, Brazil, France, Germany, Great Britain, Italy, Japan, Netherlands, Norway, Quebec, South Africa,

Spain, and United States. In an even more striking manner than the texts perhaps, the illustrations demonstrate clearly that Little Red Riding Hood is a universal icon with appeal for all ages. Like the texts, the illustrations were carefully selected for their diversity and their innovative interpretation of the tale within the context of a particular chapter theme.

Red Riding Hood for All Ages examines a wide selection of international versions of the tale published since the turn of the twentieth century. Most of these retellings have never been translated into English and therefore remain virtually unknown in the English-speaking world, even though they are often by major international authors and illustrators. The study includes works in Afrikaans, Catalan, Dutch, French, German, Hungarian, Italian, Japanese, Norwegian, Portuguese, Spanish, and Swedish. The number of countries they represent is, of course, much larger: Argentina, Australia, Belgium, Brazil, Canada, Chile, Cuba, El Salvador, Finland, France, Great Britain, Hungary, Ireland, Italy, Netherlands, Norway, Peru, Slovenia, Spain, Sweden, and United States. With the exception of a brief look at Bret Harte's 1899 poem "What the Wolf Really Said to Little Red Riding-Hood," the earliest text is a Chilean poem published in 1924 by the Nobel Laureate Gabriela Mistral. Other works from the first half of the twentieth century include Marcel Aymé's well-known French classic tale "Le loup" (The wolf), published in 1934, and the Peruvian poet José Santos Chocano's poem "El lobo enamorado" (The wolf in love), which appeared in 1937. Although a few texts are representative of the 1950s and 1960s, including Francisco Villaespesa's "Caperucita" poems, issued in Spain in 1954, and the manga "Akazukin-chan" (Little Red Riding Hood), published in 1962 by the well-known Japanese artist Shotaro Ishinomori, the majority of the texts are post-1970. The most recent work mentioned is *Érase veintiuna veces Caperucita Roja,* which appeared just as this study was being completed. The works discussed were deliberately selected from as many countries and cultures as possible to demonstrate that the rewriting of *Little Red Riding Hood* for all ages is a widespread international phenomenon. While the majority of the retellings are from the Western world, a number of works from Japan have been included, although these are all based on the Western, rather than the Asian tradition of the tale.[15] The latter is represented only by a brief mention of Ed Young's Caldecott Medal–winning picture book *Lon Po Po: A Red Riding Hood Story from China,* which was published in 1989. The re-versions selected for this study are representative of the different genres, narrative techniques, themes, voices, and visual interpretations adopted to recycle the famous tale for readers of all ages.

The first chapter examines retellings that draw on the story's tradition as a *Warnmärchen*, or warning tale. Perrault retold the story of Little Red Riding Hood as a cautionary tale to warn women and girls against predatory males. With time, the story of the little girl in red has become the archetypal tale of child abuse and rape. This study examines a diverse selection of the many authors and illustrators of the twentieth and twenty-first centuries who continue to rework the story in this vein. It includes, among other works, poems by Wim Hofman, Gabriela Mistral, and Francisco Villaespesa; tales by Francesca Lia Block and Anne Sharpe; picture books by Éric Battut, Claude Clément and Isabelle Forestier, Sarah Moon, and Yvan Pommaux; and an unpublished illustration by Roberto Innocenti. Chapter 2 looks at authors and illustrators whose versions of the tale highlight the initiatory nature of Little Red Riding Hood's adventure. Many of the recastings considered in this chapter are inspired by the oral tradition. Like the oral tale "Conte de la mère-grand" ("The Story of Grandmother") and its variants, the sexual encounter with the wolf is placed in the context of a young girl's coming of age. This is the case in tales by Bruno de la Salle and Priscilla Galloway, and novels by Carmen Martín Gaite and Viviane Julien. Sometimes the tale is even recast as a love story, as in a French picture book by Anne Bertier, a number of works by Tomi Ungerer, and Japanese manga by Shouko Hamada and Shotaro Ishinomori.

Whereas the first two chapters deal with works that retell the story from more traditional perspectives, those examined in the final three chapters adopt a more innovative approach, focusing on the wolf or "wolfhood." Chapter 3 considers the wolf's story, as told from different points of view. These versions range from homages to a wolf cast in the role of victim to accusations that put the archetypal big bad wolf on trial. Even when the wolf tells his own story in the first person, he is cast in a wide variety of roles, including seducer, sexual predator, slandered suitor, and betrayed lover. Many international authors and illustrators prefer to tell the wolf's story. The versions of *Little Red Riding Hood* analyzed in this chapter include, among others, tales by Marcel Aymé, David Fisher, and Sally Miller Gearhart; a novel by Pierre Gripari; poems by Agha Shahid Ali, José Santos Chocano, Pierre Gripari, Raúl Rivero, Gwen Strauss, and Rudolf Otto Wiemer; picture books by Elsa Borneman, Geoffroy de Pennart, José Luis García Sánchez and Miguel Ángel Pacheco, Joles Sennell and Lluís Filella; and bandes dessinées by F'Murr and Gotlib.

In chapters 4 and 5, the wolf element is an integral part of Little Red Riding Hood's own story. The complex recastings examined in chapter 4 present a Little Red Riding Hood who encounters the wolf within. Although other versions are mentioned briefly, this chapter focuses on two highly original retellings of the tale. The first is a lengthy fairy tale in two chapters that was published by the Dutch children's author Paul Biegel in 1977, while the second is a short story by the Brazilian author João Guimarães Rosa that appeared for adults in 1970 and for children in 1992. The final chapter is devoted to recyclings that present unconventional Riding Hoods who run with the wolves. Some heroines merely keep the company of wolves, while others tame wolves or become wolves themselves. The demanding, multilayered versions analyzed in this chapter often target an older audience. Although these include several picture books, notably by Christian Bruel and Nicole Claveloux, Anne Iklef and Alain Gauthier, Patricia Joiret and Xavier Bruyère, and Jon Scieszka and Lane Smith, as well as a bande dessinée (BD) by F'Murr, the majority of the works are short stories or tales, including those by Clarissa Pinkola Estés, Pierrette Fleutiaux, James Finn Garner, Tanith Lee, Pierre Léon, Annie Riis, and Luisa Valenzuela.

The story of the girl and the wolf does not just fascinate authors and illustrators. A number of scholars and critics have devoted entire studies to *Little Red Riding Hood*. Jack Zipes published his groundbreaking book *The Trials and Tribulations of Little Red Riding Hood* in 1983, and the following decade also saw the appearance of Hans Ritz's *Die Geschichte vom Rotkäppchen: Ursprünge, Analysen, Parodien eines Märchens* (The story of Little Red Riding Hood: Origins, analyses, and parodies of a tale, 1984), Alan Dundes's edited volume *Little Red Riding Hood: A Casebook* (1989), and Claude de la Genardière's *Encore un conte: Le Petit Chaperon Rouge à l'usage des adultes* (Another tale: Little Red Riding Hood for the use of adults, 1993). In 2002 alone, three books were published: Barbara Smith Chalou's *A Postmodern Analysis of the Little Red Riding Hood Tale*, Catherine Orenstein's *Little Red Riding Hood Uncloaked: Sex, Morality, and the Evolution of a Fairy Tale*, and my *Recycling Red Riding Hood*. The introduction to my first book had already announced a second volume devoted to retellings of the popular tale. Like so many authors and scholars before me, I had yielded to the fascination of the little girl in red. In a letter that begins with the salutation "Dear Little Red Riding Hood," the French illustrator Philippe Dumas humorously evokes my obsession with the fairy tale in a metafictional drawing that portrays me as Red Riding Hood wandering into the woods with my nose

"Cher Petit Chaperon Rouge" by Philippe Dumas, 2006. Used by permission of Philippe Dumas.

in a book (presumably the classic tale, a retelling, or my own book about retellings) and followed by a wolf who looks either perplexed or exasperated with my fixation. After more than a decade spent in the famous fairy-tale heroine's company, I never cease to be amazed at the sheer number and the remarkable range of the retellings she has inspired from Europe to Latin America and North America to Australia and Japan. The diversity and richness of these textual and visual *Little Red Riding Hood* narratives from around the world offer an extraordinary homage to a tale whose eternal and universal appeal knows no age boundaries.

1. Cautionary Tales for Modern Riding Hoods

My mother has warned me, warns me: watch out for the wolf, my dear little,
pure little, innocent, fragile girl, all dressed in red.

—LUISA VALENZUELA, "Si esto es la vida, yo soy Caperucita roja"

The story of Little Red Riding Hood is the cautionary tale, or *Warnmärchen,* par excellence. In her study *Little Red Riding Hood Uncloaked,* Catherine Orenstein calls the tale "the quintessential moral primer."[1] The title of Charles Perrault's collection *Contes du temps passé avec moralités* (*Tales of Times Past with Morals*), in which the first literary version of *Little Red Riding Hood* appeared in 1697, stresses the lessons explicitly expressed in rhyming *moralités* at the end of each tale. In the new translation of Perrault's fairy tales that the British author Angela Carter published in 1977, two years before her celebrated collection of reworked tales *The Bloody Chamber,* the elegant and witty verse morals of the French text are rendered in prose. Although the ingenious rhyme and rhythm of the original are lost, the prose translation allows the British author to convey the meaning of the ironic moral with greater precision.

> Children, especially pretty, nicely brought-up young ladies, ought never to talk to strangers; if they are foolish enough to do so, they should not be surprised if some greedy wolf consumes them, elegant red riding hoods and all.
> Now, there are real wolves, with hairy pelts and enormous teeth; but also wolves who seem perfectly charming, sweet-natured and obliging, who pursue young girls in the street and pay them the most flattering attentions.
> Unfortunately, these smooth-tongued, smooth-pelted wolves are the most dangerous beasts of all. (28)

The sophisticated, tongue-in-cheek moral set the tale Perrault had adapted from the oral tradition in the context of the elegant society that frequented the sumptuous court of France's Sun King, Louis XIV. The French academician actually goes further than Carter's translation indicates, as the wolves he warns against do not limit their chase to the street, but follow young girls "right into their homes, right to their *ruelles*" (14). A *ruelle* is a small, narrow street, but from the fifteenth century it also had the meaning of the free space between a bed and the wall, and during the reigns of Louis XIII and Louis XIV it came to mean the bedrooms or alcoves of the high society women who hosted the famous salons of the period. The moral of the French version refers explicitly to the sleek, slick seventeenth-century wolves who followed young women right to their beds.[2] Perrault turns the oral tale into a parable, particularly adapted for use at the court of Versailles, that warns young ladies to beware of suave and debonair two-legged wolves who would sweet-talk their way into their beds and ruin their reputations. At the same time, however, very young children can appreciate Perrault's sophisticated tale on another level. In the dedication to his *Contes,* the author claims that the tales reflect the lower class's attempt "to educate children," and he stresses the multilayered nature of the "very sensible Moral" contained in each tale.[3] Angela Carter believes that Perrault wanted to turn the fairy tales into "little parables of experience from which children can learn, without half the pain that . . . Red Riding Hood endured." In her mind, Perrault's collection was "intended for children," but she rightly points out that "these children are seen as apprentice adults" (17). At the end of the seventeenth century, the concept of childhood, as we understand it today, did not exist.[4] Twelve-year-old girls were considered women and marriageable in Perrault's day.

Perrault has been criticized for making the sexual parable too explicit in his version of the tale. In *The Uses of Enchantment,* Bruno Bettelheim is particularly critical of the French author's obvious transformation of a predatory beast into a metaphor that leaves little to the imagination.[5] Today the metaphor persists in a powerful manner in the English language, where "wolf" is a common term for a seducer of women or a lady-killer. Perrault's sexually suggestive moral, which turns the tale's wolf into a seductive Casanova or Don Juan figure, is generally eliminated when his tale is published for a contemporary audience, particularly one of young readers. However, the sexual innuendos in his tale are not limited to the moral. In Perrault's victimizing text, the little girl undresses and climbs into bed with the wolf, who tells her that his strong arms are for embracing her better. The fact that Little Red Riding Hood does not try to escape or fight back during this "direct and obvious seduction" is, according to Bettelheim, a sign either of her stupidity or her desire to be seduced. In short, the psychologist claims that Perrault turned a naive little girl into "a fallen woman."[6]

Les Contes de Perrault by Charles Perrault, illustrated by Gustave Doré, Pierre-Jules Hetzel, 1861.

In *The Trials and Tribulations of Little Red Riding Hood,* Jack Zipes shows clearly how Little Red Riding Hood is held responsible for her own rape and/or death in the first literary version of the tale. His argument is illustrated by Gustave Doré's powerful and influential engravings for the edition of Perrault's tales published by Hetzel in 1861. Doré's celebrated representation of the encounter in the woods as an intimate scene in which a very young girl, whose plump bare arms still retain some baby fat, gazes intently into the eyes of the enormous wolf that she is almost touching, has been interpreted by Zipes as a "seduction scene" in which the little girl "asks to be raped."[7] Even more damaging for Little Red Riding Hood's reputation was Doré's engraving of the little girl in bed with the wolf. The chubby flesh of one arm is bared as she holds the sheet to her bosom, while the curly locks of her long hair fall rather seductively over her shoulders. Although she seems to be shrinking back slightly from her curious bedfellow, her proximity to the wolf and her apparent lack of fear once again create an intimate tête-à-tête upon which the reader intrudes. Although the Brothers Grimm would dramatically alter the image of the little girl in red, they, too, hold her responsible for her own fate.

The Cautionary Scene

The imprudent mother in Perrault's version did not forewarn her young daughter, and so, as Carter translates, "the poor child did not know how dangerous it is to chatter away to wolves" (24). The American poet Anne Sexton underscores this ignorance in her revisionist poem "Red Riding Hood," from the well-known collection *Transformations* (1971), in which the heroine cheerfully addresses the wolf in the woods with a "Good day, Mr. Wolf" and "obligingly" tells him where she is going because she thinks that he is "no more dangerous" than "a streetcar or a panhandler" (76–77). Contrary to Perrault, whose warning is reserved for the moral at the end of the tale, the Grimms have the mother issue the admonishment at the very beginning. The cautionary scene added to the tale becomes a key scene that is generally represented by illustrators, as Zipes demonstrates when he revisits the "trials and tribulations" of Little Red Riding Hood in an essay devoted to the illustrations.[8] The mother is characteristically portrayed in the classic sermonizing gesture, wagging her finger at the little girl. Little Red Cap is warned not to "stray from the path" by her mother, who represents the patriarchal law of the straight and narrow. The mother is concerned not only with her daughter's welfare, but also with her manners, as the little girl is told to be "nice and good" in the woods and polite and well-behaved when she gets to her grandmother's ("Little Red Cap" 1:110). The preface to volume 2 of the first edition of *Kinder-und Hausmärchen* states clearly that the tales are intended to serve as "a manual of manners."[9] In keeping with the image of the Victorian child, the Grimms' Little Red Cap is expected, first and foremost, to be well behaved and obedient.

There are endless variations on the familiar cautionary scene. In many versions of the Grimms' tale, the mother tells Little Red Cap not to talk to strangers.

This advice even creeps into Carter's translation of Perrault's moral cited at the beginning of this chapter. The mother's injunctions may also include the warning to be back before nightfall, as in a version published in Arabic in 1992, where the mother reminds her daughter that the forest road is not safe after dark.[10] Illustrators of children's versions tend to offer a comical rendition of the scene, as in the American author-illustrator James Marshall's picture of a mother leaning out a second-floor window wagging her finger and shouting instructions at her good little daughter. Crossover versions, even those in a humorous mode, generally present a more complex interpretation of the scene. The rendition of the Grimms' *Little Red Riding Hood* (1993) by the internationally renowned American photographer William Wegman, like all the books featuring his Weimaraners, appeals to an audience of all ages, as the dust jacket claims. The photographer does not depict the conventional finger-wagging, or in this case claw-wagging, cautionary scene, although the mother does warn her to "go straight there and return before dark." By presenting a worried Weimaraner-mother watching her dog-daughter set off, Wegman portrays the mother in a more sympathetic manner than most illustrators, that is, as a concerned rather than an authoritative parent. Further, the Grimms' text is reworked so that instead of promising to do as her mother says, the considerate little girl tells her not to worry, although her reassurances are in vain. Like most normal parents, "her mother did worry," comments the narrator. Thus Wegman focuses on the loving and caring relationship between mother and daughter, which is overlooked in the classic versions.

In the Grimms' text, Little Red Cap promises obediently to do just as her mother says, but, as readers all know, she does not do so and therefore the wolf eats her. Unlike Perrault, however, the Grimms do not leave the heroine to her dire fate, but have her rescued from her folly by a hunter, a father figure who, in some versions, actually becomes the little girl's real father. Yvan Pommaux, the author-illustrator of the parodic picture-book retelling *John Chatteron détective* (1993), admits that the detective who rescues his Little Red Riding Hood fulfills, in part, the role of the hunter-protective father figure, as described by Bettelheim.[11] It is made quite clear at the end of the Grimms' tale that the little girl has learned her lesson the hard way. In fact, it is Little Red Cap who formulates the lesson, telling herself: "Never again will you stray from the path by yourself and go into the forest when your mother has forbidden it" (113). Wegman's witty version includes the Grimms' little-known and rarely mentioned second anticlimactic tale, a kind of epilogue or postscript, about Little Red Cap, in which a return trip to her grandmother's reveals that the little girl has learned her lesson well. As Wegman puts it in his reworking of the epilogue: "She went straight there, as her mother told her to. She did not dawdle or stray." Wegman ultimately respects the Grimms' image of a little girl who recognizes that she was responsible for her fate at the hands of the wolf and thus allows herself to be molded by prevailing attitudes toward gender roles.

In some cases, the cautionary scene and the classic sermonizing gesture of the mother are retained, but the message is replaced with an entirely new one. It is no longer a "don't stray from the path" story. The mother of the rebellious heroine in the French picture book *Le Petit Chaperon bouge* (Little Riding Hood moves, 1997) tells her complaining daughter not to argue and not to forget to phone her grandmother on the way (the cell phone that has become Little Red Riding Hood's new attribute symbolizes the modern mother's concern with her child's personal safety). An original take on the admonitory scene occurs in the Japanese chapter book *Mouhitori no Akazukin-chan* (Another Little Red Riding Hood, 1975), by the author Keisuke Tsutsui. The warning this modern Riding Hood receives from her mother is "not to touch" the precious picture book the latter had received from her mother when she was little, a book that turns out to be none other than the Grimms' cautionary tale *Rotkäppchen*. Like her predecessor, this little girl disobeys her mother, hiding the book under her apron before she leaves for her grandmother's. Older children whose grasp of the textual self-referentiality gives them a sense of superiority over the characters will appreciate Tsutsui's amusing metafictive play. Very surprised to learn how much the protagonist of her mother's book is like her, the little girl does not realize that she is in danger of sharing Little Red Cap's fate because the book has put ideas into the wolf's head. It seems entirely out of character that the resourceful and insightful grandmother, who knows the story and is ready for the wolf, does not mention his visit or warn her dreamy granddaughter, who has completely forgotten about the wolf by the time she arrives. The absence of the classic admonitory scene is especially ironic in light of the fact that the grandmother and the mother have both read the cautionary tale the little girl carries with her.

A number of contemporary retellings transfer the admonitory role from the mother to another character. Most often, it is the grandmother who assumes this function. In *Wolf* (1990), a challenging, multileveled novel for older children

Makwelane and the Crocodile by Maria Hendriks and Piet Grobler, © 2004 Piet Grobler. Used by permission of Piet Grobler.

and adolescents by the British children's author Gillian Cross, Nan sends Cassy to her mother's with instructions that summon familiar echoes: "Don't dally around now. Go straight there" (9). In a few cases, the warning is issued in duet form by both parents. The most striking example is found in *Makwelane and the Crocodile* (2004), a charming picture book by Maria Hendriks and Piet Grobler published simultaneously in Afrikaans and English to offer South African children a retelling set in a familiar landscape. The black mother and father are depicted side by side wagging a finger as they warn their daughter to beware of the cunning crocodile and to stick to the footpath. Their warning is echoed by everything around Makwelane, a rock pigeon, a yellow-billed stork, a cricket, a butterfly, even the pestle, but the excited little girl remains oblivious to it in all its forms (plate 3). Sometimes, the cautionary role is paradoxically given to the wolf. In James Finn Garner's *Politically Correct Bedtime Stories* (1994), a collection that the American author hopes will mark children as well as adults (x), the wolf warns Little Red Riding Hood: "You know, my dear, it isn't safe for a little girl to walk through these woods alone" (2). Garner's liberated, self-confident heroine, who is not intimidated by "Freudian imagery" when she encounters the wolf in the foreboding forest, merely takes offense at his "sexist remark" (2). Few contemporary Riding Hoods heed the advice, regardless of who gives it.

Although the cautionary scene of the Grimms' version does not include a specific warning about wolves, that is nonetheless the message that is often internalized. The quotation from Luisa Valenzuela's "Si esto es la vida, yo soy Caperucita Roja" ("If this is life, I'm Red Riding Hood") that constitutes the epigraph to this chapter is only one of many variations on the mother's injunction that echo throughout the story like a refrain:

> Watch out for the big, bad wolf, dear (it's the mother speaking). (105)
>
> Watch out for the wolf, says that maternal voice. . . . My mother has warned me, warns me: watch out for the wolf, my dear little, pure little, innocent, fragile girl, all dressed in red. (107)
>
> The voice of the mother warns you against the wolf. (109)
>
> Watch out. For the wolf, she says, watch out for the wolf, . . . watch out for the wolf. (110)

The mother's warning echoes obsessively in the heroine's head throughout her journey, so that the cautionary scene pervades the entire narrative. Eventually, the mother's voice is superimposed on the daughter's voice and they become one: "Red Riding Hood hears only the voice of the mother as if it were part of her own voice, only speaking in more solemn tones" (107). While she appears to heed the warning that obsesses her and causes a feeling of fear to stir within her, Valenzuela's not so little Red Riding Hood does not seem entirely convinced by the collective opinion that the fear of the wolf is "a matter of caution" because she qualifies the statement with "or so they say" (109). As the versions examined in chapter 5 show, many contemporary Red Riding Hoods throw caution to the wind, ignoring the warning "Beware of the Wolf!"

Mothers have been warning their children to beware of wolves for centuries. As we will see in chapter 2, oral versions of the tale, such as those from the Nivernais and the Morvan, sexualize the wolf's aggression.[12] However, the story of Little Red Riding Hood has its origins in medieval times when it served as a warning tale for children for whom wolves posed a very real threat, especially during the winter in the French, Tyrolean, and Italian Alps. The tale also served therefore as a warning against the danger of being killed by real wolves. The proliferation of wolves in France was due in part to the fact that until the end of the eighteenth century, hunting wolves remained a seigneurial privilege. The French film *Le pacte des loups* (*The Brotherhood of the Wolf*, 2002), set in the reign of Louis XV, shows hunting parties of noblemen seeking to kill the monstrous "wolf" that is terrorizing the countryside and savagely killing scores of women and children in a rural province of France. A character in *Possession,* the 1990 Booker Prize–winning novel by A. S. Byatt, evokes her fear of wolves as a child in nineteenth-century Brittany. However, by that time wolves evidently no longer roamed the forests of Brittany, because she admits she has never seen or heard a wolf (339). In some countries, the danger of being attacked by wolves did persist into the nineteenth century. "Wolfland," by the British author Tanith Lee, is set in nineteenth-century Scandinavia. The sixteen-year-old protagonist, Lisel, elicits the wolf's "reputation" and "the stories of the half-eaten bodies of little children with which nurses regularly scared their charges" at that time (119). Even in regions where the wolf was extinct, children were still warned to beware of the wolf. Byatt's character writes about the persistence of "the peasant's faith in wolves and in the need to put solid doors between the child and all such dangers" (339).

Despite the fact that real wolves no longer pose a threat in the twentieth century, the figure of the wolf-as-predator persists. The enduring threat is made tangible in the enigmatic, textless picture book *Vous oubliez votre cheval* (You are forgetting your horse, 1986), which was published by the experimental French publishing house Le sourire qui mord (The smile that bites), directed by Christian Bruel, who, like Harlin Quist, is known for his visually sophisticated and often controversial picture books. As the series' title, Grands petits livres (Large Little Books), suggests, the complex picture books that it includes are really crossover works that deal with difficult themes, such as sensuality and violence, in a manner that can be disconcerting even for adults. Two of the disorienting, disparate pictures that Pierre Wachs did for this innovative book are transparent allusions to the story of Little Red Riding Hood. Readers are immediately struck by the alternating black-and-white and color illustrations, which do not simply seem to be a case of distinguishing between reality and the dream world. The bear trap set inside the grandmother's living-room door in the black-and-white illustration on the verso looks unreal, even surreal, while the wolf in the color illustration on the recto appears quite real (plate 4). The viewer's gaze is drawn irresistibly through the empty room in the black-and-white illustration to the open door at the other side. The color illustration takes the viewer inside the other room, where the large, realistic wolf stands in the open door, obviously having carefully avoided the trap. In Wachs's retelling, the wolf presents a very real threat.

Hanging neatly on a hanger suspended from the doorknob is Little Red Riding Hood's hooded red coat, a clue to assist young readers in decoding the intertext. The most troubling elements of the illustration are two vulnerable-looking bare legs and feet, all that is visible of a young girl who is the object of the wolf's intent yellow gaze. As the viewer contemplates the enigmatic illustration, however, the initial sense of menace disappears. Like a well-trained dog, or even an obliging lover, the wolf brings the grandmother's slippers to the little girl with the small bare feet. The bare legs that bleed suggestively off the page conjure up images of a completely naked Little Red Riding Hood. For adult readers, even apparently innocent details tend to take on a hidden meaning. The yellow liquid spilling out of an overturned pot in the foreground closely resembles the paint on the wall and door of the room, but it is more likely melting butter, which would suggest that the girl has been in her grandmother's bed for some time. In any case, the overturned pot does not seem to be the result of a struggle. Perhaps it is a symbol of the little girl's lost innocence. Although the transparent allusions to the story of Little Red Riding Hood in these particular pictures allow readers to find the thread of a narrative, the story that emerges is fragmented, ambiguous, and disturbing, even for the adult readers of this puzzling picture book. It remains unclear whether this Riding Hood is a victim or a willing participant.

Although contemporary children need no longer fear the predatory mammal *canis lupus*, which is now extinct in many parts of North America and Eurasia, they do need to beware of the two-legged variety that can lurk in woods, on city streets, or in their own homes. Even in the nineteenth-century childhood evoked by Byatt's character, the wolves that persist seem to be of the human variety, because she writes: "Wolves come; and there are men as bad as wolves" (339). The moral of Perrault's classic tale is essentially that well-mannered, two-legged wolves are the most dangerous of all. "Le Petit Chaperon Bleu Marine" (Little Navy Blue Riding Hood, 1977), a parodic retelling of Perrault's tale from the collection *Contes à l'envers* (Upside down tales) by the French author-illustrators Philippe Dumas and Boris Moissard, expresses the moral in straightforward terms that can be understood by the youngest reader: "some men are more dangerous than wolves" (26). Although the small drawing of Hitler that follows indicates the seriousness of the moral, it is lost in the playful, lighthearted tone of the rest of the retelling. The moral that will persist in the minds of young read-ers is the same that is retained by the wolf in this very funny upside-down tale: some little girls are more dangerous than wolves. Many wolves would do well to listen to the inverted warning of the American psychologist Eric Berne: "wolves should keep away from innocent-looking maidens and their grandmothers, in short, a wolf should not walk through the forest alone."[13] In recent years, there has been a proliferation of retellings in which the story is subverted to turn it into a cautionary tale for wolves or their two-legged counterparts, warning them against dangerous females. Most wolf-friendly versions of *Little Red Riding Hood* attempt to rehabilitate the wolf, whose name has been synonymous for centuries with an irrational, primeval fear in adults and children alike.

Some critics have expressed the concern that the wolf is becoming almost over-familiar due to its rehabilitation in the name of ecology and animal rights. They feel it is important that "our inner mythology" return the wolf to its proper place, that of "a killer of children."[14] While the wolf is an endangered species whose re-habilitation in literature is essential to its survival, there is an inherent danger in casting the wolf as the victim of a dangerous female. The wolf remains an arche-typal symbol of the predatory male, and young girls need, perhaps more than ever, to be on their guard. The retellings examined subsequently in this chapter retain the tale's original cautionary function, but serve to warn modern Riding Hoods.

The Archetypal Tale of Child Abuse and Rape

The tale of Little Red Riding Hood has been used quite effectively to address the topic of violence and violation in contemporary society. It is the archetypal tale of child abuse, an association that extends well beyond the literary domain. A document on child abuse and children's rights, published by the Norwegian Om-budsman for Children in 1994, was titled "Når Rødhette møter ulven" (When Little Red Riding Hood meets the wolf). In this case, the wolf is the abuser who works with children.[15] One would expect that retellings of Little Red Riding Hood dealing with such weighty themes would be told in a serious, if not dark mode. However, that is not always the case. Some children's authors and illus-trators broach the subject of child abuse and children's rights in a playful, light-hearted manner. A few such examples will be considered before we examine retellings that adopt a highly serious tone to tell the story of the rape or attempted rape of Red Riding Hood.

In the "Little Red Riding Hood" published in 1974 by Tomi Ungerer, whose subversive children's books attract and often disturb adult readers, the protagonist is abused, not by the wolf who gallantly offers to carry her heavy baskets, but by her grandmother, who showers her with "blows and insults" (86). The little girl still bears the bruises of previous beatings, and she asks the reader to bear witness to the bite marks that persist on her shoulder from the last visit. The legal rights of children sometimes provide the main joke in humorous remakes. The enterprising Miss Riding-Hood in *The Jolly Postman: Or Other People's Letters* (1986), by Janet and Allan Ahlberg, exercises her rights and takes the wolf to court for "harassment," as indicated in the letter addressed to B. B. Wolf Esq., c/o Grandma's Cottage, from Meeny, Miny, Mo & Co., Solicitors, on behalf of their client. It was "the idea of doing a letter from a solicitor (lawyer)," which resembled "a university student's joke," that inspired the Ahlbergs to do a multilayered book with "bits for little kids, bits for bigger kids, bits for adults."[16] These reworkings of the story of Little Red Riding Hood obviously make no attempt to transmit a serious message about child abuse.

Although *John Chatterton détective*, by Yvan Pommaux, is a humorous and playful parody of *Le Petit Chaperon Rouge*, there is a dark undercurrent to this innovative French picture book, which turns the famous fairy tale into a missing child case. Years of searching for a way of retelling fairy tales without resorting to pastiche ended when the author-illustrator saw Otto Preminger's 1944 film *Laura*, which inspired him to revisit them as whodunits. The series of books star an amiable cat-detective, whose name, Chatterton, is a clever combination of the French word for "cat" (*chat*) and the name of the popular mystery writer G. K. Chesterton. The subtle play of references to the cinema and the detective genre of the 1940s and 1950s appeals to adult readers, especially movie buffs, but it is done in such a way that the books remain perfectly accessible to young readers. Children may not fully appreciate the witty intertextual play that turns the fairy-tale canon into the precedent-setting cases of Chatterton's criminal code, a volume titled *Affaires criminelles célèbres* (Famous criminal cases) that never leaves his desk. However, the intertext is established for readers of all ages when the detective links his current case involving a missing child to "that murky story in which the daughter and the grandmother are eaten by a wolf."

In Pommaux's transposition of the classic fairy tale, somber city streets replace the dark forest, and the wolf wears a stylish suit, drives a black sedan, and owns a large private art collection. In fact, he is a criminally obsessive art collector determined to stop at nothing to get *Le loup bleu sur fond blanc* (Blue wolf on a white background), the coveted Keith Haring–style painting he needs to complete his wolf collection. The remarkable double spread of the wolf's eclectic art collection appeals especially to cultured adult viewers, who are able to label many of the parodied works, including a Magritte word-image (here *loup* rather than *cheval*), a walking wolf by Giacometti, a wrapped wolf by Christo, and a wire wolf by Alexander Calder (plate 5).[17] This introduction of high art into the fairy-tale context assured the picture book's adult appeal. The wolf's art collection provoked so much interest among adults that the artist, with the help of his wife and daughter, actually created the collection, which has toured libraries in France. Although young readers can appreciate the humorous and playful treatment of past artworks and recognize the intent to parody, they are unable to identify the target paintings and sculptures and thus to decode the parody at more sophisticated levels. Recognizing these subtle references to high art is not essential to an understanding of the story, but they add a dimension that appeals strongly to adult readers and reviewers, as the traveling art collection testifies.

Pommaux's story of a Little Red Riding Hood abducted and held for ransom by a narcissistic art collector unfolds like a film noir in a series of sequential illustrations that use lighting and camera angles to create the atmosphere of a crime thriller. The silence, the elliptical dialogues, and the chiaroscuro play of light and shadow in the nocturnal scenes all combine to create the requisite dark, mysterious atmosphere. Using a landscape format that allows him to reproduce the screen effects of cinematography, Pommaux replicates close-up shots, long shots, and unusual angle shots. Sometimes textless double spreads create a vast, stationary panorama that fills a big screen; at other times, they are divided into a series of frames that are presented sequentially like the images in a film, accelerating the rhythm to a breathless pace. Suspense builds as Chatterton follows a trail of red items of clothing through a dark, public garden and along abandoned streets and alleys. The final clue is found in a powerful black car, which has become the wolf's attribute in quite a number of contemporary retellings. Pommaux parodies the lengthy striptease in oral versions of the tale, but the items shed are not intimate pieces of apparel, but only accessories. Further, the reader-viewer is not given the role of voyeur during the undressing scene. It is not clear, therefore, whether the trail of red clothing that leads the detective to the little girl is the sinister sign of a struggle with her abductor or a series of clues deliberately left by a clever captive who has borrowed a trick from Little Thumbling.

The techniques of cinematography are cleverly combined with those of the bande dessinée to create a sinister atmosphere of mystery, suspense, and dread. Pommaux represents the ransom demand scene on a page divided into two frames, which offer viewers very different perspectives: the first frame provides a close-up of the villainous wolf relaying his demand to the mother on a portable phone, while the second depicts a longer shot of his innocent hostage tied up on the floor. The helplessness of the bound victim is emphasized by her simple, cartoonlike facial features, and her fear is conveyed by lines radiating from her head, while the jagged lines of a speech balloon express her terrified scream. The horror of this frame is increased by the overwhelming presence of the wolf, who, paradoxically, is physically almost entirely absent from the scene. The forearm that alone extends into the frame is characterized ironically by the signs of a "civilized" being (a chic blue suit and a large signet ring), but projected on the wall, directly over the helpless figure of the little girl, is the huge, terrifying shadow of a wolf whose human trappings are no longer visible. The scene is reminiscent of the haunting black-and-white photograph in Sarah Moon's troubling version of Perrault's tale, in which the wolf is portrayed as a menacing, dark shadow on the wall, towering over that of the little girl. For adult readers who recognize many of the parodied art works in the wolf's priceless collection, the dangerous situation in which this modern Little Red Riding Hood finds herself is highlighted, because it becomes obvious that this wolf is a compulsive collector who will go to any ends to own the coveted painting. Pommaux, who was strongly influenced by the work of Alfred Hitchcock, manages to portray the fairy-tale wolf as a psychopath.

In spite of its dark, sinister atmosphere, Pommaux's retelling of *Little Red Riding Hood* as a story of abduction remains quite playful throughout. In keeping with the ludic tone, the story has a happy outcome that simultaneously parodies the happy ending of both the film noir and the fairy tale. Just as Dana Andrews rescues Laura in the Preminger film, Pommaux's black cat-detective saves Little Red Riding Hood by knocking out the wolf and possibly killing him with a brick. At the same time, Chatterton humorously evinces the Grimms' hunter, as he cuts the little girl free with a Swiss Army Knife. In a final ironic touch that will no doubt be missed by young readers, Pommaux pokes fun at the world of high art by showing the coveted Blue Wolf painting on the wall of Chatterton's rather seedy office, where it has been carelessly hung by the detective who is obviously not an art lover, but who has accepted it from a grateful mother as his reward for solving the case of the missing Little Red Riding Hood.

A number of authors and illustrators courageously tackle the question of child abuse and rape in a highly serious mode. One of those authors is the Chilean poet Gabriela Mistral, who published the poem "Caperucita Roja" (Little Red Riding Hood) in her popular collection *Ternura* (Tenderness). The simple songs and rounds in the collection published in Madrid in 1924 were written primarily for children, but both adults and children all over the Spanish-speaking world read them. Latin American children generally know the poem "Caperucita Roja" through school readers. As is often the case with poetry published in a collection, even if it was originally written for children, young readers generally read it at school. In this collection of moral and didactic verse written by a young schoolteacher, children's innocence is a common theme.

Mistral stresses the innocence and purity of Little Red Riding Hood, who is no match for "Maese Lobo" ("Master Wolf"), the "Traitor" with the diabolical eyes (136). She reminds readers of the girl's tender age by emphasizing her "littleness," describing her "tiny fingers" that knock on the door, her "little heart," and her "little body" in the bed. The gentleness, vulnerability, and artlessness of the heroine, which are emphasized throughout the poem, contrast with the gruffness, deception, and cunning of the wolf. The little girl yields naively to the wolf's peremptory demand for love. She answers the wolf's questions ingenuously and asks her own with equal candor. The formulaic question-and-answer sequence is punctuated with the narrator's comments concerning the actions and reactions of the two characters. Before answering the little girl's question about his ears, the "hairy deceiver" embraces the little girl. Immediately following the wolf's standard reply, readers are told that the girl's "tender little body dilated his eyes" (137). Her terror only adds to his excitement, dilating them further. This physical, sexual response provokes Little Red Riding Hood's next question about the wolf's big eyes. Mistral creates a striking and poignant contrast between the sexual arousal of the wolf and the terror of the little girl.

The tender heart of the innocent little girl, which is a leitmotiv throughout Mistral's poem, reflects the titular emphasis of the collection. The first stanza reveals that Little Red Riding Hood's "corazoncito," the diminutive of *corazón* or "heart," is "tender like a honeycomb" (136). In Mistral's verse rendition of the ritualistic dialogue, the wolf begins the familiar answers with the word "Corazoncito," this time used as the diminutive of a term of endearment meaning "my little love," as if he was addressing a lover. The poem ends with the word "corazón," as the narrator describes her death at the hands of the wolf. Unlike many retellings that only mention the devouring of the little girl, Mistral devotes the final stanza to a very disturbing description of the horrific act. The beast has crushed the trembling, soft little body under the rough hair of his body: "and has ground the flesh, and has ground the bones, / and has squeezed the heart like a cherry" (137). The graphic description of the violence and cruelty of the sweet little girl's death is shocking for readers of all ages.

Although Mistral's story is universal, it has been transposed to the rural setting of one of the Andean villages in the north of Chile, where the author grew up and began her teaching career at the age of fifteen. The powerful emotions that characterize Mistral's lyric poetry are evident in her heart-rending retelling of *Little Red Riding Hood,* as are her love for children and her compassion for women. On learning that she had been awarded the Nobel Prize in 1945, the author suggested that it was perhaps because she was "the candidate of women and children."[18] Her deep concern for women of all ages explains why Mistral's version is one of the few that deals with the fate of the grandmother. Having informed readers that the wolf hasn't eaten in three days, the poet exclaims: "Poor sick grandmother, who is going to protect her!" (137). The grandmother is as defenseless as the little girl and Mistral's compassion extends to the old lady as well. Her retelling of the story of Little Red Riding Hood expresses the "tenderness" that gave its name to the entire collection of poetry and that moves readers of all ages. It is highly appropriate that this collection of moral and didactic verse, written by a young teacher, should include the cautionary tale of "Caperucita Roja."

The Spanish poet Francisco Villaespesa wrote two poems about Little Red Riding Hood, both of which interpret the tale as a story of male violence against a young, innocent child. The two poems, published in 1954, are titled simply "Caperucita," distinguishing them from the classic tale, which is known in Spanish as "Caperucita Roja." The first poem, a sonnet, appears in a section of the first volume of *Poesías completas* (Collected poetry) titled "Canciones de niños" (Children's songs) and dedicated to the Peruvian poet José Santos Chocano, who had written his own poem about Little Red Riding Hood. Although Villaespesa is Spanish, his verse rendition of the tale, like Mistral's, is often read in schools in Latin America, where he had traveled extensively. Since these children's poems, like Mistral's, are published in volumes of collected poetry that target primarily adults, they generally find their young audience in schools.

The originality of the sonnet lies in the manner in which the tale is narrated. It takes the form of a dialogue between the narrator and several anonymous children from Little Riding Hood's village. Like Mistral, Villaespesa underscores the youth and innocence of the heroine by insisting on her small size. The narrator wants to know the whereabouts of his "smallest" friend and then tries to piece together the events surrounding her disappearance. Villaespesa exonerates Little Riding Hood from all blame. When she encounters the wolf in the woods, she is not dawdling disobediently or idly picking flowers, but diligently gathering firewood, as she was instructed to do.

The narrative situation renders the scene more dramatic and moving. The narrator, whose voice seems to be that of the poet himself, addresses the children directly, asking them a series of short, rapid questions in an attempt to find out what has happened and why there is so much crying and screaming at Little Riding Hood's house. He reports his questions and the children's answers in dialogue form with no commentary, creating a text full of suspense and tension. When Little Riding Hood did not return, everyone went looking for her in the woods, but they found no sign of her. It is not until the final stanza that readers learn, at the same time as the narrator, the fate of the little girl. The conciseness and simplicity with which her tragic end is related renders it all the more poignant: "They only brought back her little shoes . . . / They say that a wolf ate her!" (557). The collective opinion is that the wolf ate the little girl. Villaespesa approaches the well-known story from a new perspective, showing the reaction of those who loved the missing girl, notably her older friend, the narrator, and the village children who had been her playmates. The reader has the strong sense of being present at the scene and participating in the collective grief.

Villaespesa returns to the story of Little Riding Hood in a brief poem that appeared in the second volume of *Poesías completas*. Composed of a single quatrain with very short lines, this poem is even more appropriately categorized in the section devoted to children's songs than the earlier sonnet. However, even though children's nursery rhymes and songs, like the folk and fairy tales that often inspire them, frequently deal with violence and cruelty, many adult mediators may feel that the harsh reality revealed abruptly in the final line of Villaespesa's short poem is too shocking for young readers. The pathos and powerful impact of the poem is enhanced by its brevity and simplicity. The second poem can be read almost like a postscript or an epilogue to the sonnet. Time has passed and more has been learned about the events that were reported earlier. Contrary to popular opinion, "Wolves didn't eat her / Men ate her!" The original explanation that wolves ate the little girl is relegated to the realm of rumor and the new account of events is established as the truth. The Spanish poet restores the innocence of Little Red Riding Hood, portraying the little girl "asleep in the wood" (1479). The peaceful image of the sleeping girl, which is repeated in the first two lines, is cruelly and abruptly shattered in the final lines, where it becomes clear that sleep is being used as a euphemism for death. The narrator of the second poem places the blame squarely with men, absolving wolves of the dastardly crime of which they have been accused for generations.

Like Villaespesa, the Dutch author and artist Wim Hofman has reworked the tale more than once to reflect on the topic of child abuse. In fact, he has recast *Roodkapje*, as *Little Red Riding Hood* is called in Dutch, in a variety of formats and mediums. Hofman was struck by the fact that *Little Red Riding Hood, Snow White, Hansel and Gretel*, and *Little Thumbling* all have the same basic structure: one or more children are sent or taken into the woods, they end up at a house, in that house she or they must confront "Evil (Death)," in the form of a wolf, ogre, or witch. It is the presence of menace, horror, and death in these old folktales that explains their appeal for the author. His reflection on the necessity of evil as a "motor" for story led him to do a series of retellings of fairy tales, which were originally intended to be published in poster format.[19] The depiction of the four tales on a single poster, where everything would be multiplied by four, would illustrate their striking structural resemblance in the structure. Each tale consists of four rhyming verses and four small, framed illustrations that portray (1) the child/children, (2) a house in the dark woods, (3) evil, and (4) the end.

The first scene in all four tales depicts the small child/children in a clearing surrounded by tall trees that tower above her/them. Pointing out that fairy tales were intended "to train children" or "to frighten them," one and the same thing according to Hofman, he interprets the warning in these tales as "Don't go into the forest alone," since "Europe was one impenetrable forest at the time."[20] In rhyming verse, "Roodkapje" offers a succinct retelling of the Grimms' version, in which the first of the four verses focuses on the cautionary scene. This mother makes an attempt to justify the fact that she sends her daughter to her grand-mother's on her own by explaining that she is "a little tired," before warning her: Stay on the path and walk steadily on, / And do not listen to wolves! (11). The mother's admonitions contain a specific warning about wolves, which may explain why this Red Riding Hood realizes immediately that it is the wolf, and not her grandmother, in the bed in the second frame. This knowledge does not change the little girl's fate, however, as she is eaten in the third frame. In keeping

"Roodkapje" by Wim Hofman, © 1993 Wim Hofman. Used by permission of Wim Hofman.

with the Grimms' ending, the fourth frame is devoted to the rescue of Red Riding Hood by a hunter, but, as we shall see, this is not necessarily a "happy" ending according to the author.

The traumatic nature of the events that take place in the grandmother's house is the subject of another retelling of *Roodkapje* that the artist painted in acrylics on a long wooden board, a literal storyboard, in 1996. Hofman uses only what he considers the classic fairy-tale colors, that is, white for innocence, red for life, and black for death.[21] The narrative is rendered even more poignant and disturbing by the simplicity of the pictures, which seek to imitate a child's drawings, but whose stylized sophistication is that of an adult artist. The distinctive Dutch elements of this story of a Riding Hood sent into the woods on her bicycle to take red tulips to her grandmother have the effect of emphasizing the girl's innocence and youth. A bad fall from her bicycle effectively symbolizes her encounter with the evil wolf. Instead of engaging in the formulaic dialogue with the wolf in the dramatic bed scene that occupies the central frame, Hofman's Little Red Riding Hood has her back turned to the wolf and peers out at the viewer, as if making a silent appeal for help. The absence of a mouth heightens the sense of mute help-lessness of the little girl, who is depicted in the wolf's jaws in the following scene, her feet sticking out pathetically. The anonymity of Little Red Riding Hood's rescuer and the driver of the black car who takes her home at night intensifies the sense of the little girl's aloneness in the face of this horrifying experience.

As in all of Hofman's retellings of fairy tales, *Roodkapje* explores the night-mare side of childhood experience. Although Little Red Riding Hood is rescued, in keeping with the Grimms' version, the ending is anything but happy, as is sug-gested by the very dark, depressing colors of the final frames. The first and last scenes of the story are at once similar and strikingly different. Whereas the open-ing frame depicts Little Red Riding Hood in her bed sleeping soundly with her Little Red Riding Hood doll sleeping beside her, in the final frame the little girl in bed is no longer sleeping, but weeping, as is the doll that constitutes her minia-ture double (plate 6). The reassuring presence of the mother, who watches her sleeping daughter in the first scene, is replaced in the final scene by a black void that eloquently suggests the absence, if not the death, of the mother. The final scene exudes an overwhelming sense of loneliness, dread, and despair. Even with the night-light that she needs since her terrifying encounter with the wolf, the traumatized little girl is unable to sleep. In the case of *Little Red Riding Hood,* the "evil" that the child confronts in her grandmother's house is that of sexual abuse. The artist explains in categorical terms: "The most terrible thing possible has happened to her. She's a little girl who's been in the clutches of a big man who could do whatever he pleased with her." Convinced that after such an experience, "you're never really 'all right' again . . . you're never able to forget it," Hof-man believes that even in the Grimms' version, with its so-called happy ending, "things never really work out for Little Red Riding Hood."[22] The fairy-tale heroine's "trials and tribulations" do not end when she is rescued from the hands of the predatory wolf/male.

Like Susan Brownmiller, the author of *Against Our Will,* Hofman considers the story of Little Red Riding Hood to be "a parable of rape."[23] However, this underlying meaning will remain hidden from children, only adults are likely to read his various retellings in this light. A number of other contemporary authors and illustrators have told or retold the tale from this perspective in more explicit works that have stirred, startled, or shocked readers of all ages. In her controversial picture-book version of Perrault's *Little Red Riding Hood,* Sarah Moon uses photography to transpose the tale into a modern urban context. A series of sober photographs reveal the sinister events that take place during the dark hours between dusk and dawn. Awarded the Premio Grafico at the Bologna Children's Book Fair in 1984, Moon's book received a mixed reaction of profound admiration and scandalized disapproval. The controversy centered largely on the question of target audience. An Italian reader felt the jury "mistook a very refined book for adult voyeurs for a children's book" and an American reviewer and social worker thought that the Bologna Book Fair prize sticker should be accompanied by a red "HANDLE WITH CARE" stamp since the book can frighten even adults.[24] The shocking effect of the fashion photographer's black-and-white photographs of the child model Morgan is not unlike that of Anne Ikhlef's 1985 film, *La véritable histoire du Chaperon rouge* (The real story of Red Riding Hood), which casts a seven-year-old actress, Justine Bayard, in the role of Red Riding Hood. The realism of the mediums used to portray a young, flesh-and-blood girl in Moon's stark, black-and-white photography and Ikhlef's dramatic cinematography accounts for the powerful, shocking impact that these two exceptional works have on viewers.

Moon portrays the famous encounter scene as the meeting between a modern schoolgirl and the invisible driver of a large, powerful car that embodies the predatory animal.[25] In the haunting photograph of the little girl illuminated by the threatening beam of the glaring headlights of a dark car in a deserted street, Moon subverts the classic rendition of the encounter as an intimate tête-à-tête by using unusual camera angles to place viewers in the position of the anonymous driver-wolf who stares at the innocent little girl with cold, inhuman headlight-eyes. In the equally provocative picture book *Mon Chaperon Rouge* (My Red Riding Hood), by Anne Ikhlef and Alain Gauthier, the French artist imagines the encounter of a peasant girl with a well-dressed, city-slicker wolf in a gray suit who also drives a big, black car. Moon's invisible wolf is more disturbing and menacing than many of the wolves that are anthropomorphized or given a human form. A 1988 illustration of the tale by the Italian illustrator Roberto Innocenti also depicts a dangerous, dark, urban wolf who drives, not a car, but a motorcycle (plate 7).[26] Readers of Moon's book will have a strong feeling of déjà vu when they see Innocenti's Little Red Riding Hood, who bears more than a striking resemblance to Morgan running along the brick wall in the third photograph. Although Innocenti adds a few touches of color and other human beings, the scene is no less dark or menacing. On a somber, stormy night, the little girl runs through a hostile, frightening cityscape of gray metal and concrete, graffiti, garbage, and bystanders who remain indifferent to her plight. The omnipresent signs of war (gun shells, a gas mask, barbed wire, etc.) heighten the threatening atmosphere. The picture is filled with the tension of the frightened little girl's meeting with the dark, motorized wolf, a meeting that has obviously taken place seconds before in a deserted passageway at the top of the stairs. Innocenti's wolf has a human form but, like Moon's, he remains invisible, this time hidden behind his black leather suit, goggles, and helmet, as he races off to granny's, his bike light piercing the darkness. The sense of ominous foreboding that pervades the compelling picture is all the more haunting because Innocenti only did the one illustration, leaving the tragic ending to the viewer's imagination.

The final, troubling image of rumpled bedclothes in Moon's retelling confronts the reader with the sexuality and violence inherent in Perrault's tale. She eliminates Perrault's ironic moral that would have lightened the somber tone of her book and lessened the powerful impact. In the 1998 picture book *Le Petit Chaperon rouge*, the French illustrator Éric Battut, in contrast, retains Perrault's moral in his colorful rendition of the tale, which portrays Little Red Riding Hood as a peasant goose girl. In one spread, the unseen wolf casts a large, frightening shadow across the floor and the bed, reminding us of Moon's representation of the ever-invisible wolf as a terrifying shadow projected on the wall. When the wolf himself is depicted in Battut's other illustrations, he is actually rather small and comical, not the least bit frightening. Even though the wolf licking his chops contentedly in granny's enormous bed is quite tiny and funny looking, the sight of the little red clothes that the girl will never again wear, laid out in an orderly fashion at the foot of the bed, is nonetheless unnerving. It is vaguely reminiscent of Moon's final photograph of the empty bed, but the untidy bedclothes of the latter contrast with the neatness of Battut's poster bed and the methodical order in which the little girl's clothes have been placed on it. Moon's reading of Perrault's tale in 1984 led her American publisher to proclaim her "a courageous visionary" who had dared to draw out into the open the "unspeakable sin" of child abuse.[27] Her illustrations demonstrate the relevance of the classic tale, which can still serve as a cautionary tale in a world where countless children are victims of sexual violence each year. Reissued in 2002, Moon's book is no less pertinent today than it was when it first appeared almost twenty years earlier. Since its publication, however, other authors and illustrators have also used the story of Little Red Riding Hood in picture books to deal with the subject of sexual abuse.

One of the most striking examples is *Un petit chaperon rouge* (A Little Red Riding Hood, 2000), a French picture book by Claude Clément and Isabelle Forestier that addresses the question of sexual abuse and its psychological consequences and judicial implications. The book was published by a children's department, Grasset-Jeunesse, and, in spite of the delicate topic, it was targeted at children from four years of age and up. However, the picture book also has a message for adults. One is immediately struck by the sensuousness and the sensuality of the rich pastels, in which the color red dominates and often bleeds conspicuously out onto the frame of the illustration. The centering of the words on the page suggests verse, even before the reader discovers the rhythm, rhymes, and repetitions of the highly poetic text. Like a refrain, one three-line sentence is repeated with slight variations, evoking the day-to-day rhythm of life, "with its joys and its cares, in the Cité des Bergeries." The familiar phrases of dialogue from the classic text (the onomatopoeia *Toc! Toc!*, the formulaic instruction about the *chevillette* and the *bobinette*, the dramatic questions) bring a familiar pleasure to French children who generally know Perrault's text by heart. The author ingeniously integrates these familiar elements in order to create a highly original text.

A year before *Un petit chaperon rouge*, Clément wrote *La frontière de sable* (The border of sand, 1999), a novel that deals with the subject of sexual abuse in a tactful manner suitable for young readers. As the title suggests, the novel seeks to trace for young readers the fragile border between right and wrong, between what is acceptable and what is forbidden. The essential issues tackled in the novel, including breaking through the silence and shame and helping a child recover from a trauma that could ruin her life, are also addressed in the picture book. Forestier, who was familiar with Clément's novel, had already done three pastel plates based on Little Red Riding Hood before they decided to collaborate, as her own childhood nightmares had been haunted by wolves. Forestier deliberately chose Perrault's version, in which the little girl, after being invited to climb into bed with the wolf, undresses and obliges. While she acknowledges that Perrault may have addressed the tale to young girls of the aristocracy, which would give it a different meaning, in the context of the twenty-first century, when fairy tales are addressed largely to children, Forestier sees it not so much as a story about rape as "a story about pedophilia."[28]

Little Red Riding Hood by Charles Perrault, illustrated by Sarah Moon, photographs © 1983 Sarah Moon, reprinted by permission of the Creative Company, Mankato, MN.

The use of the indefinite article *un* turns the heroine of *Un petit chaperon rouge* into *a* Little Red Riding Hood among many, a representative of every child who is a victim of male violence. The blurb on the back cover distinguishes the protagonist from the heroine of the classic tale: "Once upon a time there was . . . another Little Red Riding Hood," while establishing that this Riding Hood is in no less danger than her predecessor because the wolf is still a threat in the dark forest. In a skillful manner, both the author and the illustrator have blended the old, the new, and the ageless to create a universal cautionary tale. The family situation of a single mother relying on her mother to help look after her daughter while she works is quite modern, but the close relationship of the three generations of women evokes ancient matriarchies. This Little Red Riding Hood lives in a city that has a gothic look when seen from a distance in the first illustration, but seems to be composed of modern apartment blocks when seen from much closer in a subsequent illustration. The symbolism of the rather medieval name of the isolated residential quarter on the edge of the woods is indicated by pictorial details suggesting that Cité des Bergeries (Sheepfolds City) is inhabited by sheep, for example, a boy wearing a sheep's mask or children playing leapfrog, which is *saute-mouton,* or "leap-sheep," in French. The presence of such innocent prey explains why the wolf lurks in the woods around the Cité des Bergeries. The vague ethnic background of the protagonist highlights the story's universality. This Little Red Riding Hood is a kind of Every Child, whose story is that of every abused girl or boy.

The distinctive headgear that her grandmother gives her sets this Little Red Riding Hood apart from all others. The unusual crimson velvet bonnet bears a striking resemblance to a cornucopia. In one beautiful, sensual plate, the large red bonnet actually becomes a cornucopia overflowing with lovely red and pink flowers and red butterflies. The face of the little girl holding the bonnet has been cropped to leave only a serene, enigmatic, Mona-Lisa-like smile that suggests that she possesses some new, secret knowledge. It is made clear early in the story that the bonnet symbolizes the little girl's ritual passage from child to young woman. Whereas the red bonnet lying curled up in the open red gift box initially resembles "a sleeping baby snail," according to the illustrator, it changes form as if it was "alive" when Little Red Riding Hood puts it on. The initiatory significance of the gift is obvious in an eye-catching plate of the reflection of the three generations of women in a large mirror (plate 8). The little girl admires herself in the new bonnet, while the old lady, whose gray hair retains the shape of the bonnet she had worn for so many years, watches proudly. Forestier's original idea of giving the bonnet a form suggesting the female sex was abandoned, since such a direct allusion would have been shocking in a book addressed to children. She nonetheless deliberately retained a pointed shape that psychoanalysts would interpret as a phallic symbol, and she points out discreetly in public talks that it could be a "sheath." In her view, the bonnet combines the masculine and feminine parts of our sexuality. The sexual connotations of the bonnet explain why the traumatized little girl can no longer bear to wear it at the end of the tale. Following the horrific events with which she associates it, the bonnet lies, limp and lifeless, on her bedroom floor.

The fact that the older women would allow the little girl to set out into the woods alone is justified by the fact that the mother has to work and the grandmother is ill. A striking illustration depicts an original cautionary scene in the stairwell of the apartment building (plate 9). With one finger pointed in the characteristic sermonizing gesture, the mother leans down from an upper landing to shout instructions at her daughter. The tone of this cautionary scene is different from most, as the mother's loving concern for her "darling Little Riding Hood" is combined with warm praise that expresses her confidence in her daughter because she is "a resourceful Riding Hood." The little girl is obviously not listening, as she is hurtling down the stairs and is already two flights below. Like a typical adolescent, she no doubt feels that she can manage quite well without her mother's advice. She is equally carefree when her friends, in a collective cautionary scene, echo the maternal injunctions received at home. A menacing note is introduced by the small picture on the bottom of the facing page, depicting a lone, blond schoolboy innocently dressed all in white, staring intently in the direction of the group of friends and readers from behind a sheep's mask. Although the boy may symbolize the innocence of all the children who live there, it is also possible that there is a wolf in sheep's clothing in the Cité des Bergeries, perhaps even among Little Red Riding Hood's school chums.

In Forestier's illustration of the encounter, the heads of the two figures are depicted quite close together, but there is none of the intimacy found in Doré's engraving because the proximity is merely the result of the perspective: the wolf occupies the foreground whereas the little girl eyes him uncertainly from a distance. The dark ground behind her is strewn with vivid red flowers, or perhaps even petals that have fallen from her bouquet, in an ominous portent of the deflowering that threatens the little girl. Although the sweet little girl speaks naively with the cunning wolf in spite of the multiple warnings of her mother and her friends, she refuses to undress and climb into bed with him. The ritualistic dialogue is rendered even more dramatic by the verbs used in the narrator's intervening comments. They reflect the rapid evolution of the little girl's emotions, as she moves from astonishment to insistence to alarm to panic. The unusual perspectives of Forestier's illustrations accentuate the drama of the traumatic events. From the lower left corner of one double spread and with her back to the reader, who shares her perspective, Little Red Riding Hood stares into the bedroom at the trail of red items belonging to her grandmother (slippers, dress, glasses, disconnected telephone) that are strewn ominously over the floor and right across the gutter to the wolf, who sprawls in the bed in a decidedly sensual manner. The disturbing disorder that meets her eyes undoubtedly explains why the little girl refuses to join the wolf under the sheets. It is significant that Little Red Riding Hood's bonnet no longer points happily skyward in this scene, but droops sadly toward the ground where the belongings of the wolf's first victim are strewn.

The ending of this re-version deviates significantly from the classic tale. Little Red Riding Hood manages to escape because the wolf gets tangled up in the blankets when he pounces on her, a detail that amuses children, but the frightening illustration of the wolf's enormous open jaws about to close on the point of her long bonnet demonstrates dramatically how narrowly the little girl misses being devoured. The concerned reaction of friends and neighbors at nightfall, when the little girl has not returned home, and their unsuccessful search of the woods remind us of Villaespesa's poem. In Clément's story, Little Red Riding Hood does eventually come home, but her escape from the wolf is not synonymous with a happy ending. Traumatized by the terrifying experience, the outgoing little girl has withdrawn into muteness. The psychological depth of this interpretation gives new meaning to the tale. A powerful and moving illustration depicts the little girl huddled in the farthest corner of her room, as if she is trying to hide from the world (plate 10). Although her sorrowful, haunted eyes are fixed on the red bonnet lying abandoned in the middle of the floor, the viewer's gaze is carried to the reflection of the lone bonnet in the mirror on the wall above her head, the same mirror that had previously reflected the three smiling faces. The contrast between the two images highlights the drastic change that has come over Little Red Riding Hood. The posture of the little girl sitting on the floor hugging her knees, her face hidden in her arms, is reminiscent of Donatello Berlendis's illustration of the fearful protagonist of Chico Buarque's *Chapeuzinho Amarelo* (Little Yellow Hat, 1979), who is as yellow as her hat, but the latter's withdrawal from life is the result of unfounded fears, of a wolf that does not exist. Clément and Forestier's Little Red Riding Hood, in contrast, must confront a very real fear, and it is some time before she is able to talk about what happened, thus ensuring that the imprisoned wolf is condemned for his crime. This Little Red Riding Hood must also overcome her feeling of guilt. This picture book originated from Forestier's serious reserves with regard to the moral at the end of Perrault's tale. She feels that the moral inappropriately solicits guilt when, in fact, children who have been the victims of sexual abuse at the hands of an adult are already traumatized and suffering from guilt. Clément and Forestier absolve the fairy-tale heroine of the blame that was laid upon her by the classic versions of the tale.

Although the story ends on a happy note, it does not provide a typical fairy-tale happy ending in which everything is suddenly made right on the last page. It is only because the little girl finally brings herself to speak the truth that the wolf is sentenced to be hung from his hind legs and the grandmother is restored to them. The final double spread shows the grandmother being retched up by the suspended wolf into the welcoming arms of her daughter and granddaughter, so that the three generations of women are once again united, as they had been in the mirror, although this time Little Red Riding Hood is not wearing her red bonnet. It will take some time before the young girl is ready to don once more her grandmother's gift. The grandmother, too, needs time to recuperate. The mother, who alone wears the hat that symbolizes womanhood, has her arms around the older and younger generation in a protective gesture. As they hug one another tightly and tenderly on the verso, the wolf hanging on the recto seems to be forgotten. One senses that together they will indeed overcome the traumatic events and return to a normal life in the Cité des Bergeries.

This contemporary cautionary tale is a collective warning to all children and to society in general. Instead of keeping the appalling incident secret, everyone decided to get it out into the open so that it would never happen again. That is why life in the Cité des Bergeries can resume "with its joys and its cares." The moral of this story about sexual assault and male violence is made explicitly clear, and it has a great deal of relevance for today's society. Crimes of this nature must not be hushed up, but discussed openly, so that the perpetrators can be brought to justice and the victims given the care and support they need to fully recover. Perhaps the moral of this retelling also implies a criticism of the way in which critics have often ignored the true meaning of the story of the *other* Little Red Riding Hood.

Although Clément and Forestier's picture book confronts the grim realities that face little girls alone, it does have a happy ending. When the subject of sexual abuse is dealt with in texts marketed primarily for young adults, the mood is often much blacker and the tone more pessimistic. A prime example, published the same year as *Un petit chaperon rouge,* is the tale "Wolf," by the American young adult author Francesca Lia Block. The dark, powerful story is taken from her revisionary fairy tale collection *The Rose and the Beast* (2000), which was targeted at a young adult audience but is widely read by adults as well. The anonymous protagonist is by no means the naive, innocent heroine of either the classic tale or contemporary retellings like *Un petit chaperon rouge.* As Block's protagonist puts it herself, she is "not a victim by nature" (104), and her first lines warn readers, in case they don't share her knowledge of life, that "it be a wicked wicked world out there" (101). This Riding Hood is a disillusioned, streetwise teen who has experienced life's knocks, is old beyond her years, and expects little of life. She lives in a condo in Los Angeles with her mother, a would-be actress, and her father, who has been raping her for years. The young narrator blames America's obsession with sex, the "same old boring boring story America can't stop telling itself," for the large number of runaways that are involved in drugs and prostitution on the streets in order to avoid child abuse at home (103). Her predilection for the dry, hot, barren desert, where her wise woman–grandmother lives, lies in the fact that it purifies one of thoughts of love. Block's Riding Hood is a runaway who goes to her grandmother's to escape her father, fearing he believes that she finally shared her frightful secret with her mother.

As in Gillian Cross's *Wolf,* the predatory wolf in Block's retelling is the protagonist's father. Like Cassy's terrorist dad, the heroine's father is described in wolflike terms: eyes like dark slashes, a hideous tooth laugh, and a murderous intent. In this Californian retelling, however, the protagonist associates her father with the coyote howl she hears in the night, while at the same time wishing that she could make the "deep and sad but scary" sound of the coyote so that "no one would mess with [her]" (120). When this Riding Hood encounters the wolf at her grandmother's, she shoots him with her grandmother's shotgun, or so she claims, because she believes that he has murdered her mother. The grandmother, who had taught her to use a shotgun so that she could defend herself if need be, is trying to take the blame despite the girl's insistence that she did it. "Wolf" is a dark, psychological retelling in which the anonymous protagonist tells the story in the form of a journal that is full of digressions and gaps, so that we have only her incomplete, and perhaps distorted, version of events. The narrator describes life as a long, painful, inescapable dream, and the story has the feel of a fevered nightmare. Readers may have difficulty giving credence to a narrator who begins her story with the admission that people don't believe her and think she's crazy, and ends it by acknowledging that maybe she has read "too many fairy tales" and "no one will believe [her]" (125). However, the sensuous images and evocative prose create a powerful story. Although the open ending leaves readers in some doubt, Block's retelling of Little Red Riding Hood as a troubled American teen who has been the victim of abuse for years at the hands of her own father is both moving and convincing.

Authors and illustrators who retell the story of Little Red Riding Hood for adults, young adults, or a crossover audience often interpret it as a story of rape or child abuse. A few have broached the subject of abuse in a light, playful, sometimes even comical tone. Some of these versions, including Tomi Ungerer's, have come under fire from feminists. But they also include feminist versions, such as Anne Sharpe's "Not So Little Red Riding Hood," from the Irish collection *Rapunzel's Revenge: Fairytales for Feminists* (1985), in which Scarlet, a black-belt karate expert, quickly incapacitates a would-be rapist. More often, re-versions that present a tale of rape are serious and thoughtful stories, which seek to warn both children and adults of the ever-present danger of predatory males and to assist the victims of sexual violence. Such retellings have sometimes encountered censorship, as was the case with Sarah Moon's daring photographic interpretation in the 1980s.[29] Her audacious portrayal of sexual violence certainly helped to make the taboo subject more acceptable in books addressed to children. In 1996, Jack Zipes praised Moon's book for shifting "the blame for the girl's rape and/or death to the predators or to social conditions."[30] Zipes acknowledges that the tale does not have to be interpreted "as one of rape," but, like the author of *The Trials and Tribulations of Little Red Riding Hood*, published the same year as Moon's controversial retelling, many writers have chosen to cast the tale in that light.[31]

2. Contemporary Riding Hoods Come of Age

At the magic tree, she met the talking wolf, . . . and I could do nothing . . .
When she was little, it was so much easier to keep an eye on her. But now
she's growing up.

—VIVIANE JULIEN, *Bye Bye Chaperon Rouge*

Little Red Riding Hood's origin as an initiatory tale explains much of its appeal to a crossover audience. Initiatory literature has always been popular with young readers and adults alike, as it concerns the intermediary stage between childhood and adulthood. The story of Little Red Riding Hood follows the familiar pattern of an adolescent initiation or puberty rite. The three generations of women in the tale have been interpreted as representative of the successive stages of life. This interpretation was rendered very effectively for readers of all ages in *Un petit chaperon rouge*. In female initiations, the elder women assume the responsibility for the initiatory instruction of the adolescent novice. In the short story "Riding the Red" (1997), by the Jamaican-born Canadian author Nalo Hopkinson, the grandmother warns her daughter that she has "to teach her daughter the facts of life before it's too late," but the mother feels that the girl is still too young. So the old lady tries to instruct the little girl: "listen, dearie, listen to Grandma. You're growing up." When the grandmother's lesson is interrupted by the mother, who accuses her of filling the child's head with "ghastly old wives' tales" (57), the old lady explains why that is her role: "But it's the old wives who best tell those tales, oh yes. It's the old wives who remember. We've been there, and we lived to tell them" (58). When the tale is understood in the light of a rite of passage, it is clear why the grandmother plays such an important role, while the mother is relegated to a rather minor part. Most contemporary retellings respect that distribution of roles, and many increase the importance of the elder woman in the story.

It is the grandmother who makes the ritual garment that gives the little girl a new name within her community. The heroine is sent to her grandmother's on her own, separating her from her family and her community, and, notably, from her mother, as is the case in adolescent initiations. The old lady's house, where the girl is to receive initiatory instruction that will bring wisdom and maturity, is located within or on the other side of the dark woods, which is the site for initiation rituals in many traditions. Initiation ceremonies involve a ritual death, often in the form of being swallowed up by some type of symbolic monster, followed by rebirth as an adult and return to the community. The initiatory nature of Little Red Riding Hood's experience is made quite explicit in Anne Sexton's poem. The little girl and her grandmother in the belly of the wolf are compared to "two Jonahs," who have undergone a "little death" and a " little birth" (78). The Grandma in Hopkinson's "Riding the Red" understands this as well. As she puts it, "it's wolfie who gives us birth, oh yes" (60).

Sexton also describes these events in terms of a pregnancy and delivery. The wolf, who "appeared to be in his ninth month" after devouring Red Riding Hood whole, undergoes "a kind of caesarian section," and the little girl is delivered "alive from the kingdom of the belly" (78). Barbara Swann's drawing for Sexton's poem depicts the wolf, dressed in a frilly nightgown and bonnet, sleeping peacefully with his paws resting on the pregnant-looking belly that the hunter clutches as he, in Catherine Orenstein's words, "listen[s] for a fetal heartbeat."[1] In Setsuo Yazaki's retelling of the Grimms' version, the Japanese illustrator Akane Kito portrays a very similar wolf, attired in an almost identical manner, but this time sitting up in bed, smiling blissfully with his hand on his huge belly, looking very much like a woman in labor about to give birth. The pregnant-looking wolf in James Marshall's humorous picture book *Red Riding Hood* sleeps sitting in an armchair with a paw on his huge belly, while the empty box of fancy French after-dinner mints on the floor beside him comically suggests a craving not unlike that of expectant mothers. However, few illustrators have evoked the image of a pregnant wolf with the force of the stunning double spread in the Italian artist Beni Montresor's 1991 picture book, which offers a striking sonogram of the wolf's womb. It has been suggested that Montresor's controversial picture book, with its darkly disturbing psychoanalytical interpretation, is more appropriate for adults than children.[2] The intent to appeal to adults is indicated by the fact that Luciano Pavarotti provides the introduction, but the provocative picture book fascinates young children. Likening the wolf to an expectant mother alleviates the brutality of the classic tale for children, but adult readers are aware of its much deeper meaning rooted in the initiatory significance of the earlier folktale. Perrault's literary version of the story presents a truncated initiation, since the act of being swallowed by the wolf does not lead to rebirth and Little Red Riding Hood never returns home ready to join the community as an adult.

Riding the Red

Much ink has been spilled exploring the symbolism of the distinctive red headdress that is an intrinsic part of Little Red Riding Hood's name. In fact, the color red was not associated with the fairy-tale heroine until she was given a red *chaperon* (hood) by Perrault when he penned the first literary version of the tale. Henceforth the fairy-tale heroine was to be inseparable from the red item of clothing that became her identifying trademark. The form and texture of the headgear is altered in the Grimms' *Rotkäppchen,* but the velvet cap retains the red color that has become the character's most distinctive trait. The synecdochic title of the classic tale, which uses the part for the whole and designates the little girl by her hood, has the effect of reducing her to an object. In Perrault's short tale, the expression *chaperon rouge* is repeated obsessively, recurring eleven times, twelve including the title. The function of the red hood may very well have been aesthetic rather than symbolic, as Perrault was always careful to give his protagonists an eye-catching and memorable characteristic trait, for example Puss's boots or Riquet's tuff. However, that has not prevented psychologists, psychoanalysts, critics, and writers from speculating on the symbolic significance of the red hood.

Even though it is now widely recognized that the red *chaperon* was not part of the traditional folktale, it has become an archetypal motif. The selection of Little Red Riding Hood for the cover of Christian Bruel and Nicole Claveloux's *Rouge, bien rouge* (Red, very red, 1986), which appeared the same year and in the same collection of sophisticated picture books as *Vous oubliez votre cheval,* suggests that the fairy-tale heroine is the first image that comes to mind when we think of the color red. Contemporary authors who wish to individualize the fairy-tale heroine often take care to choose a modern name that retains the "original" color symbolism, and the variety of "red" names ranges from Priscilla Galloway's Ruby to Patricia Joiret's Carmina, with its seductive connotations. Many modern Riding Hoods continue to wear the distinctive red headgear, although the cap or bonnet may be replaced with a sunbonnet, scarf, peaked cap, bathing cap, cowboy hat, or any number of forms of headdress. Often they are clothed from head to foot in red, with the addition of red capes, anoraks, leather jackets, tracksuits, jogging shorts, miniskirts, leggings, sneakers, snorkeling gear, and so forth. Moreover, authors and illustrators often play up the color and underscore the symbolism attached to it. Edward van de Vendel titles his Flemish retelling *Rood Rood Roodkapje* (Red Red Little Red Hood, 2003), and, in the predominantly black-and-white woodcuts by Isabelle Vandenabeele, the only color is a very striking blood red. In this version, it is the heroine herself who chooses her name, the most beautiful name that she can imagine, "Red! Red! Red Red Little Red Hood."

Anne Sexton also insists on the color by a redundant repetition in her description of the heroine as "a shy budkin" in "a red red hood" (77). The poet further emphasizes the red color of the girl's cape in unusual similes that do not call forth the conventional connotations. The riding hood that this heroine loves is "as red as the Swiss flag" and "as red as chicken blood" (76). Perhaps Sexton evokes Switzerland because of its reputation for passivity, suggesting the submissiveness of the classic heroine. In this case, the blood color of her cape does not take on the customary meaning of shameful or sinful behavior. The allusion to chicken blood could imply that Little Red Riding Hood is a helpless victim or that she is very timid, a chicken, just as Chico Buarque's protagonist is as yellow as her hat. Borrowing an image from the famous *Peanuts* cartoon, Sexton calls the red cape that accompanies the shy child everywhere "her Linus blanket." The suggestive image evokes a little girl who is not ready to undergo the rite of passage and clings fearfully to her childhood. In Stephen Sondheim and James Lapine's Broadway musical *Into the Woods*, Little Red Ridinghood parts with her "cape as red as blood," giving it to the Baker in exchange for freeing her and Granny from the Wolf (18). The act marks her coming of age, as is clearly indicated by the set piece she sings, "I Know Things Now" (34). One of the valuable lessons she learns on her journey of growth and self-discovery is that a cape and a hood cannot protect you.

Writers and illustrators have been strongly influenced by scholars and psychoanalysts, for whom the red hood or red cap has sexual connotations. This feature has made *Little Red Riding Hood* "one of the favourite fairy tales of the psychoanalysts," as the Swedish author Lennart Hellsing rightly claims in an article devoted to Perrault's version.[3] According to Erich Fromm, the red cap symbolizes the onset of menstruation; the little girl has become "a mature woman" ready to confront "the problem of sex."[4] For Bruno Bettelheim, the red cloak represents precocious sexuality. In his pages devoted to the fairy tale, the psychologist explains: "Red is the color symbolizing violent emotions, very much including sexual ones. The red velvet cap given by Grandmother to Little Red Cap thus can be viewed as a symbol of a premature transfer of sexual attractiveness." Concluding that the girl is too little "for managing what this red cap symbolizes, and what her wearing it invites,"[5] Bettelheim blames the grandmother for passing on the power of sexual seduction to a girl who is not yet ready to deal with two-legged wolves.

A number of authors poke fun at psychologists and researchers who have belabored the question of the significance of Little Red Riding Hood's red apparel. The French author Pef begins "Le conte du Petit Chaperon rouge" (The tale of Little Red Riding Hood, 1991) by asking *why* Little Red Riding Hood was red. Among the absurd hypotheses proposed by the narrator is one that gives a humorous twist to the sexual meaning so often attributed to the red hood: it may be the "red of disgrace melting on the little riding hood" (393). These sexual innuendos are winks at adult readers, even though the nonsensical retelling is signed Pef, the pen name that Pierre Ferrier uses exclusively for his children's books. Like all the parodic works of the provocative humorist, this one is widely read by adults. Pef's final nonsensical theory concerning the little girl's red color turns the zany story into a cautionary tale for writers and their readers: "You have to be careful what you write for it is also possible that the *chaperon* was nothing but a little red light lost among all the green lights in the forest" (393). There is an absurd logic in the playful introduction of a red light into the story of Little Red Riding Hood, since its function as a fundamental warning sign makes it particularly appropriate for a cautionary tale.

In his article devoted to Perrault's tale, Hellsing considers the color symbolism, pointing out that in the seventeenth-century bright red fabric was expensive to produce and therefore reserved for the upper class and particularly the pope and his cardinals. His hypothesis that a poor country girl who dressed like a cardinal had to be punished for her vanity by being eaten by a wolf would explain why the grandmother was also eaten, as she is partially responsible for having given the red hood to her granddaughter. However, the Swedish author also puts forward a variation on the sexual interpretation of so many other commentators, namely that the color symbolizes "the red, sinful blood flowing in the veins of lovers."[6] In her study that effectively "uncloaks" Little Red Riding Hood, Orenstein offers a similar explanation: "Perrault cloaked his heroine in red, the color of harlots, scandal and blood, symbolizing her sin and foreshadowing her fate."[7]

The French illustrator Kelek "recloaks" Perrault's Little Red Riding Hood when she transplants her to the Renaissance context of Vittore Carpaccio's *La Nascita della Vergine* (*The Birth of the Virgin*). All the innocent charm of the chubby flesh that Doré and so many other illustrators obligingly bare for the wolf and the viewer-voyeur are completely hidden under the heavy blood-red hood and long Venetian-style gown of the well-clad fairy-tale heroine who has replaced the almost naked baby Mary of the original painting. Only a few highly cultured adult readers will immediately decode Kelek's sophisticated allusions to the Italian master. While the intertextual play adds a rich, intellectually satisfying level to this unique visual interpretation, it is not essential to an understanding of the artist's take on the famous tale. Kelek's picture-book edition of Perrault's tales is intended to appeal to children as well as to the adult audience that her parodic works always attract. The artist subverts the image of a girl who invites seduction in her portrayal of a Little Red Riding Hood who is covered from head to toe with red clothing and whose back is turned to hide her emotion, as she carefully keeps her distance from the wolf gazing lasciviously at her through dark glasses from the bed.

Hopkinson's provocative retelling embraces the sexual symbolism of the hood. Remembering her own encounter with the wolf, the grandmother who narrates "Riding the Red" shows that she understands the red hood's function when she says that "the red hood was [hers], to catch [the wolf's] eye" and to set in motion "the dance of riding the red" (58). In this highly original retelling, which was published in Ellen Datlow and Terri Windling's collection for adults, *Black Swan, White Raven,* "riding the red" is a colorful metaphor and transparent euphemism for the sexual act. The old lady begins to tell her granddaughter the facts of life in the following terms: "You're growing up, getting dreamy. Pretty soon now, you're going to be riding the red, and if you don't look smart, next stop is wolfie's house, and wolfie, doesn't he just love the smell of that blood, oh yes" (57). According to this old wife, girls who have reached pubescence are in particular danger of encountering the wolf.

The grandmother in "Riding the Red" seems at first to be appropriating the mother's cautionary role, in order to give her granddaughter the same advice that she tried, years before, to give her own daughter. Like so many mothers, she, too, complains that the young never listen, explaining that "they're deaf from the sound of their own new blood rushing in their ears." It is not a warning that this old wife tries to pass along, however, but a reassurance that "it comes all right again." Inevitably, the wolf will catch the girl, just as he did the grandmother and mother before her. In fact, her implication is that Little Red Riding Hood may want to be caught. The old lady's memories question the classic version of the tale, which casts the wolf in the role of a deceiver: "Some say he even tricked me into it, and it may be they're right, but that's not the way this old wife remembers it" (58). In any case, it turned out all right in the end, recounts the grandmother, who "grew up," married a nice man not unlike the woodman, and became "the model goodwife," forgetting the wolf and the fact that "riding the red was more than a thing of soiled rags and squalling newborns." Social conventions and the pressures of life molded her into the role of wife and mother, and she renounced her erotic identity. Now the old lady dreams of riding the red one more time before she dies and showing wolfie that she knows "what he is good for" (59). In this provocative retelling, it is a lesson about enjoying her sexuality that this elderly woman would like to pass on to her granddaughter as she becomes a woman.

The red color that has traditionally been associated with the fairy-tale heroine has assumed a wide range of symbolism. Kelek gives the red *chaperon* the protective role that is expressed in the 1864 definition of the English word "chaperon," used in the metaphorical sense of "the experienced married woman [who] shelters the youthful débutante as a hood shelters the face."[8] At the other end of the spectrum, Hopkinson presents it as the lure used by a pubescent girl to ensure a sexual encounter with the wolf. Although the two interpretations are diametrically opposed, in both retellings the red garment is intimately linked with Little Red Riding Hood's coming of age. That is the case in the works of many authors and illustrators who retell the tale for adults and adolescents or for a crossover audience.

Courageous Girls

The oral folktales that predate Perrault's first literary version of Little Red Riding Hood accentuate the initiatory nature of the protagonist's adventure. They present a courageous and resourceful young heroine who tricks the wolf and systematically escapes unharmed, without any male assistance whatsoever. One of the best known of these oral versions is the rather ribald and grisly tale "Conte de la mère-grand" ("The Story of Grandmother"), which was collected in Nièvre about 1885, and published in 1951 by Paul Delarue. In this tale, a girl meets a *bzou* on her way to her grandmother's. When Delarue asked the storyteller for clarification, the latter told him a *bzou* is "like the *brou,* or *garou,*" that is, the werewolf, of which the modern French form is *loup-garou.*[9] Having learned where she is going, the *bzou* takes the path of pins, while the girl takes the path of needles, although in some variants, the girl chooses the path of pins. Yvonne Verdier argues convincingly that the path of pins marked a girl's coming of age, while needles implied sexual maturity.[10] Arriving at the grandmother's house first, the *bzou* kills the old woman and then puts some of her flesh in the pantry and a bottle of her blood on the shelf. When the girl arrives, she is invited to a cannibalistic meal of meat and wine. Then she removes her clothing one item at a time and throws them in the fire before climbing into bed with the *bzou.* Realizing her danger, she tricks the bzou by pretending that she has to relieve herself. After tying a cord around her ankle, he allows her outside, where she quickly ties the cord around a tree and escapes. Orenstein rightly points out that the oral ancestor of *Little Red Riding Hood* follows a similar pattern to that of Joseph Campbell's hero quest, and suggests that its lesson, which involves a coming of age and an act of heroism, might be the same.[11] Contemporary authors seeking to present a clever, courageous, and active protagonist who has come of age often turn to the oral tradition for their inspiration.

The French author and storyteller Bruno de La Salle draws heavily from the oral tradition to tell the whimsical story of a little girl's initiatory voyage to faraway Asia to visit her grandmother in "La petite fille qui savait voler" (The little girl who knew how to fly), published in the collection *La pêche de vigne et autres contes* (Bush peach and other tales) in 1996. As a storyteller, La Salle has collected oral versions of the tale, some of which were integrated into his own *Le Petit Chaperon Rouge* in 1986. In his unusual retelling of a little girl who flies to her grandmother's Asian home because her working parents don't have time to look after her, the French storyteller, who would certainly be familiar with Delarue's research, embeds an updated remake of "The Story of Grandmother." Although it seems a very strange power with which to endow Little Red Riding Hood, La Salle is not alone in giving the fairy-tale heroine the ability to fly. Carmen Martín Gaite's novel *Caperucita en Manhattan* was inspired by Juan Carlos Eguillor's drawings of a Little Red Riding Hood flying above the skyscrapers from Brooklyn to Manhattan. Giving Little Red Riding Hood the power to fly, a transparent symbol of freedom, turns her into an emancipated girl who is ready to try out her wings. Although the Spanish novelist did not end up creating a protagonist who could fly, Sara is an independent, modern heroine who, like La Salle's heroine, is not afraid to make the long journey to her grandmother's alone. The fact that La Salle's Riding Hood has this extraordinary skill suggests that she has already undergone a degree of initiation. During her voyage, the little girl who knows how to fly like a bird learns how to swim like a fish, thanks to dolphins with whom she plunges to the depths of the sea.

La Salle blends the old and the new to create a timeless, universal tale of initiation. The oral style relies heavily on rhythm and repetition. Certain phrases are repeated throughout like a refrain, notably the magical formula that always introduces the girl's flying: "She took the two edges of her dress and flew away in the direction of her grandmother's country" (58). The repetition appeals to children, whereas adults appreciate the highly poetic, musical quality of this written "oral" tale. In a poetic passage, the long night of initiatory time is anthropomorphized, as the narrator describes the little girl caught in "the long hair of the night, the long hands of the night, the long folds of the dress of the night" (61). Archaic terms, such as *bobinette,* contrast with anachronistic details, like the large bottle of Coca-Cola that the little girl's parents give her for the journey. Although children enjoy the comical situations such details provide, for example, the fact that the little island on which the girl stops to drink her coke turns out to be a submarine that plunges to the depths of the sea, leaving her clinging the empty coke bottle as if it was "a life buoy" (58), only adults familiar with the oral tradition of the tale can fully appreciate the anachronistic and intertextual play that results from the embedding of an oral version in a modern fantasy story.

The cautionary scene in this tale, one of the rare scenes in which the father's voice is added to the mother's, hints at the sexual nature of the encounter the little girl is being warned to avoid: "Hurry up, don't be late, try to arrive before the sun sets because the night is full of unknown animals with which you would not know how to behave" (56). These parents acknowledge that their daughter is not yet ready to deal with predatory, nocturnal animals. Like so many of her counterparts, this little girl, who is already "only a little white dot" disappearing in the eastern sky, does not wait to hear the advice and then dawdles on her way, not picking flowers or chasing butterflies, but swimming after dolphins. Her encounter with the wolf takes place in a brightly lit "nocturnal city," whose shops, noise, glittering lights, and cold crowds are frightening rather than reassuring (61).

The wolf takes the form of a man, with a limp and a nice, childlike face, who accosts her as she huddles behind a tree. Asking her if she isn't cold in such a light dress, the stranger invites her for hot chocolate, and the little girl accepts. The scene is reminiscent of Fam Ekman's *Rødhatten og Ulven* (Red Hat and the Wolf), in which the protagonist also naively accepts the wolf's invitation to go to a café for a cup of chocolate with whipped cream, but in the Norwegian picture book, Red Hat is a boy who encounters a seductive she-wolf salesclerk in a ladies' clothing store in the city (plate 11). La Salle highlights the theme of orality, which is fundamental in the story of Little Red Riding Hood and especially so in versions from the oral tradition. It is important to remember that the tale of Little Red Riding Hood finds its place in the Arne-Thompson-Uther (ATU) classification system of tales under tale type 333, "The Glutton." However, it is not only the wolf who has a voracious appetite in "La petite fille qui savait voler." The protagonist of La Salle's tale embodies the oral stage of the young child. Her gourmandism leads her to drink "one hot chocolate, two hot chocolates, three hot chocolates" (the counting rhyme effect appeals to children) and to eat all the pastries in the bakery (63). As if in a wonderful dream where all our wishes come true, the little girl has only to cast her eyes on a cake and it magically appears on her plate when the man claps his hands, but the dream soon turns to a nightmare, demonstrating the danger of accepting gifts from strangers.

In his human form, this wolf figure is even more troubling than a real wolf. The narration is focalized through the man-wolf while he watches the little girl eat, and his reaction is disturbingly like that of a pedophile: "She was so pretty with her beautiful, wrinkled dress, her muddy little shoes, her dishevelled hair, her laughing eyes and mouth, that he would have liked to laugh too or to cry, to take her hand, to touch her, but he couldn't bring himself to do it" (63). Unable to control his carnal instincts, the man's desire and frustration bring about a terrible metamorphosis, which occurs several times, turning him into an animal with the shape of a wolf. Inspired by the werewolf, or "manwolf," syndrome, the scene remains faithful to the oral versions collected by Delarue, in which the little girl meets a *bzou*. At first, he is quickly able to regain his human form by lowering his eyes from the little girl. Subconsciously, the heroine seems to associate him with the wolf because when he asks her name, she replies, in jest, that she is Little Red Riding Hood. In order to show that he is also familiar with the story, the man replies in the same joking manner: "Then I am the Big Bad Wolf" (64). This metafictive play is accessible even to small children, but it is quite possible that many readers will not decode the hypertext of this story, which begins with the unfamiliar incipit "Once upon a time there was a little girl who knew how to fly" (55), until this first direct allusion to the fairy tale. The two characters do not realize they are continuing to replay the well-known story in the following lines, as the girl volunteers directions to her grandmother's beautiful country and the wolf proposes a race to see who can get there first. The wolf's cunning is given a modern twist as the man leaves the little girl asleep at the table and tiptoes out of the bakery, turning off the electricity and locking the door as he leaves.

Interwoven into La Salle's original tale are fragments of Perrault's literary version and elements of the oral tale. He embeds the scene of involuntary cannibalism from "The Story of Grandmother" and its variants. Needless to say, the grisly scene in which the young girl eats her grandmother's flesh and drinks her blood, albeit unwittingly, shocks young readers who are unfamiliar with the oral version. The author makes no attempt to attenuate the gruesome episode; on the contrary, the horror is heightened when he personalizes it by adding the narrator's description of the wolf cutting the grandmother into pieces "like a butcher" (69). Although La Salle does not make any concessions to his young readers when it comes to violence, it is a different matter with regard to inappropriate language. He retains the cat's warning that the little girl is eating the flesh and drinking the blood of her grandmother, but the animal no longer calls the little girl a "slut" for doing so (231). The sexuality of the oral tale also remains essentially unaltered. In an elaborate striptease scene that remains relatively faithful to the oral version, the little girl removes her clothing one piece at a time, from her shoes to her undershirt, and throws them in the fire, as she is instructed to do by the wolf, who tells her she won't need them anymore. What differs is the little girl's reaction, one of increasing surprise, which does not, however, prevent her from climbing obediently into bed with the wolf. She proves to be even cleverer than her predecessor because, before she can formulate the third question in the lengthy question-and-answer sequence of the oral version, she suddenly realizes that everything about this grandmother is too big to be a grandmother. Roubeyrol's black-and-white drawing of the wolf and the heroine in bed is an obvious parody of Doré's famous bed scene, but she emphasizes the beastly side of a wolf who evinces strong reminiscences of representations of the Beast in "Beauty and the Beast."

La Salle embeds a modernized reworking of the scatological happy ending of "The Story of Grandmother" and its variants in his whimsical tale. Borrowing her early predecessor's trick, the protagonist asks to go out to relieve herself, but instead of tying the string to a tree, she ties it to the handle of the toilet, so that

La pêche de vigne et autres contes, by Bruno de La Salle, illustration by Catherine Rebeyrol, © 1996 L'École des Loisirs. Used by permission of L'École des Loisirs.

when the wolf pulls the string, the sound of flushing convinces him she will return at any moment, an act that is repeated three times to create the tripartite pattern so common in folktales. This is not the only humorous note that La Salle adds to the highly dramatic scene to delight children. Even adults will be amused by the wolf's impatience, which resembles so strikingly that of a small child: as he waits, the agitated wolf chews on the pillow, swallows the feathers, and jumps on the bed. The last frightening metamorphosis of the man-wolf occurs when he realizes the little girl has tricked him. To the ending of "The Story of Grandmother," La Salle superposes elements from another variant. Although the resourceful little girl manages to escape on her own, she then seeks the help of her godfather who is armed with a large ax and opens the belly, as does the hunter in the Grimms' version as well.[12] In the Belgian picture book *Rood Rood Roodkapje* it is the heroine who kills the wolf with an ax, and one striking woodcut depicts the little girl holding a large, bloody ax behind her back, while red blood fills her grandmother's doorway and flows out into a pool on the ground (plate 12).

Although La Salle's protagonist seeks assistance, she continues to show her intelligence and to play an important role in the final events: she manages to find her godfather, who is hiding from the invader in the woods along with many of the land's inhabitants, and she devises the plan to catch the wolf.

The little girl's heroic role is heightened by the nature of the beast that she must confront. True to ancient mythologies in which werewolves represented "generalized moral evil," warning "humans to abstain from indulging bestial appetites,"[13] La Salle's modern version of the *bzou* becomes a kind of mythical monster, "large and dark and frightening" (66), which devours, destroys, and decimates everything he encounters, leaving a trail of desolation in his wake. Like everything lovely or good, the pretty, kind grandmother, too, becomes the victim of this insatiable monster. The formulaic question-and-answer sequence is subverted to address the destruction around the grandmother's house, which includes the dead bodies of many men, women, and children. This little girl must face a beast who embodies all the evil in the world, who is, in fact, evil incarnate.

The ending of La Salle's initiatory story emphasizes the theme of rebirth. The opening of the wolf's belly is borrowed from the Grimms' version, but it is presented in a very different manner. As the little girl is not devoured, it is not her physical rebirth, but rather her grandmother's, that is described. Thus it is the grandmother, and not the heroine, who comments on the darkness of the wolf's belly, comparing it to the deepest woods. The old lady undergoes her own "metamorphosis," during which she is "rejuvenated" and "made more beautiful" (79). The final scene of rebirth in La Salle's tale takes on an original aspect because not only is the grandmother delivered, but so, too, are all the beautiful things that the monster had devoured over the years. Linking personal rebirth with cosmic rebirth, La Salle invests the tale of Little Red Riding Hood with new mythological meaning.

Wise Women

The Grimms' second tale about Little Red Cap, in which the little girl and her grandmother dispatch with another wolf, without any male assistance, by drowning him in a big trough, would be much more satisfactory if it didn't constitute merely a continuation or epilogue to the first tale, demonstrating that the disobedient girl has learned her lesson and been properly socialized. The little girl and her grandmother nonetheless demonstrate their courage and resourcefulness. Although the grandmother's role in the initiation of the young girl is essential in the oral tale, as the title "The Story of Grandmother" clearly indicates, it is through her death and the cannibalistic meal that the old lady ensures her coming of age. In contemporary retellings, the protagonist often completes her rite of passage successfully with the help of her grandmother or another elderly wise woman. The oral tradition continues to be an important source of inspiration for authors who wish to present strong women in both roles.

Like Bruno de La Salle, Priscilla Galloway is both a writer and a storyteller, and in the acknowledgments of *Truly Grim Tales* (1995), she recognizes the debt that modern retellers owe to "centuries of storytellers," both "those who have told and retold, and those who have written down and collected" (ix). Although the Canadian author pays homage to the oral tradition as well, the title of her collection suggests that she is working within the literary tradition. The clever wordplay allows readers to interpret the title as meaning that these are really *Grimm* tales, although not all of the tales are inspired by *Kinder-und Haus-märchen,* or that they are really *grim* tales, that is to say, grimmer than the Grimms'. Perhaps the perceived grimness of Galloway's stories explains why libraries catalogue the book in the adult collection, despite the fact that it was reviewed as a young adult book and considered for young adult book awards in the United States and Canada.

Although Galloway claims to tell "the truth" behind the fairy tale (ix), her retelling of *Little Red Cap* is initially disorienting for readers of all ages because the title, "The Good Mother," does not educe any reminiscences of the well-known fairy tale nor is there any allusion to the pre-text in the opening lines of the story. Furthermore, from the first sentence, readers find themselves in a strange, fantastic world. Elements are borrowed from the science fiction genre to present a futuristic *Little Red Cap* set in a post "Chem Wars" period of giant carnivorous clams and cunning beasts who attack "smoothskins," the term given to humans by the other species. Only a couple of elements in Galloway's retelling are truly futuristic, however, and the spatio-temporal setting retains much of the vagueness of traditional tales. The forest is replaced by an ocean setting, as the protagonist sets out to "Grandma's island" (74), but no details allow the reader to situate it. Paradoxically, the image that this futuristic Red Cap paints of the old lady in her unconventional setting is quite traditional: "Grandma belonged in her rocking chair in the living room of the little brown house, or nestled in the quilts of her big carved bed" (75). The familiar image of the grandmother in her bed is altered, however, by the addition of one modern detail that provides the only mildly humorous moment in the tale. The old lady wears an oxygen mask, which is later donned by the beast, who hopes the badly fitting and very uncomfortable "face" will "trick the little smoothskin" (83).

The protagonist of this initiatory tale has both modern and traditional traits. The author gives her protagonist a distinctive piece of clothing—a crimson velvet cape rather than a red cap—but the motif is later updated because Ruby's close encounter with a giant clam obliges her to substitute tight leggings and a short jacket for her "precious cape" when they go to her grandmother's island (76). Janet Woolley's striking jacket illustration for *Truly Grim Tales* depicts the huge jaws of a wolf engulfing or "hooding"[14] Ruby's head (plate 13). Although Galloway's protagonist seems to be a preadolescent, the cover portrays, not a little girl, but a young woman, whose perfect features give her a Barbie look. In a humorous, postmodern touch, an animated jar of preserves stands beside her basket with its hands over its eyes and its back to the horrible scene. In contrast, Little Red Cap herself has a serene smile on her lips, which are not ruby red, but peachy pink.

It has already been pointed out that the importance of the grandmother in the tale is explained by her initiatory role. Galloway's title, "The Good Mother," suggests a shift in focus to the maternal figure, who, at best, generally plays a peripheral role in Little Red Riding Hood stories. Adrienne Kertzer points to the relative absence of the figure of Little Red Riding Hood's mother in contemporary retellings, regardless of whether they are intended for child, adolescent, or adult readers. She finds the maternal absence strange in light of the fact that the narrative pattern most familiar to contemporary readers is one in which "the mother does indeed have a role, a gesture, and a speech."[15] For his part, Zipes remarks how illustrators continue to freeze the mother in one opening illustration that depicts her with her hand raised and her finger pointed. As we have seen, the cautionary scene that constructs the "good mother" as a spokesperson of patriarchal law is absent from Perrault's version. His mother sends her daughter into the woods without so much as a word of warning, thus presenting an image of the "bad mother" or, at the very least, an irresponsible one. Although Ruby's mother is not the "good mother" of the title, she does play a more important role in the narrative than her classic counterpart. This mother has always accompanied her daughter to Grandma's house and does so armed with a rifle in case they encounter any beasts. At first Ruby's mother, a single parent, assumes the role of the heroic male rescuer, the protective father figure. The narrator recounts how, on one occasion, she saved Ruby from a giant clam by cutting her crimson velvet cape, a traumatic incident that resulted in months of terrifying nightmares.

Initially, Galloway deconstructs the traditional maternal function, but the remainder of the narrative casts Ruby's mother in a more conventional role that confirms "traditional constructions of mothers as no more than dutiful reinforcers of patriarchal law."[16] Although the girl considers her mother's profession important, it relegates her to a support role, as she is a radio operator who alerts hunters about beast attacks. The mother will send some of these hunters to Ruby's rescue toward the end of the tale. "Mum's work saved lives," says her daughter proudly, but the statement is highly ironic because that work prevents her from accompanying Ruby to her grandmother's on this occasion, thus putting the lives of both her mother and her daughter at risk (76). Albeit reluctantly, she lets Ruby set out alone to her sick grandmother's, despite her knowledge of the grave danger. In her wicker basket, this Red Cap carries, not the traditional cake and wine, but muffins and life-saving medicine. Not only is the cautionary scene of the Grimms' version retained, but further instructions are also added, including a reminder to take her stick. Despite her mother's reservations and admonitions, it seems that Ruby, like La Salle's heroine, is now old enough to make the dangerous trip to her grandmother's on her own. However, she, too, ignores her mother's warning, dawdling and picking wildflowers for her grandmother, as had their predecessor in the Grimms' version.

As in many revisionary versions by women, Galloway questions the main binary opposition of Little Red Riding Hood and the wolf. At the same time, however, her inversion of the classic tale involves a gender change that allows her to add another female dimension. The unexpected use of the feminine possessive adjective to refer to the beast takes readers completely by surprise. The "good mother" of the title is the beast that attacks the old lady and her granddaughter in order to feed her hungry cubs, and whose maternal instincts are also aroused by the little girl. At the same time, the young girl is assimilated with the "good mother" because when the beast's injury prevents her from attending to the needs of her cubs, Ruby becomes a surrogate mother, rescuing the little creatures and feeding them soybean milk out of a baby bottle.

Like many women authors, Galloway insists on the importance of the female storytelling tradition. Ruby's grandmother tells her stories about the time "when Great-grandma was [her] age" (79). She also tells her stories about beasts that talk, but these talking animals no longer belong to a bygone era of fairy tales; they are a reality in Galloway's futuristic tale. The author also casts the grandmother in the role of a wise woman. Ruby looks to her grandmother for counsel, even after the beast has swatted the pistol from her hand and she lies "like a broken doll against the cottage" (92). Because the wise old lady realizes that the beasts are reasoning, feeling beings, a peaceful solution is found. The female "smoothskins" and the female beast show compassion for one another, resolve their conflict, and come to a mutually beneficial arrangement, but their new accord is immediately jeopardized by the arrival of the male hunters and their "fire sticks" (90). Galloway deconstructs the myth of female dependence on the protective male, the heroic hunter or woodsman, and constructs a female community that questions and defies conventional cultural patterns and seeks new solutions.

Galloway's ending presents a heroic young girl who is closer to the protagonist in oral versions than to the Grimms' Little Red Cap. The author cleverly deconstructs the ending of the conventional narrative in an open ending that concludes with Ruby looking up at the beast, who holds her after she has been accidentally shot by a hunter as she attempted to screen the beast from their guns. "The Good Mother" portrays a heroine whose courage results not from a purely egoistical desire to save herself and her grandmother, but from altruistic concern for the Other, thus bringing about important social change. With her elderly grandmother's help, Galloway's Little Red Cap completes her initiatory journey after confronting the inherent tests of self-reliance and courage. However, the outcome is not the conquering of the wolf, but the overcoming of her own fear, in order to befriend and help the beast.

The fairy-tale novel *Caperucita en Manhattan* (Little Red Riding Hood in Manhattan, 1990), by the Spanish author Carmen Martín Gaite, also presents a Riding Hood who visits her grandmother for the first time without her mother. Like Ruby, Sara accomplishes an initiatory journey that involves befriending and helping the wolf, with the assistance of a wise woman. Published in the series Las tres edades (The Three Ages), created by the publishing house Siruela for readers "from eight to eighty-eight," Martín Gaite's retelling of "Little Red Riding Hood," set in New York City, is an initiatory story that appeals to children and adults alike.[17] Within the framework of the familiar fairy tale, the author deals with the difficult period of adolescence, the passage from childhood to adulthood. In this modern retelling, the classic tale constitutes an important mise en abyme that reveals the novel's fundamental meaning. *Little Red Riding Hood* is one of the first three books that Sara received as a small child, books that have marked her profoundly because they all present a message of "freedom." Their protagonists are all out in the world on their own, "without a mother or father holding them by the hand, correcting them and prohibiting things" (22–23). This modern Riding Hood longs to have the freedom of her predecessor because, when Sara goes to her grandmother's every week, her mother always accompanies her. In her drawing of one of these weekly trips, during which Sara's mother clutches the little girl tightly by the hand, Martín Gaite illustrates the mother's fears about the dangers lurking in the city streets by drawing two dark figures of running, armed thugs in a thought bubble that emanates from Mrs. Allen.

More than one contemporary Riding Hood sets off to her grandmother's after celebrating her tenth birthday. Like many authors, Martín Gaite considers ten to be a crucial age because it marks the beginning of a child's journey toward independence.[18] Sara's tenth birthday constitutes a turning point in the girl's life. The boring, official birthday party with her parents and their friends contrasts strikingly with the exciting, intimate pre–birthday party with her beloved grandmother. The present that Rebeca gives Sara acknowledges that the little girl is coming of age and needs more independence. The insightful grandmother presents the thrilled little girl with half her bingo winnings and an elegant evening bag in which to put the money. The day after her birthday her parents are called away to her uncle's funeral, giving the little girl the opportunity to make the journey from her Brooklyn apartment to her grandmother's Manhattan suburb all by herself.

Martín Gaite deliberately set out to rewrite Perrault's Little Red Riding Hood, endowing her protagonist with the characteristics that she admired in Puss in Boots and Little Thumbling, the only Perrault characters who, in her view, refuse to passively accept their fate.[19] Subverting the classic image of the fairy-tale heroine, the author presents an active Little Red Riding Hood who takes charge of her own destiny and that of her grandmother and the wolf as well. The novelist deconstructs traditional stereotypes, turning her modern fairy-tale heroine into the clever, active protagonist of what is clearly an adventure novel (the second part is titled "La Aventura"). Along with *Little Red Riding Hood,* the other two books that Sara cherishes are adventure novels with masculine protagonists: *Treasure Island* and *Robinson Crusoe.*

With its three generations of women, the Little Red Riding Hood narrative presents a rich pre-text for an author like Martín Gaite, who generally casts women in the most important roles in her fiction. To the traditional female characters, the novelist adds the eccentric Miss Lunatic, who represents yet another generation, as she is really the 175-year-old Madame Bartholdi, maternal muse of the sculptor of the Statue of Liberty. A double of the grandmother figure, Miss Lunatic actually plays a more important role in the story than either the mother or the grandmother. The little girl rejects the conventional feminine role embodied by her mother, Mrs. Allen. This is demonstrated humorously by the traditional motif of the cake, which is cleverly reworked to become an essential theme in the novel. Sara does not share her mother's passion for cakes and has no intention of using the famous family recipe, which she will inherit, to bake cakes for her children, if indeed the aspiring actress has any children. Her mother does not know how to deal with this precocious child who, ever since she was three, has been asking very strange questions for her age, questions about death, freedom, and marriage. Grandma Rebeca would like her daughter to send the little girl to her so that she can talk to her about these important matters, but Sara's mother no doubt fears the answers she would be given by her unconventional grandmother, a former music-hall singer who has had several husbands and lovers. Sara is now of an age where these important questions need to be answered. Rebeca and Miss Lunatic, in their shared wise woman role, function as mentors and advisors, initiating this curious, modern Riding Hood.

The fear that Sara, like most Riding Hoods, must overcome on her initiatory journey is attributed, by the protagonist herself, to all the fairy tales she has read. She senses that Miss Lunatic has been sent, in the manner of a fairy godmother, to help her vanquish that fear. The old lady's advice to this contemporary Riding Hood subverts the admonitions of the mother in the Grimms' version, as Miss Lunatic recommends a leisurely stroll through Central Park on the way to her grandmother's. As if to discredit even further the cautionary discourse of the traditional tale, Miss Lunatic's advice is echoed by the grandmother, who first instilled in Sara her desire to visit Central Park. Grandma Rebeca is quite fond of strolling in Morningside Park, even though it is the notorious site of the crimes of a serial killer now known as "the vampire of the Bronx" (55). Thus it is during a nocturnal stroll in Central Park, with the blessing of Miss Lunatic and her grandmother, that Sara encounters the wolf, a millionaire cake king by the name of Edgar Woolf.

Martín Gaite recounts the crucial encounter scene in the eleventh chapter, "Caperucita en Central Park." The image of the wolf is initially connected with that of the serial killer, as Sara wonders if the vampire of the Bronx has perhaps relocated to Central Park. Mindful both of Miss Lunatic's advice and the fact that the killer is still at large, the levelheaded little girl refuses to allow the disturbing appearance and attitude of the distraught stranger to frighten her, while at the same time resolving not to allow herself to be tricked. Sara's reaction to Edgar Woolf mirrors her reaction to the wolf's picture in her favorite vignette of the beloved *Little Red Riding Hood* book, that of the encounter of the heroine and the wolf in a clearing in the woods. Identifying with the fairy-tale heroine who smiles "trustingly" at the wolf, Sara admits that she shares her sentiment and has no fear of the "likeable" animal with the "good" face (23). Despite her knowledge of the tale's tragic ending, Sara is convinced that the wolf could never eat anyone and pronounces the ending of the classic fairy tale all wrong.

The protagonist of *Caperucita en Manhattan* is referring to Perrault's pessimistic version of the tale, which is both the embedded story that haunts Sara and the pre-text of Martín Gaite's retelling. However, the author is also dissatisfied with the Grimms' happy ending, pronouncing it "a band-aid solution."[20] Martín Gaite's novel "corrects" the ending of the classic tale that neither she nor her protagonist like, offering the true "happy ending" promised in the title of the last chapter. The chapter "Caperucita en Central Park" ends with Sara and Edgar Woolf walking hand in hand through the park. Martín Gaite's drawing reworks the representation of the encounter of which the heroine is so fond: now Sara is the Little Red Riding Hood who smiles trustingly at the kindly face of the elegantly dressed Woolf. In exchange for the coveted strawberry cake recipe, the little girl asks to go to her grandmother's all by herself in one of the cake magnate's limousines, like a grown-up young lady. Sara is the agent of a classic fairy-tale happy ending for her grandmother and the wolf, who will live happily ever after. The ending remains open with regard to the heroine, however, leaving readers to imagine what becomes of Martín Gaite's Little Red Riding Hood when she leaves her grandmother and the wolf dancing to return in the dark of night to the Statue of Liberty, the symbol of her newfound freedom.

Like the protagonist of Galloway's "The Good Mother," Sara is an independent Riding Hood who proves her courage and resourcefulness in the course of an initiatory journey to grandmother's that marks her coming of age. Wise women assist both heroines; they provide the young girls with the wisdom and knowledge they need to successfully complete their initiation. These two women authors subvert the classic tale by casting both the little girl and her grandmother as strong, self-reliant females who compassionately befriend and help the wolf.

One year before Martín Gaite published her Little Red Riding Hood novel, a Quebecois author, Viviane Julien, published an initiatory novel that also casts the fairy-tale heroine as a modern young girl coming of age with the help of two wise women.

Like Martín Gaite's novel, Julien's *Bye Bye Chaperon Rouge* (*Bye Bye Red Riding Hood*) was published for a crossover audience of children and adults (plate 14). It appeared, in French in 1989 and in English in 1990, in a juvenile series by Québec/Amérique, but the series' title, Contes pour tous/Tales for All, as well as the blurb on the back cover, indicates the intent to appeal to readers of all ages. The novel is adapted from a film in the ambitious series of family films Contes pour tous, by the Quebec producer Rock Demers, whose international coproductions are often better known in Europe than in North America. Filmed in Hungarian under the title *Piroska és a farkas* and dubbed in English and French, the Canadian-Hungarian coproduction was directed by Márta Mészáros in 1989. Although Demers's childhood films are meant for a general audience, they appeal in particular to viewers aged twelve to fourteen, as they explore the psyche of contemporary adolescent protagonists and address their psychological and social problems, including peer acceptance, love, loneliness, and a variety of fears and concerns about growing up. Demers seeks to provide youth with alternatives to the violent films of American cinema, but Mészáros's film paradoxically appropriates one of the most violent fairy tales to create a beautiful, thought-provoking work about a young girl's initiation. For years, Mészáros had wanted to do a Red Riding Hood film, and she feels that all her films are essentially "about little girls who try to get to the other side of the forest unscathed."[21]

As the title immediately indicates, the novel is obviously and self-consciously a Red Riding Hood story. The words "Bye Bye," a childish corruption of goodbye (also used in French) and a child's word for sleep derived from the sound used in lullabies, suggest that the heroine of this initiatory story is taking leave of her double, Little Red Riding Hood, as she grows up and leaves childhood behind. The story begins with the familiar formula "Once upon a time . . . ," but the narrator self-reflexively questions the appropriateness of the generic incipit before proceeding to start the story again with the same ritualistic formula. Despite the narrator's initial hesitations, it seems that *Bye Bye Chaperon Rouge* is to be considered a modern-day fairy tale: "So—once upon a time, there was a little four-year-old girl who lived with her mother and father high up in an apartment building in a big city" (7). The story shifts immediately into the mode of realistic fiction, as the narrator recounts the break-up of a dysfunctional urban family through the eyes of a four-year-old girl and qualifies it as a sad story about grown-ups.[22] This fairy-tale novel published in a series of "tales for all" obviously addresses a crossover audience of children and adults.

The Red Riding Hood of this modern tale is a girl with flaming red hair, by the name of Fanny, played in the film by six-year-old Fanny Lauzier.[23] The choice of such a young actress is surprising in light of the fact that, with the exception of the odd flashback, the main action takes place when Fanny is ten. The little red cloak that the four-year-old had worn to their new home in the forest after the separation of her parents has now been replaced by a warm red cape with a hood that the ten-year-old dons on chilly days for her visits to her grandmother's. To mark her coming of age, Fanny's tenth-birthday present from her mother is "a pretty red dress, light as a spring breeze," which the girl finds the very night the wolf pays her a nocturnal visit (45).

Like the heroine's red outfit, other familiar motifs are blended with modern elements to create an initiatory tale that is at once traditional and contemporary. The faraway forest and the quaint house to which the four-year-old girl and her mother journey is described like a classic fairy-tale setting, but they take an airplane to get there and the charming house in the woods is actually the meteorological observation post where Pamela will take up her new career. Julien does not portray the terrifying dark wood of classic fairy tales, but a beloved forest that inspires absolutely no fear, and where the young girl feels entirely at home. In fact, this Little Red Riding Hood possessively considers the forest "hers" and the well-known path that leads to her grandmother's is "'her' path" (13). This familiarity is the result of her initiation to the forest and all its flora and fauna by her grandmother. But it is does not prevent Fanny's mother from worrying about her daughter when she has to go to the city on business. The cautionary scene echoes that of the Grimms', but Pamela delivers it while leaning out of their old white jeep (10). Although the little girl promises to obey, her great-grandmother tells her daughter later that day that their Fanny has not taken the forest path and has ignored "their" advice. It would seem that all the women in the family have taken on the mother's cautionary role and reiterated the same admonition.

Many women authors insist on female lineage and matriarchal bonds in their retellings of this classic tale that presents three generations of women, but Julien goes a step further by adding a fourth generation. The great-grandmother doubles the grandmother figure, but her role, like that of Miss Lunatic in *Caperucita en Manhattan,* is even more important. This deviation from the classic tale is announced in the first few lines of the novel, where *Bye Bye Chaperon Rouge* is described as the story of "a little girl, her mother, her grandmother, her great-grandmother, and a wolf" (7). Although one might expect the maternal lineage to be stressed since Fanny lives with her divorced mother, it is her paternal grandmother and great-grandmother who live in the forest. From the armchair that she hasn't left in years, appropriately described in terms of "a throne," the centenarian great-grandmother is an omniscient matriarch who, according to the narrator, "saw, heard, and knew everything that went on in the forest," especially if it concerned her little Fanny (24). This wise old great-grandmother, who always knows when the girl is in danger, appears to be a kind of witch, in spite of the fact that the author tells us in the French version that this is not a story about witches.[24] In any case, she is not the conventional evil witch of classic fairy tales. Her familiar is not a black cat, but a white owl, whose siesta is interrupted at the same moment as hers by the sudden intuition of Fanny's danger. Although the other women in the family do not share the omniscience of the centenarian, they, too, have intuitive powers that are out of the ordinary. The great-grandmother, using her exceptional telepathic powers, calls all the others to Fanny's rescue at the end of the novel.

Julien presents a matriarchal culture in which knowledge is passed, in a traditional fashion, from one generation of women to the next. Each of the women in *Bye Bye Chaperon Rouge* is responsible for a different aspect of Fanny's education, ranging from the pure sciences that her mother teaches her to a more occult science, encompassing "all the secrets of the forest," that she learns from her great-grandma (35). When a teacher and schoolchildren, who are on a field trip to the forest, express their surprise that Fanny doesn't go to school, her grandmother defiantly defends her education, obviously convinced that it is vastly superior to formal instruction. The modern concept of home schooling is linked to the traditional transmission of knowledge. Fanny looks to both her grandma and her great-grandma for guidance, but, as in the *Red Riding Hood* published by the Merseyside Fairy Story Collective in 1972, there is a particularly strong bond between the young heroine and her very old and very wise great-grandmother. Although she is already a centenarian when she dies at the end of the story, the narrator suggests that the old lady had died prematurely, "taking all her secrets with her—the vast knowledge she'd only had time to share part of with little Fanny" (111). Julien's retelling confirms the observation, in an article devoted to Jacques

Ferron's "Le petit chaperon rouge," that Quebecois authors tend to present works in which the protagonist is a young person who learns from the experience of his or her elders.[25] The powerful connection between the young girl and the older women of her family, and especially the great-grandmother, is particularly significant in the Quebecois context, reflecting the strong desire to preserve Quebec's cultural heritage. The wisdom and knowledge transmitted to Fanny by her elders will ensure the successful outcome of her initiatory journey. The grandmother assures the great-grandmother that she has taught the little girl enough so that their little lost Fanny can "find her way again" (25).

Julien's novel is a contemporary coming of age story. Like Martín Gaite's protagonist, Fanny celebrates her tenth birthday early in the narrative. The day the story really begins marks a decisive turning point in the young girl's life. That day, the great-grandmother pronounces the words that provide the epigraph to this chapter. Her observation confirms that their little Fanny is no longer so little, that "she's growing up" (24). Although she does not fully understand why, the protagonist views her life differently as of that day, "as if the sudden intrusion of the wolf, of Nicholas, and of the man in the forest had shaken her certainties" (47). Since the age of four, Fanny has led a sheltered life in the forest, with only her female family members for company, and in a single day she meets three male figures who will have a profound influence on her life. Fanny is entering adolescence and discovering her sexuality. She is at once delighted and troubled by the interest of the schoolboy Nicholas, and she feels slightly uneasy being alone with him. Likewise, she is disturbed when the wolf pays her compliments, caresses her, and wants to share secrets with her and show her wonderful things at night. In her naïveté, Fanny wants to know why it has to be at that particular time.

Other signs indicate that this day marks the end of Fanny's childhood. The cherished nightly ritual, during which her mother would sit by her bed, caressing her hair and singing her to sleep with a lullaby, is skipped for the first time. Fanny is not yet ready to give up such childish things entirely, however. Late that same night, after her mother's return from a secret rendezvous with her lover, Fanny wants to hear her favorite story and falls asleep listening to it with her hand on her mother's arm. The little girl may be growing up, but she still needs her mother. That night, the wolf's silhouette can be seen clearly outlined against the full moon above Fanny's window. Although the protagonist doesn't see him, the presence of the wolf, a symbol of male sexuality, disturbs the little girl's sleep and sends her in search of her mother.

Two stories embedded in the novel function as mises en abyme that mirror Fanny's story and mark important moments in her initiation. The first is the beloved story that she asks her mother to tell her, a narrative that begins in a similar manner to the heroine's own story on the first page of the novel. The embedded story calls to mind her happy childhood and describes the little girl's first trip to the circus, where, under the big top, she saw a very beautiful tightrope walker in a costume of red feathers, which is not unlike Fanny's beautiful new red dress, with its equally airy quality. Like the dream fragments in Gillian Cross's *Wolf*, this incomplete story (Fanny falls asleep before her mother finishes) provides a flashback to the protagonist's early childhood. Fanny's attachment to this particular narrative is ironic for readers familiar with the film version, where viewers learn that this Little Red Riding Hood is fatherless because he ran off with the attractive trapeze artist in red. The second story embedded in the novel is told to Fanny by the wolf after the little girl confesses that she can't fall asleep because her mother always gives her a goodnight kiss and tells her a story. The situation of the classic tale is thus reversed, as the wolf crawls into bed with this Little Red Riding Hood at her request, in order to tell her a bedtime story. In this scene, the male figure of the wolf replaces the mother in Fanny's life. The wolf's story is a version of *Little Red Riding Hood* that reflects and merges with Fanny's life story, but neither Fanny nor readers will ever know how his rendition ends, as once again the story is left unfinished when the heroine falls asleep. The emblematic stories embedded in the narrative self-reflexively punctuate important moments in this Riding Hood's journey toward womanhood.

The night of the wolf's visit is described as a "strange night" during which time becomes elastic, that is, an initiatory night (47). It marks the beginning of the heroine's quest for new knowledge. Subsequently, Fanny starts asking questions that she's surprised she never thought to ask before, notably about love and relationships. Unlike Sara's mother in *Caperucita en Manhattan*, Fanny's mother tries to answer her questions about love, explaining frankly how it can be both "wonderful" and "cruel" (48). She tells the young girl candidly and categorically that her father will never be coming back. Adolescence brings with it a new estrangement from her mother. Like so many adolescents, Fanny experiences a sense of loneliness and of being misunderstood and unloved by those close to her. The girl's anger and resentment come to a head one dark, cold day at the beginning of winter when her mother refuses to take her to the city and tells her to visit her sick grandmother. It is in this state of emotional crisis that the young girl sets out on her final trip to her grandmother's, a visit that adheres much more closely to the classic tale and completes Fanny's initiation.

The initiatory nature of Fanny's adventure is evident from the fact that all of a sudden the young girl starts getting lost in her familiar, beloved forest, which has now become the deep, dark, and hostile woods of tales and legends. She is no longer able to orient herself with the signs her grandmother has taught her: the direction of the clouds, the moss on the trees, and so forth. The strange sensation of being lost in the familiar setting engenders a new fear that the girl had previously never experienced in the forest. The encounter of the talking wolf at the magic tree the day her mother goes to town marks the beginning of a series of strange events that completely transform Fanny's routine trips to her grandmother's. Unlike most retellings, *Bye Bye Chaperon Rouge* does not recount a single visit to the grandmother's house, but expands the tale by superposing a number of trips over a period of several months, resulting in an intricate pattern of repetitions and variations. Julien does not limit herself to the common tripartite structure of fairy tales, but describes five different trips, each involving an encounter with the wolf and each more dramatic than the previous one, building to the climactic final visit that most closely resembles the classic version and culminates in the same terrifying events. After her escape from the wolf's den, life returns briefly to normal and a period of rather anticlimactic calm follows, during which the protagonist resumes her routine visits to her grandmother's. This narrative strategy heightens the drama of the last suspenseful visit, when the terrifying encounter with the wolf takes place in her grandmother's bed.

The traditional motifs retained in the novel are generally transfigured so that they are at once familiar and strange to the reader. The flowers Little Red Riding Hood picks on her way to her grandmother's offer a prime example. The wolf leads Fanny to a field full of extraordinarily beautiful and extremely rare flowers unknown even to Fanny's grandmother, who is an expert on the forest's flora. Variations on such well-known motifs offer new and innovative interpretations. In one scene, for example, the motifs of basket, flowers, and wolf are transposed so that the wolf carries a flower from the magic tree in his mouth to the little girl who is taking laundry off the clothesline and putting it into a wicker basket. In this initiatory novel, flowers become a symbol of the wolf's courtship of Fanny, as he consistently uses flowers to woo the girl. The wolf's first question when he meets Fanny is to ask gallantly if she would like one of the huge, red blossoms that cover the magic tree. The magic tree and the talking wolf, mentioned in a single breath by the great-grandmother, remain closely linked throughout the story. Regardless of the path she takes to her grandmother's, Fanny always ends up at the magic tree, where the wolf appears shortly thereafter as if by magic. The true magical nature of the tree lies in its mysterious red flowers, whose petals open briefly to conceal faces that seem to reflect the viewer's deepest desires. In the beautiful flowers, Fanny first sees what she believes is her father's face and then that of the ornithologist, whereas the wolf sees Fanny's face. Like all the flowers that the wolf conjures up for Fanny's pleasure, the water lilies in the mysterious pond also appear to be magical, parting of their own accord to allow the little girl to swim through.

The mysterious pond deep in the forest becomes the site of an initiatory ritual, which subverts the undressing scene of "The Story of Grandmother" and its variants. Somewhat sensually, Fanny removes her clothing one piece at a time—large red hat, blouse, and red skirt, but she does it for her own pleasure, after the wolf has abandoned her. The scene is reminiscent of a passage in the French picture book *Mina, je t'aime* (Mina, I love you), where the protagonist removes some of her clothes to wade in the stream on the way to her grandmother's, but Fanny removes all her clothes to swim in the pond. The English language edition of the novel attenuates the sensuousness of the scene for young readers by adding an item of clothing to the list, a scarlet bodysuit that she does not take off. Fanny experiences an immense happiness during this idyllic scene, which is an important step on her path to self-knowledge. Assuming the function of an initiatory tool, the pond constitutes a liquid mirror, in which the girl not only contemplates her reflection, but also into whose depths she plunges.

The absence of the father in *Little Red Riding Hood* explains Mészáros's childhood fondness for the Grimm tale and the special connection that continues to attach her to this story of a fatherless adolescent trying to cope in an alien world. The filmmaker never knew her own father, a sculptor who died in a Soviet prison as a result of Stalin's purges during her childhood. "Children who have lost their parents have fantasies about what they look like," says Mészáros, who understands this psychological phenomenon very well. As an adolescent, Fanny still suffers deeply from her father's absence. She mistakenly believes that the ornithologist is the father she has not seen since she was four. This confusion is heightened in the film, where the same actor, Jan Nowicki, plays both characters. Mészáros adds a further dimension to the father figure by having Nowicki's eyes transposed to the face of the wolf, who, in this retelling of the tale, "is both good and bad." Although the wolf is cast as "a sort of father figure," he is first and foremost the seducer.[26] The obvious father figure is the ornithologist, who has replaced Fanny's father in Pamela's life and would like to do so in the girl's as well. Like Cross's novel *Wolf*, Julien's retelling of *Little Red Riding Hood* portrays a girl who must come to terms with the past and the absence of her father. At the beginning of the narrative, Fanny studies a photograph of her father, reminding us of the heroine of *Wolf* contemplating the photo of her father, who also left her mother and her when she was very young. In both novels, the absent father remains shrouded in mystery for the protagonist. Like Cassy's Nan, Fanny's paternal grandmother disapproves of her mother, whom she blames for the departure of the heroine's father, her only child. *Bye Bye Chaperon Rouge* is a coming of age story in which the adolescent protagonist must also deal with divorce and parents taking new partners.

Julien's Little Red Riding Hood blends some of the characteristics of the active, courageous protagonist of "The Story of Grandmother" and its variants with the naive heroine of the classic tale. Like many young children today, Fanny is quite independent and often left to her own devices because her single, working mother is busy with her career and her boyfriend. To a certain extent, Julien subverts the stereotypical image of the female as the weaker sex. Contrary to Nicholas, Fanny experiences absolutely no fear wandering about the forest alone. When the little girl understands that she is really a prisoner in the wolf's den and not the victim of a joke or a game, she is frightened, but she is also angry and does not hesitate to threaten the wolf. It does not take the little girl long to realize that the wolf has brute strength on his side and that anger will not work, so she decides to try cunning. Forcing herself to smile through her tears, Fanny asks coquettishly for permission to go to the stream to wash, a trick not unlike the one used by the protagonist of "The Story of Grandmother." However, this wolf is not as gullible as his predecessor, and the little girl is not quite clever enough because her eyes light up with the hope of escaping when he agrees to bring her water, immediately alerting him to her plan. When she meets the wolf after her escape from the den, Fanny is angry, rather than afraid, and she is determined never again to fall prey to his treachery.

Fanny's courage and independence contrast with her vulnerability, which is accentuated by the fact that she has to be rescued on more than one occasion by a male character. In Julien's novel, the Grimms' hunter is replaced by two male figures, who take turns coming to Fanny's rescue when she is lost: the ornithologist, who constitutes a more ecologically acceptable variant of the hunter even though he is still armed with a gun, and the ten-year-old city boy Nicholas. When the ornithologist comes to Fanny's rescue a second time, he teasingly asks who used to rescue her before he arrived on the scene, to which the annoyed girl retorts that she never used to get lost. However, it is significant that the ornithologist and Nicholas are often acting as the great-grandmother's agents when they rescue Fanny. The wolf takes his place among the other male figures who come to the lost girl's rescue. He materializes magically at strategic moments when the adolescent is most vulnerable and in need of a confidant because she is lost or feeling lonely, depressed, neglected, or misunderstood.

Young readers easily decode many of the intertextual allusions to *Little Red Riding Hood*. When the wolf asks Fanny at their first encounter if she doesn't recognize him, and then identifies himself as "the wolf," the little girl immediately decodes the allusion and exclaims: "Just like in the story!" (15). It isn't necessary to specify the title, as they both know, as will even the youngest readers, to which story she is referring. At a subsequent encounter in the forest, the intertextual play becomes more complex, as the allusions to the familiar dialogue contain echoes of the story of Little Red Riding Hood as well as reminiscences of their previous meeting, leaving readers unsure whether they should be interpreted as intertextual allusions to the well-known tale or as intratextual references to the first encounter of Fanny and the wolf. Adults, adolescents, and children will appreciate the intertextual allusions in *Bye Bye Chaperon Rouge* on different levels. While the pet lamb that accompanies this Little Red Riding Hood everywhere is apt to evoke reminiscences of Mary Josepha Hale's popular nursery rhyme "Mary Had a Little Lamb" for young readers, adults are more likely to associate it with the fable "The Wolf and the Lamb." Curiously, even Fanny's lamb seems to have no fear of the wolf and follows docilely along behind them. Subconsciously, the little girl seems to be aware of the wolf's dangerous nature because she has a troubling dream in which the wolf suddenly appears while she is picking flowers in the meadow and devours her pet lamb, a scene reminiscent of Jean de La Fontaine's. Although not developed in the sophisticated manner of the dream sequences that haunt the protagonist in Cross's *Wolf*, Fanny's dream has the same premonitory function.

Although the protagonist is the only one who sees the wolf, he is presented as a real wolf, which, in Fanny's words, looks "a bit like a dog" (15), an image reinforced by the photos from the film, in which a malamute was cast in the role.

Unlike the anthropomorphized wolves of many contemporary retellings, he behaves like a real wolf, with the exception that he can talk. This does not prevent him from playing the conventional role of seducer, a role that is obvious to the reader, if not to Fanny, very early in the novel. As they walk together during their first meeting, the wolf solicitously compliments the little girl, telling her she is "the loveliest creature in the whole forest" (17). The wily wolf is careful not to alarm the innocent little girl or to show his true colors until he has achieved his goal of possessing Fanny and she is safely imprisoned in his den. Only when the girl rejects his advances in the den does the wolf show his menacing fangs to remind her that she is addressing a wolf. At the same time, the talking wolf gives a fairy-tale atmosphere to what is otherwise a realistic novel. In this regard, Julien's retelling is not unlike the novel *Caperucito azul* (Little Blue Riding Hood, 1975), by the Ecuadorian author Hernán Rodríguez Castello, with which it shares some of the characteristics of magic realism. While children accept without question the talking wolf and the supernatural events that involve him, adult readers will generally search for a logical explanation. Fanny is the only one who actually sees the wolf; the others, with the exception of the great-grandmother, refuse to believe that there is a talking wolf in the forest. Adult readers are likely to be skeptical as well, seeing in Fanny "the little girl who cried wolf."

Nicholas's urban world, which Fanny's grandmother has warned her against, is contrasted with Fanny's world of the forest, and an opposition is set up in the French-language edition between "his" city and "her" forest. The initial polarization gradually disappears as the two children initiate each other to their respective worlds. When Fanny initially shows Nicholas the extraordinary tree, he automatically seeks a rational explanation in technology, a hidden remote control, refusing to believe that it is magical because "magic . . . only happens in fairy tales!" (37). For a time, Fanny decides there is no sense sharing her forest's secrets, especially that of a talking wolf, with this skeptical city boy. Similarly, Fanny is initially skeptical about the wonders of the city, "cars, stores, train stations, an airport, movie theatres" (35), but her breath is taken away by the fabulous view of Nicholas's city at night, with its thousands of twinkling lights. Filled with wonder, Fanny compares the lighted central square to the magic tree, so that the city is transformed into a beautiful, glittering fairy-tale world. In fact, the city, where she was born and lived until the age of four, has haunted Fanny's dreams. Although she doesn't remember ever having gone, Fanny's subconscious is haunted by the circus, which Nicholas considers the city's greatest wonder. In a dangerous nightly jaunt in the ornithologist's jeep, Nicholas takes Fanny to the circus, where he initiates her to "another world, a magical universe beyond her wildest dreams" (93). Nicholas is initiated with equal success to Fanny's forest. At the end of the novel, Nicholas drags Fanny outside in search of the magic tree, perhaps in a solicitous attempt to take her mind off the death of her great-grandma. When they discover only a tree like all the others, its bare branches covered with snow, Nicholas reassures Fanny of the magic tree's existence. The young boy thus plays a crucial role in Fanny's initiation.

Fanny's last trip to her grandmother's stands out from the others, as she has a double encounter with the wolf in the woods. In the first instance, the wolf who pops out of the bushes turns out to be Nicholas wearing a wolf's mask. The scene is reminiscent of a passage in Cross's novel, in which her mother's boyfriend frightens Cassy with a wolf's mask. In *Wolf*, Robert admonishes his father for playing such a dirty trick on the heroine, just as Nicholas immediately realizes his joke was in poor taste. The second encounter is with the "real" wolf, who incites Fanny's anger rather than her fear. Although she does not at first notice the ominous signs at her grandmother's house, such as the unusual silence, Fanny does sense that something is wrong. She feels a pang of anguish as she approaches the vague form in the bed, because the girl no longer recognizes her grandmother. The familiar dialogue is integrated with some divergences. As the wolf becomes more excited, he begins to falter and then to deviate from the original script. By the time they get to Grandma's big hands, he replies: "The better to touch you with, dear Fanny" (105). The wolf's Freudian slip reveals his lustful desire to caress the young girl. When the covers slide down over the wolf's muzzle, the horrified little girl glimpses the wolf's fangs shining in the dark and exclaims: "Grandma, what a dreadful mouth you have!" This time the wolf's line remains unchanged, as does the tragic outcome.

All the fear and violence of the dramatic scene in the classic tale is eliminated and the initiatory nature of the event is highlighted. Rather than succinctly report that the wolf gobbled the little girl up, the narrator describes in some detail the girl's descent into the wolf's belly. As had her grandmother before her, Fanny has the sensation of passing through "a long, dark tunnel." The journey into the wolf's belly is described in transparent initiatory terms. In this Little Red Riding Hood's *descente aux enfers*, the traditional symbol of stairs is developed in an explicit manner. Fanny finds herself on "something that looked like a long stairway," not unlike the long staircase that leads to her grandmother's house, only this time it descends rapidly instead of going up steeply (108). After a seemingly endless journey through complete darkness and absolute quiet, the little girl is guided by a red light in the distance, the light in which every initiation culminates. On this journey that ends in enlightenment and the revelation of a mystery, the girl's wise grandmother is her guide. The light at the end of the tunnel is the wolf's heart, where Fanny's smiling grandmother waits for her with outstretched arms. The emphasis on the wolf's beautiful, red heart suggests that devouring Little Red Riding Hood is not just an act of brutality but also one of love, the ultimate act of love according to psychoanalysts. Julien subverts the image of the frightened little girl in the wolf's dark body, as Little Red Riding Hood herself describes the experience in the Grimms' tale. Fanny feels no fear as, nestled in her grandma's arms, she admires the wolf's beautiful heart. When the little girl asks her grandmother if they are dead, the old lady replies simply: "We're in . . . the wolf's stomach." Like Jonah in the belly of the whale, Fanny and her grandmother await an initiatory rebirth in the belly of the wolf. Death is portrayed as something beautiful and not something to be feared. Fanny admits to her grandmother that she'd "imagined death differently" (109). Julien's serenely beautiful description of the inside of the wolf's belly reminds us of Beni Montresor's controversial illustrations of a blissful Little Red Riding Hood in the red belly of the wolf. Like Montresor's picture book, Julien's novel takes the fear out of death, which, for generations of children, has been symbolized by the wolf. Julien captures the tale's initiatory meaning, while simultaneously enriching it with contemporary psychoanalytical ambiguity.

The event remains shrouded in mystery for readers, as well as for the characters, with the exception of those directly involved in the initiation. The great-grandmother's death is not explained by any specific physical cause. The wolf does not eat her, but she may have died of shock or exhaustion. Before her death, she uses her last ounce of strength to call all those who love Fanny to the little girl's rescue. In three fragmented sequences or tableaux, separated by asterisks, the scene shifts rapidly to three different parts of the forest, where Fanny's mother, the ornithologist, and Nicholas are responding to the old lady's call. The ornithologist is the first to arrive and, directed by great-grandma, goes to the bedroom and fires a shot from his rifle. The mystery enshrouding this scene is symbolized, as in *Mina, je t'aime*, by the heavy curtain that hides the bed from view. A thud is followed by a strange, unidentifiable cry, but the narrator's question

"Was it the wolf?" is left unanswered (109). When the curtain is pulled back, Fanny lies in the arms of her grandmother. The mother denies that there was ever a wolf, but the knowing look the girl and her grandmother exchange indicates otherwise. The words the ornithologist murmurs, barely heard by Fanny, offer yet another interpretation of events: "They say there's a wolf inside every one of us" (111). Interestingly, in Cross's novel *Wolf*, the mother's boyfriend also voices the same theory of "the wolf inside you" (38). Readers of *Bye Bye Chaperon Rouge* are left to draw their own conclusions about the mysterious wolf. Is the wolf real? Is the wolf merely a figment of Fanny's lonely imagination? Is he a symbol of her fear? Is the wolf a symbol of sexuality, including her own awakening sexuality? Julien's refusal to offer an answer results in an open-ended narrative. By presenting a story that can be read on different levels and interpreted in multiple ways, Mészáros and Julien oblige viewers and readers of all ages to engage in their own dialogue with both the retelling (film or novel) and the traditional tale.

Bye Bye Chaperon Rouge's open ending is a very optimistic one. All the characters are reconciled in the final, joyous reunion at grandma's house, which marks the heroine's coming of age and a new maturity in her relationships with others. Fanny warmly thanks the ornithologist, who will fill the void left by the absent father; she kisses Nicholas, who may become more than a friend; and she and her grandma are hugged by Fanny's mother, promising a new harmony between the three generations of women. The centenarian great-grandmother will be missed profoundly, but she has fulfilled her role and overseen Fanny's initiation. Julien's novel renews with oral versions of the tale that focus on the intimate relationship between the little girl and her grandmother, as in "The Story of Grandmother," whose title clearly suggests the old lady's central role.

In Perrault's version, both the old woman and the young girl are indiscriminately killed, and in the Grimms' version they are both indiscriminately saved; in oral versions, the older woman (either grandmother or mother) dies and the young girl survives. This is the ancient initiatory pattern in which the new generation must take over from the old. Although the very old great-grandmother passes away, *Bye Bye Chaperon Rouge* returns to this pattern. Mészáros and Julien actualize the traditional tale without losing the mythical meaning and sexual innuendo of the original. An increasing number of retellings, often by women, do not demythologize or demystify the traditional tale but provoke a profound emotional and imaginative response by making the mythic and initiatory elements meaningful for contemporary readers.

Little Red Riding Hood in Love

Since girls' rites of passage mark the age of puberty, and therefore a newfound sexuality, it is not surprising that the tale of Little Red Riding Hood is often turned into a love story. Some of the initiatory tales examined thus far also introduce a romantic element into the plot. This section deals with Riding Hoods who succumb to the wolf's charms and fall in love. The "very strange fairy tale," which the first-person narrator of the Slovenian poet Vitomil Zupan's poem "A Fairy Tale" claims to have witnessed and recounts in a reportage style, is an unusual version of *Little Red Riding Hood*, in which "somebody fell in love with somebody" (298). A collective "they" interferes and the poet conjures up a humorous procession in pursuit of the lovers: bloodhounds are followed by officials, and lastly come coroners in a wagon. Only then do allusions to *Little Red Riding Hood* suggest that the fairy-tale heroine is the "somebody" who fell in love. The one event retained from the classic tale is the wolf's devouring of the grandmother, told succinctly in a single line. No punctuation follows the line that dispenses with the grandmother, so the unfortunate incident is linked to the subsequent lines that recount the "accident" that "the Red-cap" had on a crossroad on her way to her grandmother's. If taken literally, the accident seems banal indeed: she has dropped a pitcher of milk, creating an analogy between Little Red Riding Hood and the peasant dairymaid who drops her milk jug in La Fontaine's famous fable "La laitière et le pot au lait" ("The Dairymaid and Her Milk-Pot"). The juxtaposition of the two accidents evokes the proverb: "There is no use crying over spilled milk." The wolf has swallowed Little Red Riding Hood's grandmother, but the girl in love does not act overly concerned. Perhaps there are sexual overtones to Little Red Riding Hood's "accident." In any case, the accident creates a diversion, and while the hounds, officials, and coroners are otherwise occupied, "somebody escaped with HER." In this elliptical poem, intended for adults, the ambiguous pronouns used throughout maintain a great deal of uncertainty about characters and events. It appears, however, that Little Red Riding Hood has eloped with the wolf. The poet clearly prefers the strange version that she witnessed to the classic tale, as she pronounces it "a nice fairy tale indeed" (298). In Zupan's revisionist version, which was first published in a literary journal for adults in 1971, it would seem that Little Red Riding Hood runs off with the wolf of her own accord.

The union of Little Red Riding Hood and the wolf provides a happy ending to Zupan's retelling, but that is not always the case when the fairy-tale heroine chooses the wolf as her partner. The Swedish author Märta Tikkanen presents a different perspective in her autobiographical adult novel, *Rödluvan*. Through the lens of the well-known fairy tale, the author offers a psychological explanation of the events of her own childhood, adolescence, and married life. The maturing young woman is drawn irresistibly to the aggressiveness and the menace represented by the Wolf, an overt symbol of male sexuality. In spite of her mother's warning, she ends up marrying the Wolf. In this case, however, the union of Little Red Riding Hood and the Wolf is not a liberating experience. Marriage to the Wolf confines the protagonist to a repressive life much like her unhappy mother's. The author suggests depressingly that young girls are fated to follow the same paths generation after generation.[27] The pessimistic interpretation of the marriage of Little Red Riding Hood and the wolf, as developed in Tikkanen's novel, is generally adopted in works addressed exclusively to adults. In versions for young readers or for a crossover audience, the characters tend to be presented as a happy fairy-tale couple.

Such is the case in *Mon Loup* (My Wolf, 1995), a charming French picture-book retelling by Anne Bertier, who uses black-and-white illustrations to tell a simple love story inspired by the inseparable couple formed by Little Red Riding Hood and the wolf. The picture book is recommended for ages six years and up, and this open-ended categorization is appropriate because, in the author's mind, it is a book is for adults as well as children. The author-illustrator rightly feels that the story can be read on several levels. If the publisher's name, Grandir, which means "to grow up," reflects an intention to provide books that help children to do that, Bertier's is certainly a wonderful addition to their catalogue. A different aspect of love had been the theme of her first book, *Un amour de triangle* (A love triangle), a playful, poetic fantasy for readers age seven to seventy-seven. When Bertier decided that she wanted her second book to deal with "the feeling of love," the idea of the wolf and Riding Hood came immediately to mind. The story of Little Red Riding Hood as it had been told to Bertier as a child, that is, the "Grimm version with stones in the wolf's belly," had always seemed to her to be "horrible and terribly unjust." Why should the "poor wolf" be punished and "the disobedient Little Red Riding Hood" be saved? Feeling a need to change this outlook, Bertier's intention in writing *Mon Loup* was to create a wolf that would make people, especially girls and women, dream. This time "it would be a different affair . . . the wolf would be seduced."[28]

The use of the possessive adjective in the title immediately suggests a personal relationship between the tall, elegant wolf on the cover and the little girl who stares up at him. However, *mon loup* is also a common expression of endearment, meaning "my pet" or "my love." The protagonist of Luisa Valenzuela's "Si esto es la vida, yo soy Caperucita Roja" also intimately calls the wolf *"My* wolf," stressing the possessive adjective, which is written in italics. She gives her wolf the nickname Pirincho, but in this case the girl's familiarity creates a distance between them and, much to her chagrin, her wolf gets away (114). Bertier's simple story begins with the meeting of a girl and a wolf that she eventually decides to keep. "One day I met a wolf," writes the first-person narrator, whose name, we later learn, is Violette. The protagonist-narrator's silhouette immediately brings to mind that of Little Red Riding Hood, as she is wearing an unusual pointed bonnet and holding a bouquet of flowers. Sometimes she is also depicted with a basket—one of the fairy-tale heroine's distinctive attributes.

Violette is a sensible girl who knows it is dangerous to talk to strangers. She attributes her precaution directly to her familiarity with the story of Little Red Riding Hood. The distance she initially kept from the charming wolf is rendered eloquently in a picture that places her silhouette on the far side of the page, where she sits aloofly, her head held at a haughty angle. Although Bertier deals with the development of a romantic relationship, it is described in simple, even childish terms that are quite accessible to very young children. Once Violette realized that he was a well-bred wolf, they "began to play together." This Riding Hood and her wolf are portrayed skipping together in a humorous picture that suggests the very tall wolf is having trouble getting the hang of it, as he has tripped on his rope. As in all relationships, they did not always play happily together, however. Violette admits that the wolf sometimes became hateful and frightened her. In the facing picture, the viewer senses her fear because the wolf has grown to enormous proportions and towers menacingly over the little girl. Unlike fairy-tale characters that are either black or white, this modern wolf is more complex and realistic, having both good and bad qualities, just like any man.

To create a book about the feeling of love, Bertier deliberately chose a medium that would provide "a simple and intense drawing in which the emotions were translated by attitudes or rather a particular position of the spinal column." The simple black-and-white illustrations, in which stencils were used to create an effect of cut silhouettes, are surprisingly expressive. This retelling of Little Red Riding Hood, in which the pictures reveal more about the characters' attitudes and

Mon Loup by Anne Bertier, © 1995 Anne Bertier and Grandir. Used by permission of Anne Bertier and Grandir.

feelings than the text, bears the distinct mark of the classes that Bertier took in her youth at Sylvia Monfort's famous mime school. The ups and downs of their relationship, in particular their lovers' quarrels, are eloquently expressed in the most basic images. In one illustration, Violette stands crying near her basket as the wolf strides off with her bouquet; in another she stands with her hands on her hips angrily admonishing the wolf who stands sheepishly among her trampled flowers. Their refusal to speak to each other is conveyed by a picture of the two figures sitting dejectedly on two chairs placed back to back. When they make up, the wolf is portrayed on his knees before the little girl. The give and take of relationships is portrayed through the appropriation of motifs from the classic tale. In a charming reversal of the classic bed scene, the wolf prepares to feed Violette, who is sick in bed. Ironically, a detail from the fatal dialogue provides the manner in which the protagonist shows her devotion to the wolf: by brushing his big ears. In order to reach the wolf's big ears, the little girl has to stand on a chair and the tall wolf has to sit on the floor. The gentle humor of the simple illustrations charms adults as well as children.

Only older readers will appreciate the more subtle allusions to the classic tale. For example, the author humorously transposes Perrault's motif of the wolf's gruff voice into a love letter, in which he explains to Violette that his voice is too gruff to express such sentiments. At this point in the narrative, the protagonist abruptly changes from the impersonal demonstrative adjective *ce* (that) to the possessive adjective *mon* (my) when she refers to the wolf. In addition, the girl now writes the word Wolf with a capital letter, suggesting the importance he has assumed in her life. In retrospect, the author thinks the capital is substituted when the wolf becomes "human." He does, indeed, seem very human as he tries to gather his courage to express his feelings to the girl he loves. When he finally gains enough confidence to do so, he initiates a variation on the familiar dialogue, which is charmingly converted into a courting scene with Violette in the role of seducer. It is nonetheless the Wolf who does the devouring; the protagonist tells us that while he recited the lovely compliments, "he devoured [her] with his eyes, his eyes only." Bertier cleverly uses the French the expression *dévorer quelqu'un des yeux*, which has the figurative meaning of eying somebody greedily, to retain the climactic act of the familiar dialogue. In this case, devouring the girl is quite clearly an act of love.

On the last page, the narrator suddenly switches to the present tense and readers are given a glimpse of the happy ending to this love story. Although the author expresses their pastimes in terms of children's play, older readers will detect erotic overtones. Now Violette and her wolf spend much of their time playing and singing "Promenons-nous dans les bois" (Let's go for a walk in the woods), which is the song associated with the game "Loup y es-tu?" (Wolf, where are you?). The song brings readers full circle, in a sense, by evoking the traditional encounter of Little Red Riding Hood and the wolf in the woods. The final illustration is an aesthetically pleasing image of the graceful wolf and the dainty little girl as a dancing couple. There is a striking choreographic element to all the pictures of this illustrator who studied dance for years. The figures often look like they are dancing and sometimes are even depicted on their toes, as if they were ballet dancers. The effect is heightened by the wolf's unusual portrayal as a slender, elegant figure, so like that of a male dancer. Bertier's anthropomorphic wolf, who skips, dances, begs forgiveness on his knees, and writes love notes, offers one of the most human and charming wolves in contemporary retellings of *Little Red Riding Hood*.

The back cover displays a metafictional scene that will be appreciated only by a few adult readers who take notice of the paratext. The small image constitutes a clever mise en abyme, in which Violette/Little Red Riding Hood and the Wolf

Mon Loup by Anne Bertier, © 1995 Anne Bertier and Grandir. Used by permission of Anne Bertier and Grandir.

are seated very close together and staring into each other's eyes in front of a book that tells, or rather retells, their own story. It begins with the same words: "One day I met a Wolf," except that this time the word "Wolf" is written with a capital from the outset. The changes to the accompanying picture in the embedded book are also highly significant. The first illustration is overlooked for the second, which depicts Violette sitting on the wall keeping her distance, but now the wolf is portrayed seated on the wall next to her. Perhaps the self-reflexive illustration humorously suggests the revised manner in which this Riding Hood

Mon Loup by Anne Bertier, © 1995 Anne Bertier and
Grandir. Used by permission of Anne Bertier and
Grandir.

and her Wolf prefer to tell their love story as one of love at first sight. In spite of
the extreme simplicity of Bertier's picture book, the adult appeal is strong. Her
charming retelling of Little Red Riding Hood and the Wolf will enchant all
those, young and old, who are, or who have ever been, in love.

In her role as a romantic heroine, Little Red Riding Hood finds her way into
Japanese manga for all ages. Little Red Riding Hood in love is particularly popular in the manga known as *shoujo,* a sentimental genre for girls. "Akazukin-
chan" (Little Red Riding Hood) is the title of a story by the famous comic-book
artist Shotaro Ishinomori, which appeared in a comic given away in 1962 by the
monthly magazine *Girls' Club.* In Japanese, *Little Red Riding Hood* is translated
as "Akazukin" (literally, Red Hood), but the suffix *-chan,* which is a term of endearment used especially with children, is often added to the title, especially in
the case of picture books. Much of the story concerns the unsuccessful attempts

of a depressive, starving wolf, who is on the point of hanging himself, to catch Little Red Riding Hood and her friends. This wolf inspires only pity and laughter as each of his traps backfires and he becomes the victim of his own machinations. In a metafictional joke that will amuse adult readers, the wolf uses a copy of *Girls' Club* magazine for bait in a rope trap; it is not a girl he catches, but an angry bear.

The unlucky wolf finally manages to catch the girl and her friends, but just as he is seasoning them in accordance with a cookbook and about to put them in a large cooking pot, they are rescued by Little Red Riding Hood's boyfriend, Peter, no doubt of *Peter and the Wolf* fame. Peter is cast in the role of the Grimms' hunter, but his appearance at the crucial moment is explained in a humorous manner. The boy has accidentally put a bullet through the grandmother's window while hunting. The romantic twist given to the happy ending—Little Red Riding Hood and Peter kiss—appeals to the magazine's female readership. The ending is not so happy for the hungry wolf whose feast has been rudely interrupted and who is portrayed on the last page howling under a dangling rope as he prepares once again to hang himself.

The romantic element is emphasized even more in comics for older readers, where Little Red Riding Hood's encounter with the wolf becomes a mere excuse for a love story. A volume of the Hakusensha Lady's Comics, a series for young women about eighteen to twenty years of age, contains a story, titled "Akazukin wa ookami otoko no yume wo miru" (Little Red Riding Hood dreams of werewolf), by Shoko Hamada. The cover illustration portrays a very young Little Red Riding Hood and a harmless, doglike wolf, but the story itself presents a sexy, Barbie-like, twenty-one-year-old university student and a wolf of the charming, two-legged variety that Perrault warns against in his moral. The title is quite misleading, as there is no allusion to a werewolf in the story and nothing remains of the terrifying image of oral versions, in which the wolf is explicitly a werewolf.[29] Unhappy with her parents' plans for a traditional, arranged marriage for her, the heroine in the sexy minidress allows herself to be seduced by a young man she encounters in the street, while on the way to meet the man chosen by her parents. The roles of the girl and her seducer are symbolized by the Little Red Riding Hood doll and the wolf that they win from a claw machine. After accompanying him to a members club called the Misty Moon, she ends up making love with him. The story has an interesting twist: her seducer turns out to be her intended. A happily-ever-after fairy-tale

"Akazukin wa ookami otoko no yume wo miru" (Little Red Riding Hood dreams of werewolf) by Shoko Hamada, © 1993 Shoko Hamada/Hakusensha, Inc. Used by permission of Hakusensha and Shoko Hamada.

ending has Little Red Riding Hood going into the wolf's arms of her own ac-cord. Like Cinderella and the other heroines of fairy tales that end in marriage, these Little Red Riding Hoods are "psychologically ready to have sexual expe-riences."[30]

The Riding Hoods in comics like Hamada's have come of age and are inter-ested in meeting the wolf. So, too, are several of the Riding Hoods Tomi Un-gerer created. Like all of the Alsatian author-illustrator's works, his retellings of the popular tale are somewhat controversial and subversive. The independent heroine of "Little Red Riding Hood," in *A Storybook from Tomi Ungerer* (1974), chooses to defy social conventions and family obligations to go and live in the sumptuous castle of an unhappy, lonely wolf-Duke with a bad reputation. The situation is somewhat reminiscent of *Beauty and the Beast*, although Ungerer's homely Little Red Riding Hood is certainly no beauty and there is nothing shy about this Beast. Ungerer's picture books are generally for a crossover audience, and more than one critic has pointed to the eroticism that is often used to subvert his fairy tales for children.[31] Although young readers may miss much of the sex-ual innuendo, it is doubtful that the bright, young heroine is totally oblivious to the meaning of the debonair wolf-Duke's seductive discourse. "Come with me and I shall share with you my secrets and more of my secrets," he invites the young girl. The secrets, vaults, and treasures of the wolf-Duke and his château evoke echoes of *Bluebeard*, whose sexual allusions are also lost on young chil-dren. The wolf-Duke seems determined to rewrite the ending of *Little Red Rid-ing Hood*, so that it respects generic conventions more closely: "I'll make you happy, you'll make me happy, as in a fairy tale" (88). In the end, Little Red Rid-ing Hood and the wolf go off "to live happily ever after" (91).

Whereas Ungerer's 1969 poster of *Little Red Riding Hood*, depicting a smiling Little Red Riding Hood offering a flower from her bouquet to the lustful wolf, an-nounces the unconventional retelling in *A Storybook*, a poster he did more than twenty years later for the exhibition *Le Petit Chaperon rouge dans tous ses états* (1992) constitutes a kind of epilogue to the story (plate 15). The sensuality and sexual innuendo underlying Ungerer's reworkings of *Little Red Riding Hood* are much more overt in this provocative poster, which certainly shows the fairy-tale heroine in one of her more interesting "states." Ungerer portrays the happy cou-ple doing laundry together in an idyllic, outdoor setting. An immodest Little Red Riding Hood, naked except for her red bonnet and long, red stockings, has her plump, curvaceous backside turned to the viewer as she hangs her red panties on the clothesline. Beside an old-fashioned washtub in the foreground, a lecherous wolf with panting tongue and ogling eyes intently scrubs the rest of her red underclothing with obvious relish. This poster causes viewers to wonder who, in fact, was the seducer and who was the seduced. It looks very much like a contented Little Red Riding Hood has caught her man, or rather her wolf, and domesticated him. She is not unlike the "Little Red Riding Hood" who announced in the *Alibi* classified ads in 2002 that she was "looking for the Big Bad Wolf," preferably a "bad wolf with attitude."[32] The image of a Little Red Riding Hood who does not shy away from sex, indeed, whose lust matches or surpasses the wolf's, is even more evident in a pornographic version published in *Tomi Ungerer's Erzählungen für Erwachsene* (Tomi Ungerer's stories for adults). In the retelling for adults, a very young Little Red Riding Hood is a hypocritically pious voyeur as her grandmother rapes the wolf.[33] Although this particular story is intended only for adults, this Little Red Riding Hood is not so very different from those in his story and posters marketed for children, who all manifest a healthy curiosity about the wolf and what he symbolizes.

In the retellings in this section, Little Red Riding Hood's meeting with the wolf takes on explicit romantic or sexual connotations. Many of these renditions of the story of Little Red Riding end in marriage, as do most fairy tales. Like birth and death, marriage is also a rite of passage. In many traditional societies, youth initiation rites provide evidence of maturity and preparedness for marriage. Thus, puberty or coming of age often coincides with marriage. The profound initiatory meaning of Little Red Riding Hood's experience is barely glimpsed, or lost entirely, in the humorous, often satiric works of the male authors discussed at the end of this chapter. In the retellings of women writers such as Martín Gaite, Galloway, and Julien, but also in that of Bruno de La Salle, the tale becomes a serious initiatory story, in which a little girl grows up as a result of her encounter with the wolf.

Like the retellings discussed in chapter 1, the versions examined in this chapter also cast the encounter of Little Red Riding Hood and the wolf in a sexual light. However, the story of Little Red Riding Hood is no longer necessarily presented as the sexual abuse of a child or nonconsensual sex with a young woman by predatory males. These authors and illustrators revisit the famous tale in order to address the subject of sexuality in the context of a young girl's coming of age. In some cases, the protagonist must still confront a predatory male, but she escapes either by her own cunning or with the help of a wise woman. Many authors use the story of Little Red Riding Hood to present a young girl's normal fears of sexuality as she grows up. Other authors depict heroines who eagerly embrace their new sexuality. Some of these Riding Hoods are willing sexual partners or actually take on the role of seducer. All of these retellings, however, portray contemporary Riding Hoods who have come of age.

3. The Wolf's Story

Ah! How sweet it is
To be the wolf

—PIERRE GRIPARI, "Le loup"

Without the wolf, there would be no story about Little Red Riding Hood. For centuries the little girl in red and the wolf have formed an inseparable couple, and their names are almost always pronounced in the same breath, even though Perrault and the Grimm brothers feature only the little girl in the titles of their classic versions. Many contemporary authors who retell the story acknowledge the wolf's major role by giving him equal billing with the heroine in a title that suggests from the outset that this is not just her story, but his as well. Generally the words "and the Wolf" are merely tacked on to either the classic title—as in the case of Roald Dahl's poem "Little Red Riding Hood and the Wolf" (1982) and José Vallverdú's play *Caperucita y el lobo* (1972)—or a recognizable variant—such as James Thurber's fable "The Little Girl and the Wolf" (1940) and Iring Fetscher's short story "Rotschöpfchen und der Wolf" (Little Redhead and the Wolf, 1972)—to constitute a compound title in which both characters have equal status.

In contemporary retellings, the heroine rarely retains the general designation and anonymity of the traditional tale, but is generally individualized and given a Christian name, which often appears in the title and puts her in the spotlight. Meike and Susann Stoebe titled their Swiss picture book *Waldtraut und der Wolf* (1996), but it appeared simultaneously in French as *Pélagie et le loup*. In some works, the wolf is also baptized with a Christian name, so that the two characters share star billing and once again have equal importance. In the case of the American author Sally Miller Gearhart's short story for adults, "Roja and Leopold" (1990), the heroine's name merely means "Red" in Spanish, so it is the wolf's name that is much more distinctive and original, indicative of his major role in the story. Leopold the Wolf, who roams the streets, parks, and freeways of Silicon Valley, is "a master storyteller" and a "closet vegetarian" in need of "A Kill" to keep up his "big bad" reputation (140). He takes on the role of a storytelling mercy killer for Roja's unconventional grandmother, who is dying of cancer. In Gearhart's modern remake, it is thanks to the Wolf that everyone "lived (and died) happily ever after" (147).

Sometimes the wolf's name actually appears first in the compound title, suggesting that the focus is being transferred to Little Red Riding Hood's adversary. However, these stories do not necessarily cast the wolf in a more important role than the little girl. The Norwegian author Annie Riis titles her short story "Ulven og Rødhette" (1986), but Little Red Riding Hood, who devours the Wolf, narrates it in the first person. Although the wolf is billed first in the title of *El lobo rojo y Caperucita feroz* (1991), by the Argentinean author Elsa Borneman, the inversion of the traditional qualifiers casts the Red Wolf as the victim of a Big Bad Riding Hood. The Spanish picture book *El último lobo y Caperucita* (The last wolf and Little Red Riding Hood, 1975), by José Luis García Sánchez and Miguel Ángel Pacheco, tells the story of a little girl whose best friend is the wolf.[1]

Even when the story is largely focalized through Little Red Riding Hood, as in *El último lobo y Caperucita,* the retelling may incorporate the wolf's story. In this reworking, the wolf is given a voice by borrowing the comic-book technique of speech bubbles. The last remaining wolf of a large pack nostalgically tells his woeful story about the good old days when there were still lots of wolves in the forest (plate 16). The last wolf becomes a kind of tragic hero, shot by a crazed hunter who claims self-defense, and mourned by a heartbroken Little Red Riding Hood who weeps uncontrollably in her grandmother's arms at the end of the story. The last wolf of another forest receives sole billing in the Catalan title *L'últim llop de la Cerdanya* (The last wolf of Cerdanya, 1994), by Joles Sennell and Lluís Filella. He, too, is given a voice and identifies himself to Anna as "a good wolf," a contradiction in terms for the little girl who is only familiar with fairy-tale wolves (9). Although this picture book tells the story of the meeting and ensuing friendship of Anna and the last wolf of Cerdanya, the final image is that of a lovesick-looking wolf under a full moon, howling goodnight to his new friend. In these picture-book retellings, the wolf is portrayed, not as Little Red Riding Hood's seducer, but as her friend or lovesick admirer.

The retellings examined in this chapter shift the spotlight from Little Red Riding Hood to the wolf, thus opening up new possibilities for renewing the age-old tale. The new focus explains, in part, the appeal of these versions with a young audience, as the wolf is an archetypal figure in children's fiction and remains a universal favorite with young readers. This is acknowledged in a French anthology devoted entirely to the Wolf and titled *Le grand méchant Loup, j'adore* (I adore the Big Bad Wolf, 1983). At the same time, the symbolic meaning attached to the wolf, in particular the sexual connotations, makes it a topic that also has a great deal of adult appeal.

When authors and illustrators transfer the focus from Little Red Riding Hood to the wolf, the wolf's role may reflect faithfully that attributed to him by Perrault or the Grimms, or it may diverge radically from any preexisting version. As we saw in the first chapter, Perrault pens the tale basically as a story of rape, in which the wolf who devours Little Red Riding Hood is clearly a predatory male. Many of his successors, particularly those writing for adults or for a crossover audience, continue to develop the symbolism of the wolf in this vein— as seducer, rapist, child abuser, or pedophile—when they retell the story from the wolf's perspective. While some of these criminal wolves feel absolutely no remorse, others seek forgiveness for their past sins. Yet others attempt to exonerate themselves, sometimes by presenting themselves as innocent victims of slander. If the rape narrative is inscribed in the retelling, the disculpation of the wolf–sexual predator becomes highly problematic, but often his story is told outside the context of sexuality. He may still be guilty of a serious crime, but it is no longer depicted as a sexual crime. Many retellings, especially those targeted primarily at young readers, portray the wolf, even the archetypal Big Bad Wolf, in a humorous light, often as a misunderstood, well-intentioned, and sympathetic character whose reputation as the baddy is unmerited. The wolf may haunt our most terrifying nightmares, but he also lends himself extremely well to a caricatural or parodic treatment that is often exploited in picture books or comics. The Big Bad Wolf then becomes a comic hero or a cartoonlike underdog.

An Homage to the Wolf

In the world of comics, the wolf is often characterized as a risible and pitiable victim. That has not prevented him from being given a starring role by some of the best bande dessinée artists in France, where the genre is truly considered an art form and is extremely popular with readers of all ages. When F'Murr[2] collected his many comics about Little Red Riding Hood and the wolf into a volume of more than fifty pages in 1974, the title *Au loup!* (To the wolf!) announced clearly that it was meant to be an homage to the wolf. The comics began appearing, under the title *Contes à rebours* (Backward tales), in the magazine *Pilote* in 1971. Later, the BD artist became the editor at Dargaud, the French publisher known for such classics as *Asterix,* which captured the hearts of readers of all ages around the world. Dargaud reedited *Au loup!* in 1979, adding eight supplementary plates in color to the original black-and-white comics. With their roots in popular culture, comics have always appealed to a crossover audience, and that is especially true in France. The mind-twisting comics that F'Murr gathered together in an homage to the wolf appeal to a very wide audience of readers of all ages. While young children delight in much of the outrageously hilarious visual humor, some of the more subtle humor may be missed even by older readers. F'Murr's use of intertextuality and metafiction, as well as his play with chronology, are often quite sophisticated and can only be fully appreciated by adults.

Although he is a leading figure in the world of the BD, F'Murr is not well known outside France, particularly in the English-speaking world. The erudite nuances of his comics are difficult, if not impossible, to translate. This is due not only to the language, but also to the assumptions about what the average well-educated French reader carries in his or her cultural baggage. Even French readers of the younger generation are apt to have difficulty with the frequent political satire. For example, the very first comic opens with the wolf blaming his species' hunger on the criminal tax imposed by Valéry Giscard d'Estaing, who is identified only as "Giscard." Adopting the wolf's perspective, F'Murr suggests that wolves would not have to resort to eating grandmothers and little girls if it wasn't for unreasonable taxes, humorously shifting the blame for the wolf's reprehensible conduct to politicians. The irony, of course, is that wolves would not have been taxed in the first place if they had not already been guilty of these crimes. The wolf's fortune has taken a turn for the better as he catches sight of Little Red Riding Hood, but at the grandmother's he is kicked out and insulted by a band of wolves, some of whom have been waiting there since the day before. They have no intention of sharing a bite with this last-minute "sponger" (3). This first comic presents the wolf as a victim of both society and his own species.

F'murr's playful metafictive discourse, which can be quite sophisticated, has particular adult appeal, although much of it is also accessible to young readers. Often one or more of the characters is familiar with the story and is quite conscious of the roles they are playing. One comic depicts the wolf talking to himself, recapping where the little girl is going and why. The joke often lies in the fact that one character has this metafictive knowledge, while a second does not.

In another comic, the wolf addresses Little Red Riding Hood directly to say that he takes it that she is once again going to her grandmother's, but the little girl wonders how he could possibly have guessed. Her ignorance allows the wolf to set about marking out a circuitous shortcut, which includes climbing an old oak and changing trains at the Concorde subway station in Paris, so that he can get to the grandmother's first. He spends so much time ensuring that the tortuous path will be sufficiently complicated that the moon is already up when the wolf suddenly realizes that his scheme has backfired and he is utterly lost. The roles are reversed in another comic, in which it is Little Red Riding Hood who has prior knowledge of the fairy tale. On finding the wolf outside her grandmother's house reading a book, she asks him angrily why he didn't go inside and wonders what's wrong with him. The characters expect each other to play their part as it was written in the script, and French children, who know Perrault's tale by heart, will understand these expectations and appreciate the metafictional humor.

F'Murr's metafictional and intertextual play also draws on the fact that Little Red Riding Hood's wolf is not the only wolf of literary fame. A misunderstanding occurs between a wolf, who seems to have forgotten his lines, and Little Red Riding Hood, who reproaches him at length, until finally she realizes it's the wrong wolf. The wolf thinks she must be the supply teacher and starts reciting Jean de La Fontaine's fable "The Wolf and the Lamb." In the first comic about the highly taxed, starving wolves, the multiplication of virtually identical wolves, who all know the story and head to the plump grandmother's to await a decent meal, increases the humor. Throughout F'Murr's book, the technique of the multiplication of the main characters is repeated, foregrounding the fictive nature of a story that is told and retold. In one comic, the wolf declares war on Little Red Riding Hood because she won't share her cake and pot of butter. The final frame shows the little girl in red leading an army of Riding Hoods against an army of wolves (plate 17). One of the most striking comics in the book is a full-page plate portraying a large, indignant wolf being attacked by scores of "filthy parasites" in the form of tiny Red Riding Hoods. The little pests are walking on his muzzle, on his feet, and up and down his legs, tobogganing off his tail, or pointing a gun at the angelic old man (present in all the comics) who is spraying the wolf with pesticide. Whether there is one wolf or multiple wolves, he is generally the victim of one or more Little Red Riding Hoods.

The wolf's difficult life is the subject of a number of the comics. F'murr's wolf wonders if he will ever succeed in catching Little Red Riding Hood. As he ad-

Au loup! by F'Murr, © 1993 Dargaud Éditeur. Used by permission of Dargaud Éditeur and F'Murr.

justs his nightcap in front of a mirror, he complains that he spends his wolf's life disguised as a grandmother. It would appear that not all wolves are fond of cross-dressing. After assuring himself that everything is "in order," in other words going according to Perrault's plan, he climbs into bed, where he is bombarded by the basket and its contents when Little Red Riding Hood, in a hurry to get to a union meeting, throws it through the door. F'Murr often presents an elderly wolf, whose advanced age gives rise to new complaints. Still dressed in the grandmother's clothes, the wolf hobbles dizzily down the path leaning on a cane and lamenting how difficult it is to be old these days. However, his chief complaint is the little pest in red who always eludes him. His futile pursuit is symbolized on the cover by the wolf howling hysterically at a moon bearing the face of the elusive Little Red Riding Hood. One comic introduces the incongruous character of Father Christmas, who explains his late arrival with the wolf's Christmas present by the fact that the wolf's letter had contained a very difficult request. As Father Christmas pulls a bound Little Red Riding Hood out of his basket, he tells the wolf that "the little nuisance" runs fast and his legs aren't what they used to be (51). This comic is one of the very few in which the wolf seems to get the better of the little girl in red.

The accumulation of comics about the two fairy-tale characters creates the impression that they never stop playing their assigned parts. The wolf expresses this himself; one comic begins with the words "Forward, to the grandmother's house for the nth time" (43). The repetitiveness of their roles is also played up by Little Red Riding Hood, who complains about what she calls her "job" (27). That does not mean they enact the story according to Perrault's well-known script. Although the wolf has been to the grandmother's house an infinite number of times, this trip is different because the old lady has relocated to a house at the top of a steep mountain surrounded by a moat with a drawbridge. For her part, the grandmother is fed up with always getting a cake and a pot of butter; she demands caviar from now on. On one occasion, Little Red Riding Hood's mother expresses her hope that their new limousine will eliminate any problems with the wolf. The little girl settles comfortably in the back seat with her basket, savoring the luxury of being driven to her grandmother's by a chauffeur. When she finally realizes that they aren't taking the right path, the chauffeur, in a series of five frames, gradually transforms back into the wolf, who has been studying mimesis. F'Murr's wolf has expanded his repertoire and is no longer limited to mimicking grandmothers. In a later comic, a perplexed Little Red Riding Hood on her way home asks readers if they understand why it was the "real" grandmother this time. The final frame provides the unexpected answer to her question: the wolf has changed his strategy and now awaits the little girl at her house, disguised as her mother. The familiar motifs of the tale are cleverly twisted and blended with the unexpected to create hilarious situations that entertain readers of all ages.

Au loup! by F'Murr, © 1993 Dargaud Éditeur. Used by permission of Dargaud Éditeur and F'Murr.

F'Murr's book is an homage to the wolf, who appears on the cover, but it is dedicated to Charles Perrault, whose caricatural bust is depicted on the title page, where a pigeon is perched irreverently on his head and Little Red Riding Hood leans against the base nonchalantly munching on her galette. The wolf remains obsessively present even on this page because the figure of a cartoonlike wolf, in a stiff, stunned state resembling rigor mortis, constitutes a repeated motif on the background of the page. Often F'Murr introduces Perrault into the story in order to poke fun at the status of the author, creating another level of metafictional play. One fine day, while strolling in the woods, Perrault is delighted to hear the sounds of a chase, promising yet another "dark drama of the forest." The author hides behind a garbage dump, but when it turns out to be Red Riding Hood again, he admits that those two are starting to get on his nerves. However, when the wolf flattens her in front of Perrault's hiding spot, the author shows new interest in the modified events, imagining with sadistic glee the "fine tale" he will be able to write about the "horrible story" of the unfortunate victim. His plans for a new work are short-lived, as the author realizes with stupefaction that the wolf is not pursuing a real girl but only a wind-up doll that has not yet been perfected (6). When Little Red Riding Hood, or "Chap' Rouge" as Perrault informally calls her, asks the author why he is carrying around a donkey skin, he begins to tell her about his new idea for a tale. He is, of course, referring to his tale *Peau d'Âne* (*Donkeyskin*), which is not as widely known in the English-speaking world as most of his other tales. When Perrault opens up the donkey skin to show Little Red Riding Hood what the prince will find inside, instead of an attractive princess, it contains a grinning wolf (39).

None of Perrault's characters seem happy with the role they have been given. A very ugly, mean-looking grandmother feeds a potion from her cauldron to the other characters, one after another, until Little Red Riding Hood, her mother, and the wolf are all transformed into exact duplicates of the grandmother, who wants to steal the show. When Perrault encounters the gruesome grannies, he wants to tell them "a new version" of the fairy tale, presumably based on the events he witnessed from behind the garbage dump, but he finds himself pinned to the ground with a funnel in his mouth and about to become a character in the grandmother's new version. The renowned classic tales, which Perrault did not take very seriously, are demystified by F'Murr. In this comic, the terrified author promises the gang of grandmothers never to write another "idiotic tale" (17). The characters all have their ideas about how the tale should have been written. One day the wolf arrives at Perrault's house with a group of the author's largest, ugliest monsters to inform him that they have formed a Union of the Characters from Ch. Perrault's Tales (Syndicat des Personnages des Contes de Ch. Perrault or S.P.C.C.P.). The union members have come to demand that the author make some changes to the endings of his tales. As the author is having the wolf arrested for stealing his manuscripts and rewriting the endings with his union, Little Red Riding Hood stands innocently by thinking what a coincidence it is that she had entertained the same idea. While Perrault tells Bluebeard categorically that he will not change the ending of his story, a bold Little Red Riding Hood, who has heard of his monstrous reputation as a wife murderer, appears and tells him that she would like to marry him when she grows up, so that they can spend their time "tearing each other's guts out" (24). Little Red Riding Hood would like to rewrite the tale of Bluebeard as well as her own. The author of the tales is as discontent as his characters. Overcome with frustration by the madness of all his characters, Perrault wonders why he ever set about writing fairy tales. The lunacy of Perrault's fairy-tale characters is reminiscent of the madness of the novelistic heroes in *Dialogue des héros de roman* (Dialogue of the novelistic heroes), by Perrault's contemporary, Nicolas Boileau. Only adult readers will decode such sophisticated intertextual allusions.

F'Murr often uses anachronism to create a comically incongruous situation. Sometimes this is the result of clever intertextual play. Perrault has Little Red Riding Hood and the wolf rehearse a text they both find quite hopeless. When the author admits that he did it on purpose to annoy them, he is accused of thinking he's Ionesco now. Although the seventeenth-century academician is pastiching the work of the twentieth-century playwright in order to vex his characters, F'Murr's warped reworkings have more in common with the Theatre of the Absurd than with the classic repertoire of fairy tales. In another comic, F'Murr apparently inflicts the famous classic author with Alzheimer's disease. Looking rather undignified without his peruke, a doddering and disoriented Perrault scratches his bald head, wondering what to tell his characters in the face of his memory lapse. Dressed only in his robe and slippers, the forlorn author stands, holding a sheet of paper with a large inkblot, amid reams of discarded sheets of spoiled or crumpled paper. He is surrounded by his characters, who seem to be taking advantage of the author's quandary to unwind and engage in their own pastimes. Much of the playful distortion of chronology will be lost on young readers.

F'Murr also pokes fun at the codes and conventions of the fairy-tale genre. Installed in the grandmother's bed, the wolf recognizes what he calls the "Toc Toc Toc Rouge" ("Red Knock, Knock, Knock"). It is obvious that the color red refers here to Little Red Riding Hood's leftist political affiliation. The wolf massacres the archaic phrase by replacing the *chevinette* with the "moulinette," which is a vegetable mill, and then, at a complete loss for the *bobinette*, substitutes the catchall word "le truc" (the thing) (21). On one page, the wolf is using the fairy tale as a guide to ensure that he does everything according to the book. The familiar lines are abbreviated in a humorous manner ("Tire la bob . . . et la chev. cherra"), as if the tale was in fast-forward. As the wolf climbs into the grandmother's bed, he congratulates himself on a successful operation, completed "in 5′ 19″ 7′ " with "scientific exactitude." When Little Red Riding Hood knocks on the door, everything seems to be going according to schedule. However, it isn't the little girl, but her huge, ogrelike big brother, with an ax in his belt, who enters carrying an incongruous little basket for his grandmother (36). In another comic, F'Murr has fun with the conventional fairy-tale setting. Little Red Riding Hood's forest is now a classified site with its own reference number, as the wolf and the little girl angrily remind a developer who has managed to build a skyscraper right in the middle. In a clever play on words, the shady businessman tells dear Little Red Riding Hood that her motto could be "galette et pot de beurre" (cake and pot of butter), but that his would be "galette et pot-de-vin" (49). The literal translation of *pot-de-vin* is pot of wine, evoking the bottle of wine in the Grimms' version, but the expression means a "bribe." Like so much of F'Murr's humor, the wordplay is not always accessible to children.

F'Murr's dynamic storytelling style is particularly suited to these parodic revisions of the fairy tale. Readers never tire of returning to the tale time and again, as it is continually recast in an entirely new manner and constantly takes the most unexpected turns. Often the narrative is multilayered, presenting several parallel storylines. Although much of the plot is based on total nonsense, the tone ranges from the absurd to the profound. The comics are witty and sophisticated, and one is particularly struck by the well-defined personality of the wolf/wolves, who come to life under the artist's pen. *Au loup!* is F'Murr's homage to the fairy-tale character who, in today's retellings, is so often the underdog, with little or no chance of outwitting Little Red Riding Hood. Although F'Murr also portrays the wolf as the underdog figure so familiar in cartoons, the BD artist nonetheless makes him the hero of this memorable book. The majority of the comics are told from the wolf's perspective, and it is his figure that remains in readers' imaginations as they close *Au loup!*

In light of F'Murr's large adult audience in France and his wide range of parodic, intertextual play with the Perrault version of *Little Red Riding Hood*, it may seem surprising that he does not exploit the French academician's ironic portrayal of the wolf as seducer in any of his comics. However, that would obviously have cast the BD artist's wolf in a less comical, as well as a less sympathetic light. Many authors of contemporary retellings that turn the wolf into the eponymous hero deliberately portray him in an unsympathetic light.

The Wolf's Perspective: From Seducer and Sexual Predator
to Slandered Suitor and Betrayed Lover

The attribution of the narrative voice to the wolf is a strategy often adopted in contemporary retellings for all ages. Using the wolf's first-person narrative allows authors to lay bare the wolf's soul, to expose his thoughts, his feelings, and his aspirations. Authors have found ingenious ways of approaching the story from his perspective, adopting the form of an homage, monologue, ode, elegy, or postscript. This interiority is often associated with the latent sexuality in Perrault's tale and may even be used to foreground the sexual violence, but it is sometimes connected only with a pure love or a naive infatuation. It may also explore other emotions, such as pride, sorrow, remorse, and guilt.

The wolf may still be cast as a seducer, rapist, or pedophile even when the story is told from his perspective in first-person narration. Some wolves readily admit to being sexual predators and feel no remorse whatsoever for their crimes. In other cases, the wolves confess their guilt, but express their regret; they may even seek forgiveness for past sins. Although interpretations in this vein are often addressed primarily to an adult audience, a number also target a younger audience. A large number of authors and illustrators who retell *Little Red Riding Hood* for children or for a crossover audience present the wolf not as a sexual predator, however, but as a well-intentioned admirer or even an innocent victim. Many wolves, whether they are accused of sex-related crimes or simply the murderous act of devouring a girl and her grandmother, attempt to disculpate themselves by claiming to be the victims of slander. The wolf may even represent the slandered opposition to a repressive regime. Often wolf-narrators retell the story with the intention of establishing the "true" version of events. However, the reliability of first-person narrators is often questioned, and in the case of a fairy-tale character reputed for his cunning and ability to deceive, it becomes even more problematic.

The use of the wolf's first-person narrative to renew the story is not a new phenomenon. As early as the nineteenth century, the American poet Bret Harte had already told the story in the first person, from the wolf's point of view, in a poem titled "What the Wolf Really Said to Little Red Riding-Hood." As is often the case in works focalized through the wolf, this one claims to "correct" the classic tale. The wolf reinterprets the formulaic answers, explaining to the "puzzled and fair" maiden that his eyes only wish to behold her beauty and his arms only wish to protect her. To the traditional dialogue's familiar list of physical features, the wolf romantically adds his sighs and his silence. In the final line of the poem, the wolf reluctantly confides to the "wondering maiden" the "truth" behind his surprising appearance and behavior: "I am not your grandmother, Riding-Hood dear!" (248). In his poem, Harte subverts the image of the wolf who deceives the girl in order to seduce her. Albeit reluctantly, this wolf admits to the girl that he is not her grandmother. It seems that he only wishes to be her admirer and protector. The climactic dialogue, the tale's most famous scene, is cast in a new light by presenting it through the eyes of the wolf who is supposed to have devoured Little Red Riding Hood, but the wolf conspicuously avoids mentioning that act. The deliberately ambivalent ending leaves the possibility that Harte offers the perspective of a wolf who, as the French would say, merely devours Little Red Riding Hood with his eyes, but readers tend to suspect that there may be more to this wolf's story than he is willing to say.

Like the wolf in Harte's poem, the wolf who narrates the retelling by the Peruvian poet José Santos Chocano also addresses Little Red Riding Hood to express his love. A descriptive adjective in the title of "El lobo enamorado" (The wolf in love, 1937) immediately establishes the amorous state of the wolf, who confesses to the little girl:

I am in love with you, Little Red Riding Hood . . .
A wolf in love? Yes, a wolf. And why not? (64)

The wolf's rhetorical question acknowledges the collective disbelief or surprise with which the story of a wolf in love would be met in light of his reputation. When the wolf's story is told as a love story, it is generally a sad, if not tragic tale. Both the subject and the tone of Chocano's retelling are clearly announced in the title of the posthumous collection *Poemas del amor doliente* (Poems of sorrowful love), which was published for adults in Chile in 1937.

The wolf in love portrays himself as a sad, suffering creature who deserves the girl's sympathy. Using the possessive adjective, he implores Little Red Riding Hood to "take pity on [her] wolf" (63) Contrary to Anne Bertier's *Mon Loup*, in which the little girl uses the possessive to refer to "her" wolf, this is not a mutual love story with a happy ending. While the wolf in picture-book retellings that target young readers, such as *El último lobo y Caperucita* and *L'últim llop de la Cerdanya*, is portrayed, not as Little Red Riding Hood's seducer or lover, but as her friend or lovesick adorer, sexual overtones creep back into this poem intended primarily for adults. The wolf feels he should be pitied because he is in love with a girl whom he has met too late and cannot devour because he lacks the force. In very sensual terms, the wolf imagines the feast that he would have had "in the enchantment of [her] divine body," if only he had met her on his path earlier in life (63). While the wolf's sexual desire is intact, he is apparently too old to engage in the sexual act. He suggests that he would be content just to hold Little Red Riding Hood and that things would go no further. The girl's help is solicited to convince her grandmother to let the wolf just rest in her bed, so that he can hug her to his heart. While the wolf acknowledges Little Red Riding Hood's physical attractiveness, the quality he particularly praises is her goodness, especially toward him. Although the wolf appears to be sincere, he is possibly still the deceiver, playing on the girl's tenderness and compassion.

Chocano's wolf casts himself in the role of a romantic lover who throws himself at the feet of Little Red Riding Hood to confess his love. He shares with her the literary aspirations she inspires in him. The self-reflexive stanza constitutes a mise en abyme, mirroring the poem we are reading. The wolf has indeed become a poet and penned the tale of the "sorrows of a wolf in love." As in Harte's poem, the ending is ambiguous. If this wolf doesn't devour Little Red Riding Hood, it is only because he is too old and weak to play the seducer. Yet the last stanza suggests that the well-known tale of Little Red Riding Hood has been replaced by the tale of a peaceful wolf who describes himself as "the wolf brother of Francis of Assisi" (64). By likening himself to the legendary fierce wolf of Gubbio, who preyed upon men as well as animals before he was tamed by St. Francis of Assisi, the wolf-narrator attempts to convince Little Red Riding Hood of his own reform, but this sudden transformation remains highly questionable to readers. In "El lobo enamorado," Chocano portrays a wolf who is determined to convince Little Red Riding Hood of his sincere love and good intentions. However, the wolf's words indicate that if he has indeed changed, it is only because he is physically incapable of pursuing his old crimes. Perhaps it is only in old age that the wolf can curb his predatory sexual appetite.

The wolf in the American songwriter Robert Blackwell's "Lil' Red Riding Hood," released by Sam the Sham and the Pharaohs in 1966, is a young, two-legged wolf, who clearly makes his sexual desires known. The song begins with a long wolf whistle, which is repeated throughout to underscore his lustful desire. The wolf who narrates this popular version is the male out to pick up a fully grown Riding Hood, perhaps with the hope that their date will end in consensual sex. The encounter scene of the classic tale is turned into a courtship scene, in which the wolf woos a big Little Red Riding Hood. The wolf does not deny his carnal desires, but he is determined to repress them and be on his best behavior until he has managed to charm the girl. Admitting that he would like to hold her, he resists the temptation out of fear that she will take him for a big bad wolf. Substituting a big heart, which is all the better to love her with, for the big body parts of the classic dialogue, the wolf assures Little Red Riding Hood that bad wolves can also be good. A lot of wolves use this line, but with varying degrees of sincerity. Blackwell's big bad wolf is on his best behavior, in the hope of persuading Little Red Riding Hood to go out with him before they get to her grandmother's place.

The topic of the wolf in love has inspired more than one Latin American poet. In a very intimate verse retelling for adults by the Cuban poet Raúl Rivero, the wolf also confides to readers that he was "a wolf in love." The unusual love poem, written in two parts—"Version libre" (Free version) and "Version libre . . . 2"—in a Cuban jail in 2004, has political overtones.[3] Forbidden to write anything but love poems while he was in prison, the dissident Cuban journalist and poet tells the woeful story of a wolf who was in love with Little Red Riding Hood. The re-version appeared in Spain in the collection *Corazón sin furia* (*Heart without Fury*, 2005), along with the other love poems that Rivero's wife had managed to get out of Cuba while he was still in prison.

The surprising subversion of the formulaic fairy-tale opening hints at the wolf's death: "I was a wolf once upon a time." The protagonist immediately qualifies himself as "a good wolf," adding later that he had no "wolf instincts." Casting himself in the role of protector, he claims that he was Little Red Riding Hood's "personal escort." The wolf in the song sung by Sam the Sham and the Pharaohs thinks that he should also play that role in order to protect the girl from other wolves. The surprising life story the wolf shares with readers becomes increasingly intimate. Little Red Riding Hood returned his love and their sexual relationship was consensual. Their lovemaking in the grandmother's cabin is described quite sensually.

Whereas the love story of Chocano's wolf is merely sad, that of Rivero's wolf is quite tragic. While walking in the woods one day, Little Red Riding Hood denounced the wolf to a woodcutter who, in the company of several hunters, came to kill the wolf. Rivero is not the first author to use the story of Little Red Riding Hood to denounce a repressive regime, but his story of a wolf betrayed by his Little Red Riding Hood–lover is more than just a political allegory; it is also a tragic love story. This retelling could almost be considered an elegy to the wolf, composed by the wolf himself. In the second part of the poem, the wolf's sad voice continues to speak from beyond the grave, although the deceased narrator admits that he does not know what ensued. The remainder of his narrative is based on speculation. The betrayed wolf suggests that Little Red Riding Hood is perhaps very happy. With a touch of the macabre, he imagines his large dry, gray, and "stupid" head hanging on the wall of one of the hunters. Rivero's dead wolf does not seem to be familiar with Perrault's tale, which ends with the death of Little Red Riding Hood, as he claims: "My death has always been the end of this tale." The grave, tragic tone of this wolf's first-person narrative tends to add credibility to his story. Perhaps readers feel more inclined to believe a dead wolf-narrator, who has nothing to gain by falsifying his heartrending story. Unlike many of his counterparts, Rivero's wolf does not attempt to convince his audience, but merely to share his tragic story for posterity.

The wolf narrators discussed thus far all make some attempt to portray themselves in a positive light, casting themselves in the role of Little Red Riding Hood's admirer, well-intentioned suitor, or consensual lover. Some wolf narrators, in contrast, are quite content, if not eager, to admit their guilt and to present themselves in the role of sexual predator or murderer. Not only do they remain entirely unrepentant, but they also rationalize their dastardly crimes by claiming they are merely fulfilling their role in life. They may even congratulate themselves and proudly vaunt their exploits to readers. Somewhat surprisingly, such a portrayal is even found in retellings marketed for children.

In his collection of poems for children, *Marelles* (Hopscotch, 1988), the French author Pierre Gripari, who wrote for both children and adults, includes a poem, titled simply "Le loup," that is narrated in the first person by the eponymous protagonist. In addition to changing the perspective, the poet chooses a gap in the story and has the wolf recount his thoughts and actions prior to his encounter with Little Red Riding Hood in the woods. Gripari's wolf makes no effort to hide his true intentions or to paint himself other than he is. The short, rhyming lines of this lyrical recasting give a light and playful tone to the wolf's monologue, but there are disturbing undertones. The first verse contains a self-portrait, which presents, at a different moment and through the wolf's eyes, several of the physical traits from the ritualistic dialogue. As in the famous exchange, the self-portrait culminates with his sharp teeth, which give him a "sinister" look. When the wolf-poet sets the stage in the second stanza, the anthropomorphic terms in which he describes the wind, as it "whistles, molests and slaps" the stroller, reflect the violence that the wolf will inflict on the little girl. The nature of the wolf's desire is indicated by the fact that the enticing odor on the wind speaks not to his stomach, but to his heart. Although she is referred to subsequently as a walking "meal" that makes him salivate, it seems that she will assuage his sexual appetite (13).

Young readers may not immediately guess that the wolf is stalking Little Red Riding Hood. References to the intertext are initially rather vague. The little girl is first referred to ambiguously, in the masculine gender, as a "stroller" (13). The "meal" metaphor offers a more helpful clue for young readers who are still in the dark. Subsequently, the wolf refers to the fairy-tale heroine in an ever more precise manner. In the following verse, he calls her a "kid," and the French noun "gamine" now indicates her true gender. The image of a little girl coming through the woods, alternately "dilly-dallying" and "trotting along," should be familiar to even the youngest readers, although it is the tarrying trait and not the faster gait that is normally associated with Little Red Riding Hood. The first words of the next verse identify her specifically as "un chaperon" (a riding hood), which is qualified as "all red and round." This Red Riding Hood is a toddler who still retains her baby fat. Readers see Little Red Riding Hood through the eyes of the wolf, who describes both her physical and mental traits. There is a cheeky or saucy look about her, according to the wolf, who calls her a little "chattemite," that is, a person who pretends to be sweet and modest to fool those around her. Licking his lips, the wolf hurries off to "accost" the little girl, whom he now refers to as a "doll." In many illustrations of the famous encounter of Little Red Riding Hood and the wolf, the little girl is portrayed with doll-like features, and in Aofumi Horio's Japanese version she is actually represented as a china doll. However, the use of the term here takes on the derogatory colloquial sense of a pretty, rather useless female who is seen merely as an object to be used for man's pleasure.

Although they are not expressed explicitly, the sexual connotations in Gripari's poem are evident to adult readers. In spite of the playful, humorous tone of the poem, which amuses young readers, many adults will sense a sinister, misogynist overtone. In "Le loup," the crucial scene of the encounter in the woods is left to the reader's imagination. The poem ends with the philosophical reflections of the wolf as he races expectantly toward the dramatic meeting, thinking how sweet it is to be the "guardian" (Gripari uses the evocative term "garde-fou," which means a railing or parapet to prevent people from falling) of "the good children" who wander into "the wild wood" (14). Gripari's wolf justifies his behavior by casting himself in the role of a moral enforcer who prevents good little children from erring by eating the ones that do. This line of reasoning is not unlike that of the wolf who narrates Agha Shahid Ali's "The Wolf's Postscript to 'Little Red Riding Hood,'" a poem published for adults in 1987, one year before "Le loup." Ali's wolf puts it in pedagogical and literary terms, claiming to have done it "for kindergarten teachers" and "a clear moral." This wolf does not deny his actions or claim that the reported facts are incorrect, as his story is presented as a "postscript" to the classic tale. He nonetheless insists that he was "no child-molester."

Even in retellings narrated by the wolf, authors sometimes foreground the sexual violence latent in Perrault's tale, particularly in works that address primarily adults and/or young adults. The American poet Gwen Strauss presents a disturbing image of a predatory male in "The Waiting Wolf," from *Trail of Stones* (1990), a collection of verse published for adults. The volume was a collaboration between the poet and the British author-illustrator Anthony Browne, who were both interested in approaching fairy tales "from a new perspective."[4] Better known for his award-winning picture books for children, Browne had just published his modern fairy tale *The Tunnel* (1989), in which transparent as well as more sophisticated pictorial allusions to Little Red Riding Hood and the wolf offer a revisioning of the classic tale that appeals to adults as well as children. In her preface to *Trail of Stones*, Strauss insists on the fact that a fairy tale read aloud to her as a child is not the same as the fairy tale she reads as an adult. "Forgotten details" suggest new perspectives and new voices to adult readers who return to the cherished bedtime story of their childhood. The combination of Browne's drawings and Strauss's poems was intended to provide "a collection of portraits" that would reveal some of the startling, secret moments that are obscured in the tales.

The verses devoted to the "portrait" of "The Waiting Wolf" reveal him, as do Gripari's, in a moment that is not exploited in the classic tale. In this case, it is the time he spends lying in the grandmother's bed awaiting the arrival of Little

Red Riding Hood. Strauss seems to have taken her image of the waiting wolf from Perrault, who mentions the wolf in the bed waiting for the little girl, but does not elaborate. The Grimms' version does not even allude to the period that must have elapsed before the dallying little girl finally arrives at granny's door. Like the other fairy-tale characters from whose perspective Strauss had chosen to write her poems, the wolf "demanded certain props." Her waiting wolf is not content to dress only in the conventional costume of nightgown and cap, but also dons granny's "lace panties," a detail that strongly suggests sexual deviation. He is not without some resemblance to the wolf "dressed in frills" that Anne Sexton describes in her poem "Red Riding Hood." However, Sexton's "deceptive fellow" is evoked in the more sympathetic light of "a kind of transvestite" (76), whereas Strauss develops the more sinister image of a pedophile.

Strauss's search for the "private voices" of well-known fairy-tale characters led to the discovery of intriguing "private details" and gradually she began to appreciate the depth of their personal stories, which had often remained untold. Like all the characters in Strauss's and Browne's portraits, the wolf is "compelled to turn inward" during a time of "solitude" and "private crisis." Gripari's wolf is also portrayed in a solitary moment, awaiting the arrival of Little Red Riding Hood in the woods, but he does not have a guilt complex and feels no qualms whatsoever with regard to his impending actions. Strauss depicts the calculating wolf in a moment of unaccustomed weakness, when his troubled conscience forces him to confess: "at this moment I do not like myself." The weight of his guilt is expressed in a premonitory metaphor that alludes to the form his punishment takes in the Grimms' version, as the wolf describes his lies as being "strangely heavy in [his] belly like stones" (14). It is the wolf, rather than Little Red Riding Hood, that Strauss places, as she does all her characters, in "a dark wood where they must either face themselves, or refuse to." During this privileged moment of self-revelation, the wolf is given the opportunity to choose to change. Instead of doing so, he rationalizes his behavior, suggesting that it is his role to "stalk" Little Red Riding Hood. He goes even further than Gripari's wolf when he claims that the little girl is to blame because she had led him on: "she placed herself on my path, / practically spilling her basket of breads and jams" (14). The language of this "dark lurking pedophile of a wolf, with his creepy, self-rationalizing approach to his soon-to-be sexual offense" is, as Catherine Orenstein points out, "the familiar language of men who accuse women of leading them on."[5] Although narrated in the third person, Anne Sharpe's "Not So

Little Red Riding Hood" focalizes on the wolf to offer a glimpse of the twisted thoughts of another perverted stalker who believes that all women, especially those dressed in red, are provocative seducers. Scarlet's rejection of his invitation is seen as part of her ploy by the two-legged wolf, who confides that "this wasn't the first time that a girl in a brilliant scarlet cape had led him on" (47). So great is the delusion of this predatory male that he portrays himself as the "abused," rather than the abuser (49).

In Strauss's poem, the wolf's final lines seem intended to justify his actions to himself, as well as to readers, because he intimates, as does Gripari's wolf, that the young girl has been aware of his true identity all along. Strauss's wolf presents the psyche of a sexually aggressive male while at the same time adopting a manner of expression that is in keeping with his species and natural habitat. The wolf's evocative metaphors are drawn from the only world he knows, that of the forest. He imagines Little Red Riding Hood's fingers unfurling "like fiddle heads in spring." Then he tries to put himself in the place of the little girl and to see himself through her eyes, but still his terms of reference are those of a nocturnal forest animal: "My matted fur will smell to her of forest / moss at night." He foretells her musings about his ears, eyes, and nose, but in different, more sensual terms than those of the classic tale. They now involve senses other than sight and imply the intimacy of a scene in which the girl knows his ears are "soft as felt" and feels his "leather nose on her belly" (16).

Anthony Browne's single striking black-and-white drawing in pencil and pen-and-ink for "The Waiting Wolf" is somewhat reminiscent of nineteenth-century engravings, and in particular the celebrated Doré illustration reproduced at the beginning of this book. Browne deliberately refers to what is undoubtedly the most famous iconographical representation of Little Red Riding Hood and the wolf. At the same time he sets up a striking contrast with the well-known engraving by the conspicuous absence of the little girl in the bed (plate 18). There is a deliberate, parodic alteration of certain elements of Doré's illustration. The bedsheet is now pulled up over the wolf's muzzle; all that is visible of the waiting wolf are his piercing eyes, which stare out at the reader from an indefinable, menacing blackness between the prominent white nightcap and bedsheet. In a masterful manner, Browne's eye-catching illustration visually reinforces the focalization of Strauss's poem, which is told through the eyes of the wolf who awaits his victim.

As the poems by Gripari and Strauss demonstrate, retelling the story from the wolf's perspective does not necessarily entail casting the wolf in a more favor-

Rubrique-à-brac by Gotlib, © 1970 Dargaud Éditeur.
Used by permission of Dargaud Éditeur and Gotlib.

able light. When the wolf bares his soul, it may still be as black as Perrault painted it. Although Strauss's wolf suffers from a bad conscience, he does not repent and change his ways. And Gripari's wolf is quite proud of his role of predator. In "The Wolf's Postscript to 'Little Red Riding Hood,'" Ali's intellectual wolf asks only that he should be granted his "sense of history" (he did it "for posterity") and his "generous sense of plot" (he could have gobbled the heroine up much earlier). In many retellings, however, authors who give him the narrative voice paint the wolf, or at least let the wolf paint himself, as a sympathetic character with good intentions.

The well-known French humorist Gotlib casts a mild, long-suffering wolf in the role of patient in his hilarious BD "Une ordonnance maladroite" (A tactless prescription, 1970).[6] The conventional image of the wolf as carnivorous predator is subverted in the lengthy, descriptive subtitle that announces "The sad story of the vegetarian wolf marked by his heredity." The tormented wolf is portrayed telling his doctor about his terrifying nightmares, in which he is the victim of fictional characters once victimized by wolves. The most obsessive of these dreams is an inversion of the story of Little Red Riding Hood: the wolf is on his way to his grandmother's with a basket when he meets a little girl all dressed in red. The hearts around the wolf's head indicate his infatuation with the girl. He offers her one compliment after another, in a humorous reworking of the traditional

Rubrique-à-brac by Gotlib, © 1970 Dargaud
Éditeur. Used by permission of Dargaud
Éditeur and Gotlib.

CE N'EST PLUS UNE VIE, DOCTEUR! JE VOUS LE RÉPÈTE, J'AI HORREUR DE LA VIANDE. SI TOUS CES BRAVES GENS ONT SUBI DES SÉVICES DANS LE PASSÉ, JE NE SUIS TOUT DE MÊME PAS RESPONSABLE DE LA MAUVAISE CONDUITE DE MES ASCENDANTS!

QUE VOULEZ-VOUS MON PETIT, QUAND LES PARENTS MANGENT, LES ENFANTS TRINQUENT!

MAIS JE PENSE QUE LA *CAUSE* DE VOS ENNUIS EST JUSTEMENT VOTRE RÉGIME VÉGÉTARIEN. VOTRE CONSTITUTION RÉCLAME DE LA VIANDE. VOUS LA LUI REFUSEZ, D'OÙ, DÉRÈGLEMENT...

AH BON ?

Rubrique-à-brac by Gotlib, © 1970 Dargaud Éditeur. Used by permission of Dargaud Éditeur and Gotlib.

Rubrique-à-brac by Gotlib, © 1970 Dargaud Éditeur. Used by permission of Dargaud Éditeur and Gotlib.

dialogue that appropriates Little Red Riding Hood's lines for the wolf and substitutes the word "nice" for the word "large." She has a "nice nose" and "nice
hair," but also a "nice stick" that is "All the better to hit [him] with!" (116). The
wolf's nightmare always ends this way.

Gotlib presents a sympathetic wolf who is painfully aware of his mental, as well
as his physical, problems. The troubled wolf, a vegetarian who detests meat, doesn't
understand why he should have to pay for the sins of his ancestors. Addressing
the wolf paternalistically as "mon petit" (my boy), the doctor preaches a version
of the scriptural lesson about the sins of the fathers being visited on their children:
"when the parents eat, the children pay!" (117). Convinced that all his wolf-
patient's troubles are due to his vegetarian diet, the doctor confidently predicts
that as soon as the wolf starts eating meat, he will regain his mental equilibrium
and nightmare-free sleep. "Une ordonnance maladroite" offers an excellent example of the absolute logic and unbridled absurdity that are inextricably interwoven
in Gotlib's comics. The final frame shows a potbellied, burping wolf exiting the
office of the plump doctor, who has been reduced to a stethoscope, a white coat,
and a pile of bones. Ironically, the mild-mannered wolf has merely followed the
doctor's orders that he should not put off a change of diet.

In comics and cartoons, the wolf often finds himself in a doctor's office. A
cartoon by Mali depicts a wolf lying on the psychiatrist's couch with the caption:
"I like to dress up in old ladies' clothes and eat little girls."[7] In Mali's cartoon,
which is meant for an adult audience, the sexual connotations are manifest. Here
the wolf's psychological problems make him the victimizer, and he is portrayed
as a transvestite pedophile. In Gotlib's crossover BD, in contrast, the wolf's mental problems are those of a victim of physical violence and unrequited love. With
reluctance the vegetarian wolf finally eats, not an innocent little girl, but an in-
considerate doctor, who dictated his own end with his tactless prescription.

The first-person wolf-narrator generally seeks to exonerate and redeem himself by presenting himself as the victim of slander, that of Little Red Riding
Hood, her grandmother, the woodsman, the collective public, or even the storyteller. Critics have often pointed out the wolf's excellent rhetorical powers in the
classic tale; he skillfully dominates the little girl by his persuasive discourse. Many
of his contemporary successors follow in his footsteps; some even attempt to use
their persuasive powers with the audience. When the protagonist of the metafictive parody *Archie, the Big Good Wolf,* by the Australian picture-book team of Allan Baillie and Jonathan Bentley, introduces himself to readers, he admits that he's

"the Big *Bad* Wolf," according to "the muck that scrawny Mother Goose wrote about [him]," but he is determined to convince readers that he is not the bad guy in the story, but the unfortunate victim of a "scribbler goose" who got the facts all wrong. It is a different storyteller who is blamed in Jane Yolen's "Happy Dens, or A Day in the Old Wolves Home" (1985). Wolfgang, an aging, toothless, vegetarian wolf tells Nurse Lamb how he had shared a carrot cake intended for Grandmother with Little Red Riding Hood, whose real name was Elisabet Grimm. If we are to believe the old wolf, the classic tale is the invention of a little girl who called herself a storyteller and assured the wolf that she would think of some way of explaining the missing cake to her mother. Readers are tempted to suspect, however, that Wolfgang is just another wolf who has been forced by old age to reform and who therefore invents a story proclaiming his innocence.

The German children's author Rudolf Otto Wiemer presents another old wolf in his poem "Der Alte Wolf" (The Old Wolf), published in 1976. A third-person narrator suggests that the wolf has reformed in his old age and he is "now piously old and good" when he meets Red Riding Hood again in the woods. While the third-person narration may give more reliability to this story, the wolf's voice quickly replaces the anonymous voice. Whereas Little Red Riding Hood is given only half a line, the wolf narrates six of the poem's twelve lines. The wolf goes further than the third-person narrator, implying that he was never bad, or at least never as bad as the stories about him made out, stories that he dismisses as "wild." He blames the Brothers Grimm for the "lie" that is told about "a dark murder affair of old." The wolf wants Little Red Riding Hood to corroborate his version of the story and bids her "confess" that "it wasn't half as bad as they claim." The little girl acquiesces, but her stammered reply is given under duress, as she is very much aware of the wolf's menacing "bite" (255). Little Red Riding Hood's visible fear on this occasion suggests strongly that the Grimm brothers had not exaggerated the facts, but the wolf seems determined to play down the sin of his youth. The heavy sighs induced by the little girl's confession may reveal the regrets of a pious old wolf who has mended his ways since their first meeting. However, they could also be the nostalgic sighs of an old wolf who regrets the good old days of his youth. Wiemer's poem ends with the wolf giving his kind regards to Granny and waving good-bye. What resembles a happy ending is, in fact, a highly ambiguous open ending. After all, the first meeting in the woods ended in a similar manner. Who is to say that there is not more to this story as well!

The reliability of first-person wolf-narrators is highly questionable in most of these tongue-in-cheek parodies. But does the third-person narration of the British picture book *The Small Good Wolf* (1997) really give any more reliability to Mary Rayner's cautionary tale about "the big bad human" that has been passed down through generations of wolves, contradicting the classic version that *"Little Red Riding Hood and her family, and her children, and their children's children, have been telling . . . in their own big bad way"* for centuries? Many of the comical parodies mentioned thus far are targeted primarily at children. As we shall see in the next section, however, quite a number of authors writing for adults or for a crossover audience have fun with the wolf's big bad reputation in playful, humorous works that attempt to establish, in a tongue-in-cheek manner, the wolf's guilt or innocence.

The Archetypal Big Bad Wolf on Trial

Little Red Riding Hood's wolf is often confused with other fairy-tale wolves, so that he becomes merely one incarnation of the mythical figure of the notorious Big Bad Wolf of the fairy-tale world. There is only one wolf in the Kingdom of Fairy Tales, explains a character in Pierre Gripari's novel *Patrouille du conte* (Guardians of the tale): "It's the same archetype which is used for all the stories" (55). Not only is one wolf blamed for all the crimes committed by wolves in fairy tales, folktales, and fables, but wolves also continue to live under the shadow of their big bad reputation. As the narrator of Tomi Ungerer's "Little Red Riding Hood" points out, the wolf's reputation is often "even worse than his deeds" (84). Later in his story, Ungerer's wolf defines the word "reputation" for Little Red Riding Hood: "A reputation is what people think you are. Reputations come in all sizes. Some are good, some are bad or very bad, like mine" (88). Agha Shahid Ali's wolf realizes that readers are going to call him "the Big Bad Wolf," as that is now his "only reputation." Wolves in contemporary retellings have to contend with a legacy of centuries of negative wolf propaganda. Gotlib's BD shows the negative effect this grim legacy has on the health of one wolf, who, like so many of his counterparts, is unable to shake off the reputation of the Big Bad Wolf. His story is that of an innocent wolf being punished for his ancestors' sins, sins that include the demise not only of Little Red Riding Hood and her grandmother, but also the lamb, the three pigs, and so forth. Like Gotlib, many authors portray the wolf, even the archetypal Big Bad Wolf, in a humorous light, turning him into a sympathetic, misunderstood character whose evil reputation is unmerited.

In the collective imagination, the wolf has already been found guilty. The retellings examined in this section depict the persecution and criminal pursuit of the wolf in a playful manner, outside the context of sexuality. In some cases, the wolf may still be guilty of a serious crime, but it is no longer depicted as a sexual crime. The wolf is constantly being brought to task for his numerous crimes of folk tale, fairy tale, and fable. In some cases, he is pursued and brought to trial. In a number of instances, he is merely cross-examined by other characters. Sometimes he is punished by his own guilty conscience. Many contemporary authors choose to subvert the stereotypical image of the Big Bad Wolf by turning the classical fairy-tale world upside down and making the traditional victimizer the victim.

In 1934, Walt Disney superposed the two best-known fairy-tale wolves in the Silly Symphony *The Big Bad Wolf,* a sequel to *The Three Little Pigs* (1933), in which the pigs join forces with Red Riding Hood to vanquish the Big Bad Wolf. This bricolage of fairy tales (and wolves) has become a widespread strategy in contemporary literature, and it is particularly popular with young readers. According to many stories for all ages, a single, infamous wolf has terrorized the worlds of both fairy tale and fable. The newspaper headlines announcing the wolf's return in the French picture book *Le loup est revenu!* (The wolf has returned! 1994), by Geoffroy de Pennart, causes all his alarmed, former victims to gather under one roof: Little Red Riding Hood, the three pigs, Mrs. Goat and her seven kids, the little lamb, and Peter and his goose. When the hungry wolf knocks at the door, his former victims attack and overpower him and then invite him to join them for dinner, provided he promises to be good. The ending is deliberately ambiguous. Is the wolf forced to reform simply because he is outnumbered and overpowered when his former victims band together? Is the wolf's bad reputation, which haunts the collective unconscious and which is fanned by the sensationalism of the press, based solely on rumors and hearsay? Readers are left to decide whether they should give credence to the front-page headline of an embedded newspaper that reports the wolf's words: "Really, I am not so bad" (37). The question of the wolf's guilt or innocence is even more ambiguous in the sequel, *Je suis revenu!* (I have returned! 2000), in which the same story is narrated in the first person by the notorious wolf himself. *Le loup est revenu!* is a picture book for young children, but it was the author's talks with adult mediators, as well as children, that gave Pennart the idea for the sequel written from the wolf's perspective.[8]

The archetypal wolf is literally put on trial by David Fisher in "USA V. Wolf," one of the tales in his very funny adult collection *Legally Correct Fairy Tales* (1997) written in tongue-in-cheek legalese. The wolf who appears in court to make his deposition is named Thaddeus Wolf, but he is apparently "known among his associates by the nickname of 'Big Bad.'" Thaddeus is not, however, the only Wolf being charged. The government of the United States of America is bringing its charges of "corruption, fraud, and illegal control of specific building trades unions" against "both named and unnamed individuals known collectively as 'the Wolf Family'" (33–34). Whereas many authors attribute all the crimes of fairy tale and fable to one wolf, Fisher humorously makes his Mr. Wolf a member of "an organized crime family" (34).

The wolf is portrayed as a jocular character seeking to downplay the charges by turning everything into a joke. He solicits laughter in the courtroom by asking if the Court gets its jokes from "the Grimm Brothers" (37). While the primary intertext is the story of the Three Little Pigs, the Court also alludes to other criminal activities by the Wolf Family. The accused is asked if he has ever heard of a Peter, an obvious reference to *Peter and the Wolf,* or if he or any other members of his family "dress in sheep's clothing" (36). At an early stage in the proceedings, the Court wants to know if Mr. Wolf is familiar "with an individual known as Little Red Riding Hood." Fisher alludes wittily to the masculine gender of the French name "Le Petit Chaperon Rouge," when Mr. Wolf, ever the jokester, asks facetiously if the "gentleman" is "any relation to Robin Hood" (35). Metafictive play provides another source of tongue-in-cheek humor that appeals particularly to adults. Mr. Wolf seems to be quite familiar with fairy tales, including all those in which a wolf plays the role of the villain. Despite his denials and lighthearted banter, the accused in this story does not come across as an innocent victim, even though he may not personally be guilty of all the crimes mentioned by the Court. Although Thaddeus, alias "Big, Bad," Wolf is presented as one of the named members of a large Wolf Family, the Court implicates him in all the crimes committed by wolves in fairy tales.

The title character of Marcel Aymé's tale "Le loup" is also *the* wolf of fairy tale and fable fame, responsible for the demise of Little Red Riding Hood as well as the lamb and quite possibly a number of other fictional characters. "Le loup" is the opening story in the first volume of the timeless French classic, *Les contes du chat perché*, first published in 1934. Although Aymé's tales constitute one of the most popular French children's books of all time, the author denies having written them for young readers. These tales "for children from 4 to 75" were penned for his own pleasure, without a thought to his eventual audience, although he undoubtedly had his granddaughter, Françoise, in mind when he began writing them.[9] This crossover work was an immediate success with children and adults alike. In the 1930s, the tales appeared separately in small, softcover books suitable for a very young audience, as well as in Gallimard's adult series, the Collection blanche. Unfortunately, Aymé's tales are not well known in the English-speaking world, even though the first volume to appear in translation, under the title *The Wonderful Farm*, is the first children's book illustrated by Maurice Sendak, in 1951. In light of the wolf's universal appeal in children's literature, it is surprising that "Le loup" was overlooked in the first volume, appearing only in the 1954 sequel, *The Magic Pictures: More about the Wonderful Farm*, under the more descriptive title "The Wolf Who Turned Good."

Aymé's tales relate the adventures of two little girls, Delphine and Marinette, who live on an enchanted farm of talking animals. The genre of the fairy tale is explicitly mentioned in the title, so that readers begin Aymé's tales with certain expectations dictated by the codes of the genre. Marc Soriano rightly designates these tales as "anti-contes" (antitales),[10] however, because Aymé borrows the structures and characters of the traditional tale, while playfully subverting them. These tales about talking animals also echo the fable, which has a long and illustrious tradition in France thanks to La Fontaine. As with the fairy tale, however, Aymé adapts the genre of the fable to his own purpose. Although many of the animal characters are common barnyard and domestic animals, as the English title *The Wonderful Farm* suggests, Aymé also presents some of the wild animals popularly portrayed in fables, the wolf being a prime example. None of the characters, or for that matter the readers, question the fact that the animals talk or that they all speak the same language. This suspension of belief seems to be in stark contrast to the skepticism of young readers of the postmodern age, as witnessed in a cartoon by Bill Keane, in which a young boy listening to his mother read the story of Little Red Riding Hood interrupts impatiently to object: "But wolves can't talk."[11] Through the sententious sayings of moralizing animals, Aymé pokes fun at social conventions, prejudices, preconceived ideas, and human foibles. The wolf and the other talking animals do not hesitate to criticize the parents, who are portrayed in a rather caricatural manner. Contrary to his more

1. *Rotkäppchen* by Jacob and Wilhelm Grimm, illustration by Susanne Janssen (© 2001 Carl Hanser Verlag München Wien)

2. *Érase veintiuna veces Caperucita Roja*, illustration by Kaori Tsukuda (© 2006 Kaori Tsukuda; used by permission of Media Vaca)

3. *Makwelane and the Crocodile* by Maria Hendriks and Piet Grobler (© 2004 Piet Grobler; used by permission of Piet Grobler)

4. *Vous oubliez votre cheval* by Christian Bruel and Didier Jouault, illustration by Pierre Wachs
(© 1986 Le sourire qui mord; used by permission of Christian Bruel)

5. *John Chatterton détective* by Yvan Pommaux (© 1993 L'École des Loisirs; used by permission of Yvan Pommaux)

UNIVERSITY OF WINCHESTER
LIBRARY

6. *Roodkapje* by Wim Hofman, 1996 (used by permission of Wim Hofman)

7. *Cappuccetto Rosso*, Roberto Innocenti (© 1988 Roberto Innocenti; used by permission of Roberto Innocenti)

8. *Un petit chaperon rouge* by Claude Clément and Isabelle Forestier (© 2000 Éditions Grasset and Fasquelle; used by permission of Éditions Bernard Grasset)

9. *Un petit chaperon rouge* by Claude Clément and Isabelle Forestier (© 2000 Éditions Grasset and Fasquelle; used by permission of Éditions Bernard Grasset)

10. *Un petit chaperon rouge* by Claude Clément and Isabelle Forestier (© 2000 Éditions Grasset and Fasquelle; used by permission of Éditions Bernard Grasset)

11. *Rødhatten og Ulven* by Fam Ekman (© 1985 Cappelen; used by permission of Fam Ekman)

12. *Rood Rood Roodkapje* by Edward van de Vendel and Isabelle Vandenabeele (© 2003 by Uitgeverij De Eenhoorn; used by permission of Uitgeverij De Eenhoorn)

13. *Truly Grim Tales* by Priscilla Galloway, jacket illustration © 1995 Janet Woolley (used by permission of Janet Woolley and Lester Publishing)

14. *Bye Bye Chaperon Rouge* by Viviane Julien (poster © 1989 Alain Thomas/Avant-Première; used by permission of Rock Demers)

15. *Le Petit Chaperon rouge dans tous ses états,* by Tomi Ungerer, Musées de Strasbourg, Collection Tomi Ungerer. Photo by Nicolas Fussler. (© Diogenes Verlag, Zurich; used by permission of Diogenes Verlag)

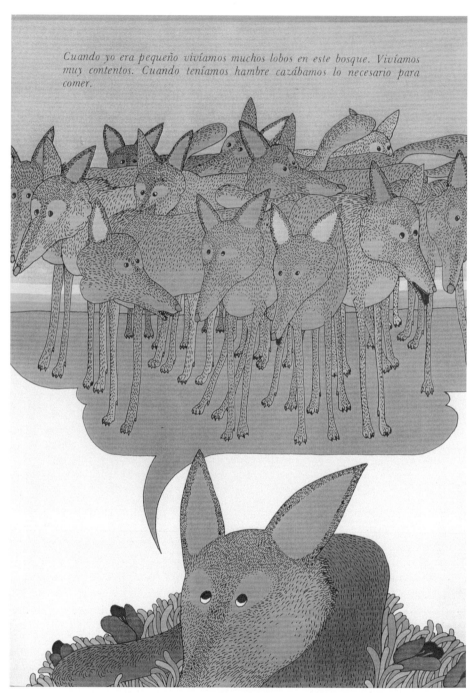

16. *El último lobo y Caperucita* by José Luis García Sánchez and Miguel Ángel Pacheco (illustrations © 1975 Miguel Ángel Pacheco; used by permission of Miguel Ángel Pacheco)

17. *Au loup!* by F'Murr (© 1993 Dargaud Éditeur; used by permission of Dargaud Éditeur and F'Murr)

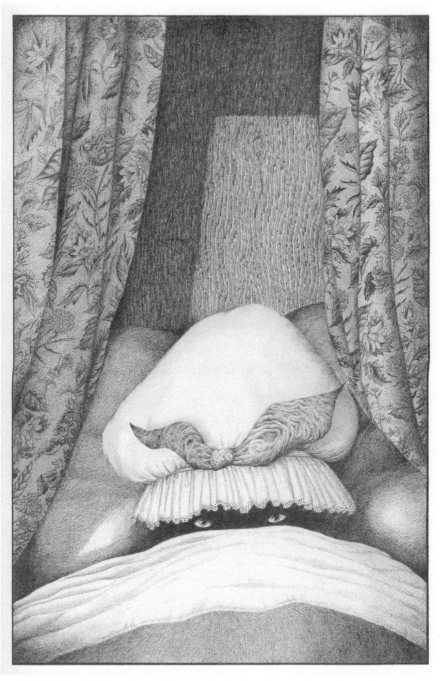

18. *Trail of Stones* by Gwen Strauss, illustration by Anthony Browne (© 1990 by Anthony Browne; used by permission of Anthony Browne)

19. *Wie je droomt ben je zelf* by Paul Biegel, illustration by Carl Hollander
(© 1977 Carl Hollander; used by permission of Uitgeverij Holland and the
Hollander family)

20. *Wie je droomt ben je zelf* by Paul Biegel, illustration by Carl Hollander (© 1977 Carl Hollander; used by permission of Uitgeverij Holland and the Hollander family)

21. *Wie je droomt ben je zelf* by Paul Biegel, illustration by Carl Hollander (© 1977 Carl Hollander; used by permission of Uitgeverij Holland and the Hollander family)

22. *The Stinky Cheese Man and Other Fairly Stupid Fairy Tales*, by Jon Scieszka and Lane Smith, illustration by Lane Smith (illustration © 1992 Lane Smith; used by permission of Penguin Group UK and Penguin Group USA)

23. *The Stinky Cheese Man and Other Fairly Stupid Fairy Tales*, by Jon Scieszka and Lane Smith, illustration by Lane Smith (illustration © 1992 Lane Smith; used by permission of Penguin Group UK and Penguin Group USA)

24. *Mon Chaperon Rouge* by Anne Ikhlef and Alain Gauthier, illustration by Alain Gauthier (© 1998 Éditions du Seuil; used by permission of Éditions du Seuil and Alain Gauthier)

L'enfant saute sur le lit et
dévisage la gueule noire
du loup. Elle frémit !

« Que vous avez de grands
yeux ! »

« C'est pour mieux te voir mon
enfant ! C'est pour mieux te voir ! »

Puis elle se laisse glisser sur le
corps sombre :

« Oh ma grand que vous êtes poilouse ! »

« C'est de vieillesse mon enfant !
C'est de vieillesse ! »

« Que vous avez de grands bras ! »

« C'est pour mieux t'embrasser, mon enfant !
C'est pour mieux t'embrasser ! »

« Que vous avez de grandes jambes ! »

« C'est pour mieux courir, mon enfant !
C'est pour mieux courir ! »

L'enfant se redresse tout à coup et
met sa main dans la gueule du loup :

« Que vous avez de grandes dents ! »

« C'est pour te manger ! »

25. *Mon Chaperon Rouge* by Anne Ikhlef and Alain Gauthier, illustration by Alain Gauthier (© 1998 Éditions du Seuil; used by permission of Éditions du Seuil and Alain Gauthier)

26. *Mon Chaperon Rouge* by Anne Ikhlef and Alain Gauthier, illustration by Alain Gauthier (© 1998 Éditions du Seuil; used by permission of Éditions du Seuil and Alain Gauthier)

27. *Mon Chaperon Rouge* by Anne Ikhlef and Alain Gauthier, illustration by Alain Gauthier (© 1998 Éditions du Seuil; used by permission of Éditions du Seuil and Alain Gauthier)

28. *Petits Chaperons Loups* by Christian Bruel, illustration by Nicole Claveloux (© 1997 Éditions Être; used by permission of Christian Bruel)

29. *Petits Chaperons Loups* by Christian Bruel, illustration by Nicole Claveloux (© 1997 Éditions Être; used by permission of Christian Bruel)

30. *Mina, je t'aime* by Patricia Joiret and Xavier Bruyère (© 1991 L'École des Loisirs; used by permission of Xavier Bruyère)

31. *Le Petit Chaperon rouge* by Maud Riemann (© Maud Riemann; used by permission of Maud Riemann)

32. *Rotkäppchen* by Eleanor Marston (© 2004 Eleanor Marston; used by permission of Eleanor Marston)

realistic works published only for adults, the social satire in *Les contes du chat per-ché* is not biting, but adopts a much lighter tone of tolerant amusement. While the fantasy and ludic element of these tales appeal spontaneously to children, they can also be read on another level as serious moral and sociopolitical allegories for adults.

The opening lines of the tale focus on the title character, who waits patiently behind the hedge for the parents to leave. In the original edition, Nathan Altman's first illustration of a large, intimidating animal, who stares disquietingly at the house with his long tongue hanging out of a large open mouth full of sharp teeth, reinforces the stereotypical image of the Big Bad Wolf. Rather than depicting the wolf realistically, Altman offers a highly theatrical representation, which bears the mark of his work as a set and costume designer for Russian avant-garde theater. The wolf's starring role in the story is emphasized by the format of the illustrations, which depict him within a circular shape like a stage actor in the circle of the spotlight. All but one of Altman's illustrations portray the wolf, and even in those that include Delphine and Marinette, the animal continues to occupy center stage. The wolf is present in all eight of Philippe Dumas's more recent drawings in the popular Folio Junior edition,[12] whereas the little girls appear in only two, unless we count the one that depicts an arm sticking out of the wolf's mouth. Contrary to Altman, Dumas subverts the traditional image of the ferocious wolf by presenting a comical, friendly looking wolf, who often resembles a good-natured dog. Like Altman's first picture, Dumas' initial drawing also focuses on the wolf, but this time it is a smiling, playful wolf. Aymé's illustrators are ever mindful of whose story is being told in "Le loup."

The tale is full of clever intertextual play. The opening is reminiscent of the Grimms' tale *The Wolf and the Seven Young Kids*, as Marinette and Delphine's parents leave them at home alone with the warning not to open the door to anyone. The parents are thus given a cautionary role not unlike that of the mother in the Grimms' version of *Little Red Riding Hood*. After the little girls have disobeyed their parents' injunctions and let the wolf in, Aymé adds a second cautionary scene in which the classic tale is embedded. After a lengthy lecture on the greediness and wickedness of wolves, the mother begins the oft-told exemplum of *Le Petit Chaperon Rouge* with deliberate cautionary intentions. The cautionary role of the classic tale is undermined, however, when Marinette interrupts to correct it in accordance with the version told to the girls by the wolf. Initially, Aymé seems to set out to deconstruct the stereotype of the wolf that pervades children's literature by using as intertexts the very works that are responsible for that cultural construction. He has fun with the powerful, mythic fear of the wolf that has haunted the collective unconscious for centuries. When the wolf taps on the window to get the sisters' attention, Marinette, the younger and more spontaneous of the two girls, seems, by virtue of her age, to be less affected by social conditioning than her older sister, as her immediate reaction is not fear, but laughter. The older, more sensible Delphine recognizes the wolf and dictates the requisite collective response:

> "It's the wolf."
> "The wolf?" said Marinette. "Are we afraid then?"
> "Of course, we're afraid."

Only then do the two girls begin to tremble and to clutch each other tightly.

Aymé's tale deals with the reform of the wolf, telling the story, according to the descriptive English title, of "The Wolf Who Turned Good." Touched by the sight of the pretty little blondes, the wolf realizes that he has suddenly become good, "so good and so gentle that he could never again eat children" (11). The contrasting images of the big bad wolf of once upon a time and this newly reformed wolf, who is so good that he can't believe it himself, is quite humorous. Even the wolf's voice is appropriately altered; his "gentle" voice, so unlike the gruff voice that attempts to imitate the grandmother in Perrault's tale, takes the girls completely by surprise. In this metafictive text, the wolf is conscious of the role he plays in the cultural imagination, commenting sadly on his reputation and insisting that you can't believe all the tales people tell about wolves. Like so many of his modern counterparts, Aymé's wolf feels that his public image is undeserved. There is some doubt as to whether he refers to himself since birth, or only to the wolf who turned over a new leaf minutes earlier, when he insists: "The truth is, I'm not really bad at all." On several occasions when he is sorely tested, the wolf congratulates himself on how "unbelievably" good he can be (18). The wolf still has difficulty believing in his transformation, long after the two girls, and probably most young readers, no longer have any doubts.

While the wolf's sad words and deep sighs are enough to win over Marinette, Delphine is not so quick to forget the wolf's infamous literary reputation. Admitting that the wolf looks "very good" at the moment, she reminds her younger sister of "the wolf and the lamb" (12), a direct allusion to La Fontaine's fable. Although Aymé's wolf is not brought to trial, he undergoes a rigorous cross-examination by a little French girl who knows her fairy tales and fables extremely well. In a witty exchange typical of Aymé's comical dialogue, Delphine first cross-examines the wolf about the innocent little lamb he ate. The wolf does not deny the accusation; in fact, he calmly asks which one and readily admits to having eaten lots of lambs. In his eyes, this is not a crime. In fact, he reminds his accusers that they also eat lamb, a fact the girls cannot deny because, as the narrator interjects humorously, they had just had a leg of lamb for lunch that very day. According to the wolf's logic, that fact should settle the question and prove to the girls that he is not really bad. The indulgent Marinette points out that the wolf cannot be expected to let himself starve to death, but Delphine, who disregards their own carnivorous appetites, insists that the wolf could have eaten potatoes. Aymé humorously suggests that there is one law for humans and another for wolves.

After the case of the lamb, the wolf is cross-examined about Little Red Riding Hood. Aymé's clever intertextual play with the famous tale announces the many metafictional retellings of the postmodern period. The classic tale constitutes far more than just a passing allusion or a simple "parenthesis," as one critic calls it;[13] indeed, it structures the entire tale. Initially, however, the characters somehow overlook the most obvious wolf story of all. It is only when Delphine is about to break down and let the wolf in that she suddenly remembers *Little Red Riding Hood*. This time the wolf is aware of his guilt. Hanging his head, he shamefacedly admits having eaten Little Red Riding Hood, but assures the girls that he's been tormented by regrets ever since. Aymé paints the comical portrait of a repentant wolf thumping his chest just over his heart in the classic mea culpa gesture and solemnly swearing that if he had it all to do over again, he would rather starve to death. He even resorts to theological discourse to vindicate himself, calling it "a sin of youth," and then humorously quoting scripture: "Every sin can be pardoned" (14). Readers have to question the sincerity of his remorse when the wolf adds that eating that little girl has given him no end of trouble. Apparently, what the wolf really regrets is the bad reputation he gained by the infamous act.

Aymé's wolf undermines the classic tale by ridiculing people who go so far as to say that he first ate the grandmother. He categorically denies having committed that crime, but his reason increases his guilt: he was not fool enough to eat a tough old grandmother when there was a tender little girl just waiting to be eaten. The more the wolf tries to vindicate himself, the guiltier he appears. At the memory of that meal of "fresh flesh," the wolf can't resist "licking his lips several times," thus revealing his long, sharp teeth. The wolf's instinctive gesture causes the observant and judicious Delphine to call him a "liar," because, as she puts it, he wouldn't be "licking his lips that way" if he truly felt remorse. In light of his reputation as a deceiver, the wolf is often accused of being a liar in contemporary retellings. Aymé's wolf admits sheepishly that lying is a bad habit he inherited from his family, which prompts Delphine to ask if "eating little girls" is also "a family habit." Apparently, hereditary flaws plague quite a number of literary wolves. It would seem that Aymé's wolf is unable to escape his past and that the memory of Little Red Riding Hood constitutes an insurmountable obstacle.

Few wolves in retellings of *Little Red Riding Hood* are endowed with such a distinctive personality or come to life with the power of Aymé's wolf, who alternately pleas and apologizes, flatters and threatens, laughs and sobs. He even plays on the girls' guilt, warning them that if he starts eating children again, his regression will be entirely their fault. The sad reflections of the sobbing wolf—about how, with the girls' friendship, he would have become better and better and even give up eating lambs—are no longer spoken aloud to persuade the girls, but said mournfully to himself, thus humorously illustrating the wolf's sincere conviction that he is reformed. Eventually he convinces both girls that his is "the voice of truth" (16).

The Big Bad Wolf's reputation as a prevaricator undoubtedly explains his frequent casting in the role of a master storyteller. In Aymé's tale, one of the wolf's ploys to gain admittance is the promise to tell the girls stories. True to his word, the wolf has an extensive repertoire of animal stories, along with a gift for telling them. Dumas' comical drawing of the wolf sitting comfortably in a chair in front of the stove telling stories reminds us of the storytelling wolf that he drew ten years earlier for the parodic retelling "Le Petit Chaperon Bleu Marine" (Little Navy Blue Riding Hood). Dumas and Boris Moissard carefully distinguish their storytelling wolf from the archetypal Big Bad Wolf, but nonetheless establish his relationship to more than one famous fictional wolf. He is the great-great-nephew of the one from Perrault's tale and a distant descendant of the one from La Fontaine's fable. The well-read wolf, who knows his great-great-uncle's story by heart and has no desire to share his fate, prefers an audience of wolves to one of little French girls. Dumas depicts the wolf-storyteller leaning against a

large tree stump on a snow-covered Siberian plain and surrounded by an attentive audience of wolves, undoubtedly telling the story of Little Red Riding Hood
or the one about Little Navy Blue Riding Hood, both of which are to be found
in his repertoire. As a storyteller, the wolf can cast himself in a better light or
even in an entirely different role.

The wolf plays a major role in children's culture, not only in literature but
also in games and songs. The importance of child's play and games in Aymé's
tales is announced in the French title, since *chat perché* is off-ground tag, and it is
unfortunate that this emphasis on ludic activity is lost in the English title. After
the storytelling session, the girls start teaching the wolf their games. We are reminded of other Riding Hoods playing games with the wolf, notably Violette in
Mon Loup. Like Bertier and so many other authors, Aymé integrates the game
"Loup, y es-tu?" During their games, Delphine sticks her little hand "dans la
gueule du loup," an apposite play on words because the French expression has
the figurative meaning of throwing oneself into the lion's jaws. Aymé's inventive wordplay and verbal acrobatics, along with his particular brand of fantasy,
have led to comparisons with Lewis Carroll. Although she does not do so inten-
tionally, Delphine seems to bait the wolf. While her hand is in his jaws, she can't
refrain from borrowing a line from Little Red Riding Hood: "Oh! What big teeth
you have . . ." Very ill at ease, the wolf overcomes temptation and "tactfully"
avoids mentioning the "big hunger" in his belly (perhaps an allusion to the ritualistic dialogue in which all the wolf's body parts are described as "big"). During his first visit, the wolf turns out to be the perfect playmate and, for his part,
thoroughly enjoys human games. On his next visit, they play "Loup y es-tu?" to
take the wolf's mind off the distressing fact that the parents refuse to believe he
has become good. Even very small children will appreciate the irony in the fact
that the wolf, who is logically chosen to play the wolf, has to be taught the rules
of the game. The reformed wolf gets completely carried away with his role and
plays the game so well that he unintentionally gobbles up his two playmates.

As one becomes older, the cultural construction of the wolf becomes more ingrained and difficult to change. The parents refuse to entertain the idea of the
wolf's reform. When they detect the distinct odor of wolf after his first visit,
Delphine allays their suspicions by borrowing a convincing, "adult" argument
with which her father is unable to argue: "If the wolf had come into the kitchen,
we would both have been eaten." Little Marinette comes immediately to his defense, denying that he eats children or is bad. In the end, both girls ardently take

Les contes du chat perché by Marcel Aymé, illustration by Philippe Dumas, illustrations © 1987 by Éditions Gallimard. Used by permission of Philippe Dumas.

up the wolf's defense, interrupting each other in their eager attempt to convince their parents of the wolf's innocence. The sisters humorously reiterate the wolf's arguments and even borrow some of his religious terminology. Aymé often satirizes the unshakable, preconceived ideas of adults, and in this case Delphine and Marinette's closed-minded parents stubbornly present the collective view of the Big Bad Wolf. The girls are eventually sent to bed without dinner for their "scandalous defense" of an animal that will never change (22).

Since children and animals generally represent the voice of wisdom in Aymé's tales, readers tend to disregard the parents' negative opinion of the wolf. However, the unsympathetic parents are not the only ones who doubt the wolf's reform. Some of the forest animals also express their doubts. As the wolf heads off to visit the girls, a chattering old magpie taunts the wolf, saying that he has undoubtedly chosen "very plump and tender" friends (24). According to the angry wolf, who congratulates himself on his clear conscience, exactly that kind of gossip creates bad reputations. As in La Fontaine's fables, the satire in Aymé's tales is full of delicious irony. When the girls express their desire to visit the woods with him in the spring because they wouldn't be afraid in his company, the wolf tells them that by that time he will have "preached" so well to his forest companions they will all have been converted to gentle behavior. Ironically, the first

Les contes du chat perché by Marcel Aymé, illustration by Philippe Dumas, illustrations © 1987 by Éditions Gallimard. Used by permission of Philippe Dumas.

animal he attempts to convert is the fox, a most unlikely candidate if one considers the incorrigible unscrupulousness of his literary reputation. The amusing encounter casts the two animals in the stereotypical roles of the fox and the wolf that date back to the famous medieval epic *Reynard the Fox*. The ingenuous wolf does not recognize his artful companion's irony when, at the end of his sermon, the fox assures him that he would like nothing better than to follow the wolf's example. Although the wolf is now convinced of his reform, his difficulty in persuading others will perhaps create some doubt in readers' minds. In the end, Delphine and Marinette's father might have been right when he stated categorically that "the wolf would always be a wolf" (22).

Whereas Altman avoids illustrating the shocking scene in which the two girls are devoured, Dumas revels in depicting a huge-bellied wolf with one anonymous arm sticking out of his mouth and blood dripping into a puddle on the floor, where a pair of wooden clogs is all that remains of the two girls. The rather gory scene will certainly shock some readers, probably mostly adult mediators concerned about violence in children's literature. However, it is so overdone that most readers will find it absurdly funny. More appalling than Dumas' illustration of the dramatic scene is the fact that Norman Denny felt it necessary to eliminate it entirely when he translated "Le loup" into English. The watering down of the crucial, climactic moment of the classic tale undermines Aymé's parodic reworking. Perhaps it was because the original scene was considered too violent for an English-speaking audience that "Le loup" was not included in the first collection published in English. In his visual interpretation of the scene, Dumas chooses to highlight the violence and exaggerate it in a parodic manner that renders it purely comical. It is rather surprising that Denny felt obliged to alter this scene so drastically, because, contrary to many of Aymé's tales, "Le loup" ends happily. Modeling his ending on the Grimms' more optimistic version, Aymé replaces the woodsman with the parents, who, on their return, open the wolf's belly to deliver the two little girls.

In Aymé's tales, animals may be cruel and display human faults, but even the most shocking and reprehensible conduct retains a certain innocence. Animals remain true to their own nature. The wolf cannot really be blamed for his voracious appetite, and the compassionate little girls forgive the wolf for eating them. Aymé's contrite wolf stoically assures the girls that he deserves the pain caused by the stitches, and he swears that in the future he will be less "gourmand" and run in the opposite direction when he sees children. Although a certain amount of ambiguity remains at the end, evidently this time the wolf has indeed reformed. The narrator concludes with a kind of epilogue, informing readers that it is generally believed that "the wolf kept his word." At any rate, since his adventure with Delphine and Marinette, the wolf has not been known to eat "any little girls" (28).

Aymé's retelling is not the only one that deals with the question of the wolf's redemption. In 1974, Roque Jacintho published the children's book *O Lobo Mau reencarnado* (*The Big Bad Wolf Reincarnate*, 1981), a continuation of the Grimms' version in which the drowning wolf dies full of remorse for gobbling up Little Red Riding Hood and her grandmother. At the Institute of Moral Reform in the Spirit World, the Spirit in charge of "Bad Wolves" assures the wolf that he will become good. Although he is tired of being "a Big Bad Wolf," the wolf is convinced he is a hopeless case entirely beyond help. "I'll always be a wolf, a Big Bad Wolf who eats grandmothers and little red riding hoods wherever I find them," he says despairingly. In this retelling published for the purpose of proselytization by the Brazilian Spiritual Federation, the "ex-Big Bad Wolf" is set on the path of redemption, undergoing a series of reincarnations that give him the opportunity to prove to the other characters in the fairy tale that he has mended his ways.

In his novel *Patrouille du conte* (Guardians of the tale, 1983), Pierre Gripari portrays a wolf whose reform, unlike that of Aymé's and Jacintho's wolves, is not of his own free will, but forced upon him by society. Whereas the wolf in Gripari's poem "Le loup" is seen only in his role as devourer of Riding Hoods, chapter 5 of the earlier novel, also titled "Le loup," presents another reworking of *Le Petit Chaperon Rouge,* in which the eponymous character ate the three little pigs and the lamb as well. *Patrouille du conte* was published for adults, but the author, who claims not to distinguish between writing for children and writing for adults, uses the novel to illustrate what he calls the "intermediary space" that can be frequented by both child and adult audiences. In actual fact, Gripari never really considered *Patrouille du conte* a children's book, although he admitted it could be if it didn't contain such precise political references. The proposal to turn it into a children's book didn't meet with Gripari's approval because it would have been at the price of a "reduction" that would have impoverished rather than enriched the novel. For example, it was suggested that he would need to eliminate the controversial three little pigs who denounce the "antiporcinisme" (antiporcinity) of an unnamed Arab province and end up eating the wolf, but the author was fond of the little pigs, who were also a big hit with readers.[14] Moreover, young readers seem to appreciate the vicious, greedy, wolf-eating little pigs at least as much as adult readers.

Gripari's novel is a hilarious bricolage of fairy tales and nursery rhymes in which the newly created Ministry of Fairy Tales and Cultural Environment in the French Republic of the real world gives a patrol of eight boys, commanded by a young lieutenant and an adult captain, the task of keeping law and order in the Kingdom of Fairy Tales. The Ministry has decided that only young people can be entrusted with the job of cleaning up fairy tales for children because their purity and innocence will ensure that Perrault's *Contes* is not turned into a pornographic book. The lieutenant doesn't even know the meaning of the word *pornographic,* and issues of a sexual nature are generally beyond the comprehension of the other young members of the patrol, just as they go over the heads of young readers. Their mission is "to moralize and democratize" fairy tales for children by purging them of everything harmful from "a moral, social, or ideological point of view," including murder, cruelty toward animals, fraud, and injustice (10). In light of the fact that the book was targeted at adults, it is surprising that the crimes of rape, child abuse, and incest are overlooked. Acknowledging that a culture dating back several centuries cannot be democratized overnight, the Ministry charges the patrol to begin with the most urgent cases, by putting an end to bloodshed and abolishing barbarous acts against "animals, children, and men" (12). One is consistently struck by the fact that women's rights are not high on the French Ministry's agenda. Not surprisingly, feminists have taken Gripari to task. Tales that cannot be ideologically corrected, even with the most radical modification, are to be deleted from the canon. The clever metafictional play in the novel is particularly humorous for older readers. Each mission modifies Perrault's *Contes*, so that new editions are continually coming off the press, leaving the patrol as well as readers constantly wondering how the tale will be revised or if it will even make it into the next edition.

Le Petit Chaperon Rouge is at the top of the list of fairy tales to be dealt with by the patrol after the completion of a simple initial mission involving a popular French song, "La Mère Michel" (Mother Michel), in which a cat is slaughtered. It seems that the murder of a cat is more important than the double murder of a little girl and her grandmother. In a tongue-in-cheek comment on the social conditioning of classic fairy tales, Gripari has one little boy pronounce Perrault's tale morally justified because the little girl dallied, wasting time, as he puts it, "running after flowers and picking butterflies." In this scene, the author humorously points out the absurdity of holding Little Red Riding Hood responsible for her fate. In an attempt to demonstrate that the punishment of death hardly fits the crime, the captain retorts that the boy would be long gone "if all the scatterbrains who dawdled while doing errands were to be eaten by wolves" (19). Further, the captain reminds the boy of the innocent grandmother, who had done absolutely nothing to deserve her fate, and later rebukes the boy for dismissing the grandmother because of her age, since the elderly also have their rights in a democratic society. The innocence of the victims in Perrault's tale is clearly established. After recounting the ending of the German tale, Gram (the similarity with Grimm is probably not fortuitous) pronounces the happy ending implausible but quite moral, while another young member of the patrol disagrees, claiming that although the wolf doesn't have any right to eat people, people don't have the right to kill the wolf either. Little Red Riding Hood, her grandmother, and the hunter are also guilty. The adult captain informs the patrol that the tale has to be rewritten because there has been "an abuse of power and a violation of the rights of animals" (21). The author of *Pa-*

trouille du conte perversely puts the rights of animals before those of women and children.

As the chapter title "Le loup" indicates, the mission involving the story of Little Red Riding Hood is focused on the wolf. The little girl in red is sidelined and does not even make an appearance in this chapter. The wolf seems to acknowledge his archetypal role. His surprise is evident when the patrol asks him to identify himself, as he thinks it is quite obvious that he is "the wolf" (22). Further, he is not at all pleased at being cross-examined by the patrol. In a humorous parody of the classic tale, the question the wolf asks of Little Red Riding Hood is now put to the wolf, but, unlike the naive little girl, the wolf insists it is none of their business where he is going. Unimpressed by their policing role, the wolf only admits that he is going to Little Red Riding Hood's grandmother's house after they threaten him with a gun, as he has a deep aversion to firearms. When he fails to admit that he was going there to eat the grandmother, this wolf is also accused of being a liar. Confident in their knowledge of the plot, the patrol proceeds to tell the wolf his own plan, paradoxically providing him with a good one if, as he claims, he had intended no such thing. Perrault's volume of *Contes,* which provides the patrol's guidebook throughout the novel, is produced to prove that they know everything, but it bears no weight whatsoever with the wolf, who is unfamiliar with the cultural artifact called a book and couldn't give "a damn" if it is not something edible (23).

Gripari gets away with a defiant disregard for decorum by putting the four-letter words into the mouth of the big bad wolf. Gripari pokes fun at the hypocrisy of adults in this regard. The captain's displeasure at the new version of "La Mère Michel," is largely due to the fact that Mère Michel's vulgar language is "inadmissible" in a book intended for young people, yet the captain uses equally crude language with the young members of the patrol when he refers to Mère Michel as a "bitch" (29). The captain could in fact do with the same dressing down that he prescribes for the Mère Michel. In this highly metafictive work, the patrol attempts to precensure the language of the tales by warning characters not to use coarse words, since they don't know which of their words will be written down for posterity in the official version of the tale.

As is often the case in retellings of Little Red Riding Hood, the episode of "Le loup" is peppered with legal jargon.[15] When playing innocent gets him nowhere, Gripari's wolf ends up confessing his "criminal plans," but he "defends" himself with a speech about his ecological role (27). The wolf insists on his niche in the food chain, that of the "regulator of mankind" whose role is to prevent the degeneration of the human race by getting rid of "undesirable elements" such as old, sick grandmothers and disobedient little girls (23). The wolf's discourse is not unlike that of his counterpart in Gripari's poem "Le loup," whose role is described in moral, rather than ecological terms. The threat of being shot stone dead if he eats a single human being prompts the wolf to propose replacing humans with "the three pigs . . . the lamb . . ." This archetypal wolf would undoubtedly have added some of his other fictional victims to the list if the patrol had not interrupted his enumeration with a ban on that "grub" as well. More down to earth than the Ministry, the boys realize that the wolf's sharp teeth do not belong to a grazer but to a carnivore, and that there is no point preaching to the wolf unless they can find a way of feeding him. Gripari has a great deal of fun spoofing idealistic, impractical government policies. The lesson learned from the wolf has a marked impact on future missions. Before sending the patrol out to fix the tale *Little Thumbling,* the captain warns the members that ogres, like wolves, are "a recognized, legal, catalogued, classified species," and therefore cannot be prevented "from eating children." The Ministry's lowered expectations, since their dealings with the wolf, are evident when the patrol is instructed to convince the ogre to eat only "naughty, egoistic, fascist, ideologically harmful children" (36). Child abuse is to be allowed, as long as it is only perpetrated against those who have not been properly socialized!

Irony and satire pervade Gripari's text. Since the patrol has the good fortune of dealing with a talking wolf, they are instructed to reason with him and convince him to change his violent plan. At the same time, the patrol is given leave to resort to threats and force if the wolf refuses to listen to reason. Violence and bloodshed are morally justified if the Ministry of Fairy Tales and Cultural Environment gives its blessing. Gripari's pointed references to politics in the real world account to a great extent for the book's success with French adult readers. The grandmother turns out to be harder to reason with than the wolf. When she is told that the wolf agrees not to eat either her granddaughter or her provided that she gives him a mash containing meat twice a day, the old lady quibbles and haggles, questioning the good faith of the "hairy villain," complaining about the cost that she will incur, and demanding some kind of compensation (25). In exchange for his mash, the wolf will assume the role of a guard dog, so the grandmother will no longer have to bother securing her door with the *bobinette.*

The patrol must await the latest edition of Perrault's *Contes* to find out if *Le Petit Chaperon Rouge* has become a moral story that can be retained or whether it has been deleted. Although the patrol is opposed to deleting fairy tales from the canon, the captain points out that in the particular cases that concern them—those in which the main subject of the story is a murder—once the crime has been eliminated, there is no raison d'être for the rest of the story. The example of *Le Petit Chaperon Rouge* is used to illustrate the point: "What do we care about the grandmother, the little pot of butter, and the cake, if the wolf is no longer dangerous?" (34). When a member of the patrol expresses his consternation at the idea of eliminating this particular tale, one of his favorites, the captain uses typical socialist discourse to insist that these small sacrifices are sometimes necessary for the common good. The captain evidently does not know any of the numerous, successful re-versions that rehabilitate the wolf and turn him into a sympathetic, even endearing, character.

As it turns out, the tale is not deleted, but the ending is rewritten in a most unexpected manner. One day Little Red Riding Hood arrives at her grandmother's to find her preparing to cook the wolf, a cruel plan the old lady rationalizes by the fact that they have nothing left to eat and that the old wolf has outlived his usefulness now that he is lame and almost blind. Little Red Riding Hood's tears and pleas, as well as the cake and little pot of butter that will keep the wolf from the door or, in this case, from the pot, for another few days, convinces the grandmother to postpone her beastly plan. The grandmother underscores the subversion of the traditional roles when she says the wolf is very lucky to have a defender like Little Red Riding Hood and an old "bête" like herself for a mistress. Although the grandmother is undoubtedly calling herself an old "fool," the more common meaning of *bête*, "beast" or "animal," is perhaps more to the point. In this retelling, the wolf turns out to be a far more likable character than the grandmother. The boys' increasing sympathy for the wolf is evident when they refer to him as a "fellow" (24) or address him as "monsieur le Loup" (25), which is in stark contrast to the insulting names used by the grandmother. Fearing that the "old bitch" will put him on to boil in the middle of the night, the wolf decides that he will be safer in the forest, but the domesticated animal is no longer able to survive in his natural habitat (52). Weak, starving, and half-frozen, the poor old wolf has his throat slit before being torn to pieces and devoured by the three pigs. In a highly absurd manner, Gripari applies the common strategy of turning the fairy-tale world upside down to make the traditional victimizer the victim.

Gripari's intertextual play and clever bricolage is an unending source of humor. In a pastiche of Perrault's verse moral, Gripari cautions wolves to beware of grandmothers and little girls and little pigs. Whereas the patrol finds this ending absolutely appalling and is convinced they have merely substituted one crime for another, the captain prefers to downplay the tragic and violent events, qualifying the new ending as merely "sad." Again, adults will appreciate the political satire. It is clear that the captain's mitigated reaction is politically motivated. The three pigs are a politically sensitive issue because their history is one of suffering and they claim to be the victims of prejudice, including "acute antiporcinity, congenital misohogony, and inveterate pigophobia" (123). The porcine neologisms provide an excellent example of the insolent wordplay that has so much appeal to children. The author ingeniously weaves the different tales together into a very funny and increasingly complex plot. In the mission devoted to *Little Thumbling*, readers learn that the boys are not afraid of the wolf in the forest because they know he's fed twice a day by the grandmother, but because of his small size, the protagonist is terrified of the three pigs, who would gobble him up in a single bite.

The wolf continues to play a lead role, even in the climactic scene that brings together all the characters who star in this fairy-tale bricolage. A huge, double republican wedding, which is to be the crowning achievement of the Ministry's cultural policy and to mark the total alignment of the fairy-tale realm with the real-world French Republic, brings together all the reformed fairy-tale characters, including Little Red Riding Hood and her grandmother. The celebration is interrupted by a manifestation led by the wolf, the she-wolf, and several cubs. The latter carry a huge banderole bearing the words: "*Our animal proteins,*" and the wolf and she-wolf's signs read: "*We are the regulators of children*" and "*Free movement of Petits Chaperons rouges*" respectively (147, author's italics). Many other familiar fairy-tale characters unhappy with their lot and carrying signs with similar slogans follow the activist wolves.

Gripari's subversive novel turns the fairy-tale world completely upside down. The utter pandemonium of the hilarious climax delights young readers, while adults appreciate the underlying political irony. The outcome is revealed in a top-secret report to the Minister that is embedded toward the end of the novel. After intervening, against orders, when the wolf cubs started mauling the humans, the patrol ended up joining the dissidents, "the werewolves and . . . all the darkest, most disturbing and dangerous forces of the world of fiction" (154). Soon they were joined by some of the wedding guests, reluctant converts to the Fairy Tale Republic. Gripari insists on the violence unleashed by the government's attempt to reform fairy-tale characters like the wolf. According to the report, officials are still trying to establish the list of dead, injured, and unaccounted for. Also embedded in the novel is a news bulletin reporting the unexplained events that followed the fateful wedding and caused an influx of "fantastic creatures in the real world" (151). One of the reported incidents concerns wolves attacking "lone strollers" in the Morvan, the Pyrenees, and the Vosges (152). Gripari alludes tongue in cheek to historical events in certain regions of France that gave birth to medieval oral versions of the famous tale.

The wolf's political activism has far-reaching results. The President decides that the patrol is to be abandoned in the imaginary world, with which it had sided, and that henceforth its members will belong to folklore. As far as History is concerned, the Tale Patrol is to be a deletion or a torn-out page. There will be a return to the status quo ante and Perrault's *Contes* is to be reprinted "in accordance with the original edition" (155). In stereotypical politician fashion, the Minister belatedly recognizes, although not publicly of course, their error in wanting to interfere in a world that does not belong to them and whose laws they do not understand. The government is forced to acknowledge that evil (violence, cruelty, etc.) has "a purifying function" in the imaginary and must therefore be allowed to survive "in tale and legend." Moreover, its "pedagogical importance" must be officially recognized. The Minister has perhaps been reading or consulting psychologists such as Bruno Bettelheim, whose influential book *The Uses of Enchantment* was published in French a few years before *Patrouille du conte*. The paradoxical message of this postmodern novel, constructed by subversively deconstructing classic tales, seems to be that it is best not to tamper with the world of fairy tales. However, the author's warning is really directed at those who would sanitize the classic tales and use them for ideological purposes to acculturate children. At the same time, Gripari's *Patrouille du conte* takes *Little Red Riding Hood* and other fairy tales to "the limits of subversiveness."[16] Perrault's wolf has been turned into a political animal who now publicly claims his right to eat little girls. Furthermore, he will be allowed to do so.

The attempt to reform the wolf, regardless of whether the reform is initiated by others or by the wolf himself, tends often to backfire. The good intentions of the wolves created by Gotlib and Aymé do not prevent them from committing or attempting to commit the crimes of which they or their ancestors have been accused. At the same time, the wolf's guilt is mitigated in these humorous retellings. Gotlib's wolf only eats humans reluctantly, on the advice of his doctor. Readers are led to believe that Aymé's wolf really did reform after the regression brought on by playing wolf. When the laws of society impose the reform, as in Gripari's novel, the result is equally unsuccessful. In this provocative parody, society is forced to acknowledge that the wolf has the right to eat Little Red Riding Hoods. When the wolf's crimes are viewed in a nonsexual context, his criminal pursuit and persecution are generally the excuse for humorous works that appeal to readers of all ages.

When contemporary authors shift the focus from Little Red Riding Hood to the wolf, his story takes as many different forms as hers. Some authors of retellings for all ages spotlight the wolf in order to explore further the latent symbolism of the wolf as seducer and sexual predator that was present in Perrault's tale. Even in books that target principally young readers, some authors push this interpretation still further to expose the wolf as child abuser or pedophile. However, in many retellings, especially those marketed primarily at young readers, the wolf's story is told outside the context of sexuality. This makes it possible to turn the wolf into a sympathetic, or at least a less odious character for the purpose of developing new interpretations in both serious and humorous modes. Many authors disculpate the wolf, feeling that it is time to deconstruct the stereotypical image of the wolf as aggressor. A large number of parodic retellings in a humorous mode subvert the stereotypical image of the Big Bad Wolf by turning the classical fairy-tale world upside down and making the traditional victimizer the victim. Focusing on the wolf or adopting his perspective allows authors and illustrators to renew the story of Little Red Riding Hood by questioning and subverting more conventional interpretations of the tale. Whether he is depicted as seducer, sexual predator, pedophile, or lover, as criminal or innocent victim, in contemporary retellings the wolf holds as much fascination for many authors and illustrators as does Little Red Riding Hood.

4. The Wolf Within

The wolf is your own fear.

—PAUL BIEGEL, *Wie je droomt ben je zelf*

As we have seen in the preceding chapter, the figure of the wolf possesses tremendous symbolical power in children's literature and popular culture. The wolf is an obsessive presence in the folk and fairy tales and nursery rhymes that have saturated the collective conscious. The animal carries with it a world of anguish, dread, and fear that is incarnated in the wolf of *Little Red Riding Hood*. Knowing this particular wolf haunts the dark corners of the child's imagination, the Canadian author-illustrator Mireille Levert alludes to the tale in one of her picture books in order to express the child's "universal fears," she writes in a 27 February 2001 letter. The wolf does not only haunt the imagination of children, however. Authors like Angela Carter and Tanith Lee show how the wolf lurks in the subconscious of adults as well. It would seem that the fairy-tale wolf is the primordial, archetypal Fear. The wolf's obsessive presence in literature and culture for all ages is due to the fact that the figure of the wolf crystallizes human fears. In the story of Little Red Riding Hood, the little girl's terror has a concrete source and takes a specific form: the wolf. In the retellings discussed in this chapter, the dangers represented by the wolf are internalized. In the heroic quest, as well as in any form of initiation, the encounter with a monster symbolizes not only physical danger but also the inner demons of fear and self-doubt. In the recastings examined here, Little Red Riding Hood encounters the wolf within.

Many contemporary authors who retell the story of Little Red Riding Hood seek to demystify the powerful, mythic fear of the wolf that haunts the collective unconscious and pervades the field of children's literature. Often the wolf is no longer depicted as an embodiment of fear but as a source of ridicule or pity, as we saw, for example, in the works of F'Murr and Gotlib. Philippe Dumas and Boris Moissard adopt a different approach in "Le Petit Chaperon Bleu Marine," where the public's fear of the wolf is ridiculed by exaggerating it to absurd proportions. The unknown whereabouts of a single harmless wolf, released from the zoo by Little Navy Blue Riding Hood in order to reenact the story of her grandmother, the ex–Little Red Riding Hood, causes widespread terror. The press fans the collective hysteria, according to Dumas's comical drawing of Parisians congregating at a newspaper kiosk plastered with papers, whose headlines all scream the story of the wolf at large.

A significant number of authors are, on the contrary, intent on preserving the wolf's primeval, mythical power. The British author Tanith Lee achieves this in a memorable manner in "Wolfland," from *Red as Blood: Or Tales from the Sisters Grimmer* (1983), a collection of retold fairy tales that the back cover blurb warns are not for children. Like Francesca Lia Block, Lee writes young adult fiction that is also read by adults, and her retold tales appeal to a wide crossover audience of teens and adults.[1] The protagonist of "Wolfland" feels that it is not just the cultural image of the wolf, but its actual reality, from its appearance and movement to its howling, that belongs to "the stuff of nightmares" and accounts for the "primordial fear" she experiences in her grandmother's château that stands in what, since ancient times, has been the Wolfland (119). The spontaneous fear aroused by the wolves provokes in Lisel an overpowering physiological reaction: her hair stands on end, her arms are covered in gooseflesh, and her bones turn to liquid. The protagonist's fear is transmitted to readers, evoking their own primordial fear of the wolf.

Retellings for all ages use the story of Little Red Riding Hood and the wolf to explore our deepest fears. In her novel *Wolf*, Gillian Cross sets out to subvert the stereotype of the wolf that has terrified children for centuries. The titular wolf in Cross's disturbing and multilayered novel is a metaphor for the protagonist's fear. A character in the novel explains to Cassy that the topic of the wolf concerns "the nature of fear" (23). Like so many children, the wolf haunts Cassy's dreams. The tale of Little Red Riding Hood resurfaces from the girl's subconscious before she even knows she is in danger. A disturbing, recurring dream, which weaves its way obsessively through the narrative, constitutes a fragmented mise en abyme of the classic tale. Toward the end of the novel, Cassy's fear is no longer about a "story" or a "dream," but involves a "real danger" (128). As in Francesca Lia Block's "Wolf," Cross casts the protagonist's father in the role of the wolf. Cassy is being stalked by her father, Mike Phelan or Mick the Wolf, an IRA terrorist also known as the Cray Hill bomber. The father-wolf deliberately exploits the girl's fear to his own ends, beginning his threatening letter with "*Dear Red Riding Hood*" and signing it "*The Big Bad Wolf*" (114, author's italics). Cross presents a modern Little Red Riding Hood who learns to conquer her fears and to vanquish her wolf. Fully aware of the danger, Cassy bravely sets out on her own to rescue her grandmother, who is being held hostage. Like the other books discussed in this chapter, *Wolf* uses the themes and motifs of the story of Little Red Riding Hood to offer a profound psychological exploration of the protagonist's fear.

The Wolf in the Mirror

The popular Dutch children's author Paul Biegel offers a highly original psychoanalytical interpretation of *Little Red Riding Hood* in *Wie je droomt ben je zelf* (You are who you dream about). When Biegel was commissioned to write a book in 1977 for Children's Book Week, he decided to realize an idea that had been in the back of his mind for years, that of a story of Little Red Riding Hood written from the point of view of each of the different characters.[2] According to the author, the text is far too difficult for children, but he believes that Carl Hollander's illustrations appeal to a young audience. Although Biegel may feel that the story did not specifically target young readers to the extent it should have, the book's success with that audience is demonstrated by the fact that, after tens of thousands of copies had been given away, it was reprinted in 1990. Adults appreciate the psychological depth of this retelling by an author known for his difficult and challenging children's books. Although he is conscious of his young readership, Biegel never deliberately addresses himself to children, and he repeatedly points out that his works can be read on many levels. His innovative and thought-provoking retelling of *Little Red Riding Hood* speaks to both children and adults due to its multilayered narrative.

In his fantasy works, Biegel often uses the characters, themes, and motifs of fairy tales to address the universal problems and aspirations of the human condition. He concurs with Bruno Bettelheim's belief that fairy tales "state an existential dilemma briefly and pointedly" in a form accessible to the child.[3] The author explains his intentions to readers in a short preface, titled "Ben jij het zelf?" (Is it you?).[4] In a simple manner, Biegel points out to young readers what psychoanalysts have believed for many years: fairy tales as well as dreams use symbols to express fears and forbidden desires that have been repressed into the unconscious, and can therefore tell us about our innermost selves. One of the "disguises" adopted in fairy tales by these hidden feelings is that of the wolf (7). The author obviously expects his readers to interpret his retelling of *Little Red*

Riding Hood in a personal manner, journeying into their inner selves to explore their subconscious and discover the wolf within. Biegel's preface prepares readers for a recasting that relies heavily on a psychoanalytical interpretation of the tale.

The multilayered intertextual play offers levels for readers of all ages. The enigmatic title of Biegel's retelling provides no hint of the relationship to the famous tale. However, young readers should easily decode the cover illustration of the disguised wolf, even though the wolf's feminine apparel consists of a white dress and summer bonnet rather than the customary nightgown and cap. The illustration inside the book replaces the dress with the more familiar nightgown. Young readers are alerted to the intertextuality in the preface, where the author insists that familiarity with the pre-text is essential to understanding the new story. Readers must be aware that "the wolf" has been deliberately drawn out of the depths of the classic tale and exposed in the retelling. It is a sign of the complexity of the text that the author feels obliged to explain the symbolism of the wolf so explicitly: "*The wolf that you are so scared of, that you struggle against, that you flee from, is not a wolf in the woods. It is something from your inner self, disguised as a wolf*" (8–9, italics in original). It is to be hoped, however, that children, as well as adults, forgo the explanatory paratext and let the poetic tale speak for itself. The preface's concluding remark merely echoes the story's title, implying that those whose nightmares are haunted by wolves are actually wolves themselves.

The fundamental theme of identity is cleverly represented in Hollander's cover illustrations. Holding his bonnet in one paw and a fan in the other, the wolf on the front cover admires himself coquettishly in a large mirror. Anne Sexton's description of the wolf as "a kind of transvestite" comes to mind (76), as this wolf obviously takes great pleasure in cross-dressing. Hollander's double image on the cover evokes at once the disguised wolf of the tale and the *other* wolf, the wolf that lurks in our subconscious, the wolf of our dreams, the wolf within. The illustration of the dancing wolf inside the book, where he is doubled, not by his image in a mirror, but by his dark shadow projected on the wall, strengthens this interpretation. The entire cover illustration is enclosed within an oval frame, which gives the impression that the "real" wolf is also an image in a mirror. On the back cover of the book, a somewhat blurry young face is framed in an identical manner. Although it could be that of Little Red Riding Hood, the face does not resemble in the least the illustrations of the heroine in the book. Perhaps the vague, androgynous portrait represents the reader of the book. The identical gold frame that surrounds the two portraits, on opposing covers of the book, suggests that the wolf and the child are merely two reflections of the same being.

Biegel explores the different voices in the classic tale, and this plural self-reflexivity revitalizes the story in a unique manner. Rather than competing with each other, the different stories are complementary. The first part of the narrative is focalized on the grandmother, who, in this re-version, is not merely sick, but dying. Death is a prominent, if not obsessive, theme in this powerful retelling by an author who never hesitates to explore uncomfortable universal truths in books targeted at children. The formulaic fairy-tale opening is eliminated and the story begins abruptly: "There was an old grandmother who lay dying in her down-filled bed" (11). The rusty hinges of the door, like the extinguished fire and the still hands of the clock, create an atmosphere of neglect, old age, and pending death. Biegel's recasting of *Little Red Riding Hood* reflects his predilection for the bizarre, the fantastic, and the unexpected. The visitor that the grandmother awaits is not the wolf, as readers expect, but death. The grandmother is depicted in Hollander's first illustration as a very frail old lady lying in bed awaiting death, as images of her life pass before her eyes (plate 19).

In the first scene, the wolf is a transparent symbol of death: the grandmother's door opens to reveal "death, black as a wolf." The old lady recognizes death, in spite of his unexpected appearance: "I didn't know that you looked like a wolf." For the grandmother, death takes the form of the wolf. The wolf denies, however, that he is anything but a hungry wolf: "I look like who I am" (14). Biegel portrays the grandmother as an old lady on her deathbed. The fact that the wolf intends to start with her while waiting to devour the granddaughter confirms the old lady's original impression: "Then you are death, the grandmother thought, and that was her last thought because everything around her became black and wolfish" (15).

The second section is focalized through the wolf and begins in an almost identical manner to the first: "There was the wolf, lying in the down-filled bed." Like Gwen Strauss, Biegel develops the neglected moment in the narrative when the wolf awaits the little girl's arrival in the grandmother's bed. Biegel does not portray the traditional "big bad wolf." No longer the lone, asocial figure presented in the classic tale, this wolf is a rather loveable, highly sociable creature with buddies. One of his chums bears the illustrious name of Gubbio, and the name comes obsessively to the wolf's lips, even though he remains anonymous. Like so many of his contemporary counterparts, Biegel's wolf also aspires to be a storyteller. He imagines himself in his future role of storyteller of a version of *Little Red Riding Hood* that has a happy ending for the wolf. The metafictive play in this scene is quite humorous, as the wolf lies in bed imagining the "magnificent story" that he will be able to tell his buddies. The would-be wolf-storyteller even imagines the enthusiastic reaction of his wolf-audience, who will "howl with laughter, as wolves do at the full moon" (20).

Despite his reprehensible actions, the wolf is a sympathetic, playful character. His thoughts, feelings, and actions are quite childlike, and they give him a very individualized personality. The wolf enjoys immensely the game of dress-up and playacting; he dances merrily about the room. It is painfully obvious that he wants to impress Gubbio, the wolf equivalent of the most popular kid at school and the object of a blend of hero worship and envy. Eating a little girl and her grandmother is the daring feat by which he hopes to earn Gubbio's admiration. The waiting wolf's mood swings from bragging overconfidence to anxious fear. Like a cocky schoolboy, the wolf prances swaggeringly about the room, claiming to be the only one capable of pulling off such "cunning tricks" and calling Gubbio a "coward" (16). Struck by the thought that the "tender morsel" might have gotten wise to his plans and warned the hunter, the confident, carefree wolf becomes suddenly fearful and vulnerable (18). The wolf then begins to reflect on death, which, for him, takes the form of a hunter. Seen from the wolf's perspective, the hunter is ironically qualified as "sneaky," a term usually reserved for the wolf. He nonetheless retains the customary descriptor "sly" as his self-assurance returns, but his arrogant defiance of the hunter/death is a dangerously provocative summons.

In the next scene, the narrative shifts at last to Little Red Riding Hood. Biegel highlights the traditional fairy-tale setting of the deep, dark woods into which so many fairy-tale protagonists venture. Mysterious, fascinating, and eerie, the dark woods assume a symbolic dimension in the fairy tale, where it represents the unknown and the subconscious. Bettelheim suggests that fairy-tale forests represent the place where we must come to terms with ourselves: "Since ancient times the near-impenetrable forest in which we get lost has symbolized the dark, hidden, near-impenetrable world of our unconscious."[5] It is only necessary to say the word "woods" or "forest" in order to "set the wood's psychic aspects swirling within our imaginations," writes one critic.[6] In his illustration of the dark forest of huge oaks that tower over Little Red Riding Hood, Hollander portrays the forest as a living, metamorphosing being and home to supernatural creatures. It is a place of awe and wonder, but also of apprehension and fear. Both Biegel's text and Hollander's illustrations capture the mythic meaning of the forest as it is described in the *Encyclopedia of Magic and Superstition:* "The uncanny quality of the woods is part of the lore of childhood. In the forest you are far from home, . . . In the forest you are lost. In the forest the trees put out roots to trip you, and reach out for you with crooked, skinny fingers."[7] As seen through the eyes of the little girl, the forest is a fascinating, but frightening place inhabited by all kinds of supernatural creatures. The little girl is portrayed politely greeting all the trees as a precaution, just in case they are giants. This Riding Hood's imaginative vision of the forest offers an original explanation of her reason for straying from the path. Deeper in the woods, she hopes to discover fairies and dwarfs who perhaps prefer to avoid the paths used by humans.

Although elements of the traditional dialogue are faithfully retained in Biegel's encounter scene, they are interspersed in a very original exchange, full of witty repartee. The subtle eroticism that is playfully introduced into their conversation is not unlike that found in Tomi Ungerer's "Little Red Riding Hood." The absurd idea that she is a wolf provokes the little girl's innocent protest: "No way! If I take off my clothes I am still a little girl" (26). The sexual innuendo in the wolf's reply that he would like to see that will be obvious to many children. The little girl does not understand the sexual meaning behind the wolf's remark, yet her instinctive modesty gets her out of the awkward situation when she insists that he go first.

Biegel reworks the story of Little Red Riding Hood to address the themes of identity and self-knowledge. His retelling is a philosophical story that is accessible to young children but that also enchants adults. The encounter with the wolf is turned into a humorous scene centered on the philosophical subject of identity and the *être* and the *paraître*. The wolf questions the true identity of the wolf, the girl, and the grandmother, which demonstrates how difficult it is to define someone. This Riding Hood's fascination with the fairy-tale theme of metamorphosis allows the classic motif of the wolf's disguisement to be introduced into the story right from their first encounter, where it provides the excuse for a witty philosophical discussion. The scene is an excellent example of the skillful manner in which the author deals with a serious theme while retaining a sense of enchantment and a childlike view of reality. The playful sense of humor and imaginative use of language delights readers, as the wolf tries to convince the little girl that he might really be a dwarf or a fairy, and that she is disguised as "a lit-tle human," although she is perhaps really a wolf, a wolf in little girl's clothing. Although she refuses to be taken in by the idea of a disguise because she can't see any buttons on the wolf, the little girl is willing to entertain the idea that the wolf is bewitched, perhaps a bewitched prince. This is not a new theme in Biegel's works. In *The Gardens of Dorr,* which is his only book for young adults and con-sidered by some to be his best work, a princess engages in a quest to find the an-tidote for a spell that has bewitched her city and turned her lover into a flower. The wolf, who has a penchant for storytelling, spins a sad tale about a witch's spell, which is, in essence, a werewolf story.[8]

The little girl denies vehemently that she is a wolf and identifies herself: "I am just Little Red Cap." Her nickname leads to a philosophical question: "Yes, that is what they call you, but who are you really?" (32). The wolf is not refer-ring merely to her real name, but to her inner self, with its hidden fantasies, as-pirations, and fears. The little girl's anger at the wolf for suggesting that she is perhaps really "a bewitched wolf" reflects society's negative image of the Big Bad Wolf. However, the thought the author leaves unfinished is obviously that it might also be rather fun to be a wolf. That explains her earlier curiosity about whether it was "very bad" to be a wolf, to which the wolf replies enigmatically that "it gnaws at you." This outwardly good and obedient little girl seemingly has hidden aspirations of being very bad. At the end of the encounter, the wolf teases the angry little girl, saying that she is already beginning to resemble "a bad wolf." The transformation will be completed in her dream.

The section devoted to Little Red Cap begins with a parodic, exaggerated ver-sion of the cautionary scene, in which the harping mother's long enumeration of dos and don'ts is left unfinished by the author. The mother's authoritarian atti-tude is underscored by the fact that the poor little girl has trouble getting an an-swer in edgeways; her obedient reply responds to all her mother's admonitions in one breath: "Yes mother, no mother, okay mother" (20). The complete lack of communication between the two generations is accentuated when the narra-tor adds the thoughts of the daughter and her mother after their rather one-sided exchange: "She never remembered that she should always . . . and mother al-ways sighed because she never . . ." (21). The scene ends with another hu-morous parody of the cautionary scene. In a scene full of irony, the wolf takes on the mother's admonitory role, advising Little Red Cap to go quickly to her grandmother's and warning her that the forest is a dangerous place for a little girl because she might "meet up with the big bad wolf" (33). Little Red Cap is no longer the docile little girl who had replied obediently to her mother's admonitions. In the wolf's presence, her rebellion surfaces; she stamps her feet in rage, tramples flowers, and kicks trees. The little girl does indeed have a wolf within. As Bettelheim reminds us, the wolf in *Little Red Riding Hood* represents "all the asocial, animalistic tendencies within ourselves."[9] She begins to experience the gnawing the wolf had alluded to: "Inside of her something started to gnaw: mind that you never, mind that you always, mind that you don't, mind that you do . . ." The mother's earlier admonitions echo like a refrain, but the little girl's reply is no longer one of docile obedience. Instead, she explodes in rebellious disobedience: "No mother, no mother, NO!" (34).

The scene shifts back to the down-filled bed, which is now occupied by the grandmother-wolf. The wolfishness that had engulfed the grandmother at the end of the first scene provides the link to this scene. As if she has undergone a metamorphosis, the grandmother has now become "wolfish" or rather "completely wolfized," as she lies in bed "like an old wolf with pointy ears" (34). The state of disorder in which Little Red Cap finds her grandmother's house does not alarm her, as it did the heroine of *Un petit chaperon rouge,* because the little girl obsessed with disguises merely assumes her grandmother has been dressing up. This provides an original explanation for the fact that Little Red Riding Hood could mistake a wolf for her grandmother, as the grandmother-wolf continues to play the game by admitting she "dressed up as a wolf." The familiar dialogue is altered appropriately, as Little Red Cap begins: "Grandmother, what big ears you put on" (36). After the question about the mouth, which immediately provokes the fatal ending in the classic version, this Little Red Cap is given time to add another body part, the claws that allow her to see his true identity. The wolf still insists on playing the game, although his actions confirm that he is indeed a real wolf: "No child, a bewitched wolf, and he is going to grab you. NOW!" The final sentence of this section echoes the last line of the section focalized through the grandmother: "So it is true, the little girl thought, and that was her last thought, because everything around her became black and wolfish" (38). The truth is revealed to Little Red Cap, as it is to her grandmother, when the wolf devours her.

The opening scene of the second chapter is once again focused on the down-filled bed, but it is now occupied by all three characters: the very full wolf and, inside him, the grandmother and the little girl, who are all snoring and having disturbing dreams. The entire chapter is devoted to the nightmares of the three characters. With the exception of his general preliminary remarks in the preface, Biegel leaves the interpretation of the dreams to the readers. Because the wolf's dream has a familiar pre-text, it is much easier to interpret than those of Little Red Cap and her grandmother.

Initially, the wolf's dream reflects quite faithfully, with a few new humorous touches, the ending of the Grimms' tale: the wolf's stomach is cut open, the two "human morsels" jump out alive, and his stomach is filled with stones and sewn shut. Like Wim Hofman, Biegel incorporates into the Grimms' version the variant that ends with the drowning of the wolf, although there is a slight deviation. When the wolf goes to the creek for a drink, Gubbio and his other buddies are there, taunting him from the far side. The derisory reaction of his buddies, who roll on the ground with laughter in the dream, reflects the wolf's fear of being a laughing stock, rather than a hero, in their eyes. The helpless state so often experienced by the dreamer prevents the wolf from answering them.[10] The water in the creek constitutes a mirror in which the wolf gazes at his reflection and gains self-knowledge. For the wolf, revelation also comes at the moment of death. When the wolf's premonitory dream repeats itself in reality, it has a happy ending. As he waddles toward the creek, the heavy, thirsty wolf struggles to remember his dream, which he thinks of in terms of another funny "story" he must tell his friends (56). As in a fun hall of mirrors, the movement of the water distorts the wolf's reflection this time, as if he was making fun of himself. Although his image triggers something deep in his subconscious, the dream remains out of reach. His buddies are all there laughing uproariously, as they were in his dream, but this time Gubbio saves the wolf's life. His advice to "spit out" the stones (58) echoes the advice the grandmother offered to the little girl. The characters must purge themselves of things hidden deep within. Like Gubbio and the other wolf buddies, the grandmother is doubled over with laughter when she reveals the truth to Little Red Cap. Biegel's characters do a great deal of laughing at one another, as one character sees the truth that another is unable to see about his or her self.

While the wolf dreams of his death, the grandmother dreams that she is death: "black death who is not afraid of anyone or anything" (42). Because she is disguised as an old lady, no one believes that she is death. The familiar motif of the basket of cake and wine is introduced into the grandmother's dream in a convincing imitation of the way events from our real lives are curiously transformed in our dreams. The people making merry, drinking wine and eating cake out of a basket by the bed, "chok[e] on their wine and cake" when the grandmother's veil falls away from her face to reveal her true identity (44). Hollander's illustration of this scene captures the moment when the veil falls away from the grinning skull of the gaunt grandmother, dressed from head to toe in black, but the three villagers, engaged in the pleasures of this world, have not yet noticed, as they are all looking in another direction (plate 20). One fat peasant is licking his lips as he stares ecstatically at the slice of cake he is about to bite into, another peasant holds up his glass of wine in a toast directed ironically at the grandmother, and a young woman stares at the two men with an indulgent or provocative smile on her lips. Readers are left to imagine the moment when the three villagers turn back to see the terrifying figure of death, in the form of the grandmother, smiling down at them.

Biegel calls forth the collective fear of death in a humorous manner. The vision of the grandmother as death causes all the villagers to flee in terror. The door scene of the classic tale is subverted, so that now the grandmother knocks at doors, but no one calls to her to come in. Only the pastor agrees to open his door to the grandmother in a scene full of irony. Although he initially appears unafraid and ready to confront death, when he is invited to dance with the grandmother/death (the church organist is ordered to play a waltz), he escapes from her grasp and runs away. Biegel engages in a little mild social satire. The pastor is only able to deal with death as an abstract idea, but when it enters his own life, he is no less terrified than his parishioners. The dream ends, as did the wolf's, with the grandmother gazing at her reflection. The coat and hat disguise has been removed and, in the mirror, the old lady recognizes death. As she addresses her reflection as death, it suddenly becomes "light" (45). The darkness the grandmother had experienced in the wolf's belly disappears when the old lady confronts and accepts death.

Little Red Cap's dream is the last to be related. Paradoxically, this fairy-tale heroine is no different from real little girls who dream of being princesses. Since Little Red Cap had admitted to the wolf that she thought it would be fun to be a princess, it is not surprising that the little girl in the wolf's belly dreams that she is a princess. As is generally the case in dreams, however, the recognizable threads are interwoven with strange elements. The wolf's claim to be a bewitched prince obviously inspires Little Red Cap's strange dream, in which her prince has been turned into a wolf, but there is no logical explanation for the stilts, the clown, or the search in the stars. Hollander's illustration of the dream sequence, which depicts the little girl falling off her stilts and tumbling through space, elicits reminiscences of Alice falling down the rabbit hole. Earlier, the little girl had been afraid to evoke a crow, because in her system of transformations, crows become witches. In her dream, the metamorphosis takes place in reverse: the witch who has cast a spell on her prince is a crow high up in a tree. The little girl can't reach the witch/crow because she has lost her stilts, which is yet another example of the characteristic helplessness experienced in dreams. The witch/crow merges with the mother, cawing out the cautionary scene: "Mind that you don't . . . mind that you never . . . mind that you always . . ." (46). In fairy tales and dreams, the mother often takes the form of the wicked stepmother or the witch, allowing the child to vent some of her negative feelings.

In her dream, Little Red Cap's dark, hidden wish is fulfilled. The spell is not broken but reversed: the prince is changed back into his former self, but the little girl is simultaneously transformed into a wolf and as such, she devours her beloved prince. Inspired by psychoanalysts, Biegel equates the wolf's devouring of Little Red Riding Hood with an act of love. Little Red Cap howls to the moon that, as a wolf, she has "to devour everything that [she] love[s]" (48). In a humorous role reversal, Little Red Cap becomes the wolf that knocks on the door of her grandmother's house deep in the woods. When this wolf claims to be Little Red Cap, he truly is. The familiar dialogue is completely inverted, as it is the grandmother who comments on Little Red Cap's big ears, nose, and mouth. The granddaughter-wolf's replies are focused on the magic word that would break the spell, beginning with her big ears that would be "the better to hear the magic word with." When her grandmother tells her, as the little girl had earlier told the grandmother-wolf, that she has claws and is therefore a wolf, her reply echoes the wolf's: "No, grandmother, I am a bewitched wolf" (51).

When Little Red Cap asks her grandmother if she will then become human again, the answer is to be found in the old lady's eyes, which are likened to "mirrors." Like the wolf and the grandmother, Little Red Cap also gazes at her reflection, but this time her image is reflected in a dual mirror. In one eye Little Red Cap is reflected as a wolf and in the other, as a human. Now the little girl asks the philosophical question that the wolf had asked her: "Who am I?" In the belly of the wolf, the darkness is dispelled and it becomes "light," just as it had for her grandmother (51). The light into which the little girl is reborn after the initiatory night in the wolf's dark belly symbolizes her enlightenment and newfound wisdom. Thus each of the three main characters regards his or her reflection in a mirror, at the end of the dream sequence, in order to gain self-knowledge. Little Red Cap has recognized the wolf within the little girl.

The opening of chapter three focuses on the hunter. Biegel playfully reworks the pre-text, so that the loud snoring heard by the Grimms' hunter is explained by the fact that it is the cumulative snoring of the wolf, the girl, and the grandmother. A knife is substituted for the conventional scissors and, as in Sexton's poem, the hunter performs "a cesarean section" and delivers the little girl and her grandmother (52). Another humorous detail is added when the narrator informs readers that the hunter held Little Red Cap and her grandmother under the pump to wash them off and wake them up. Significantly, the hunter alone gathers the stones (exactly twelve), puts them in the wolf's stomach, and then sews him up. Little Red Cap and her grandmother do not take part in the wolf's punishment. Biegel subverts the stereotypical image of the hunter-rescuer. While the hunter sees himself as a hero, the other characters see him differently through their enlightened eyes. His heroism is questioned parodically when the narrator informs readers that "the brave hunter" hid in the deepest corner of the closet when the wolf began to wake up (55). Although Biegel also tells the hunter's story, he does not share the same status as the other three characters and remains an outsider. While the hunter speaks of their traumatic experience, the grandmother and Little Red Cap describe a positive initiatory experience that is beyond his understanding. Having known death, the grandmother can now truly live because she need no longer fear death. Little Red Cap's description of her experience is equally enigmatic for the hunter. Having dreamed that she was a wolf, now the little girl can truly be a human being. Many of Biegel's works portray characters who gain self-awareness through initiatory journeys.

The final scene shifts from the grandmother's down-filled bed to the mother's sheepskin sofa in order to tell the mother's story: "There was a mother who fainted onto her sheepskin sofa." The authoritarian role of the mother in the Grimms' version is underscored, as she repeats her admonitions after the fact. This time the child's answering "yes" is followed by a "but" and the explanation that she has merely been herself. She thus justifies the disobedient behavior for which Little Red Cap has been reprimanded since the Grimms' penned their version, vindicating all her counterparts who have been punished for straying from the path.

Biegel's ending is a parody of the celebration that reunites all the characters at the end of so many versions of the tale. Readers are told that "the brave green hunter" had come along "to celebrate the happy ending." The scene is full of irony. The hunter assures the fearful mother proudly that the wolf is "stone-dead," but readers know differently. Little Red Cap questions the closure the hunter is determined to impose on the story. She and her grandmother understand the significance of the splashes they hear in the creek at the precise moment the wine is being poured for the celebration, whereas the patriarchal hunter disdainfully considers the women's idea that the wolf might have survived sheer nonsense. Hollander's illustration of the happy ending portrays a jovial, smiling hunter with his arm consolingly, perhaps paternalistically, around the old lady's shoulders while she pours wine with a knowing smile on her face (plate 21). The hunter's blitheness and self-satisfaction are short-lived. When the unperceptive hunter is unable to hear the wolf and his buddies "howling with laughter at the humans," the wise grandmother tells him, in an appropriation of the ritualistic dialogue, that he needs big ears to hear the wolf, a big nose to smell him, a big mouth to taste him, and four claws to grab him. Even the uncomprehending hunter is able to deduce that if that were so, then he would be a wolf. He does not realize, however, how deadly serious the grandmother is when she declares that he is indeed a wolf. The wise old woman provides the key to Biegel's retelling when she explains to the mystified hunter: "The wolf is your own fear" (62).

Readers get a glimpse of the reunited characters' reactions to the grandmother's enlightening words, as the old lady hands wine "to the mother who was silent, and to the child who knew, and to the hunter who was trembling" (62–63). The mother's endless admonitions have been silenced; her daughter has come of age. The illustration of this scene depicts a mature-looking Little Red Cap, who stares boldly and knowingly out at the viewer. She looks much older than in the preceding illustrations, indicating that she has come of age during her initiatory experience and is now a young woman. Little Red Cap and her grandmother have overcome their fear, whereas the brave hunter has just recognized his. The one character who is generally missing from the happy celebration appears at the very end. As "they toasted and drank and ate cake to celebrate the happy ending," the latch is lifted and the creaking door opens to reveal the wolf (63). The wise grandmother has obviously been expecting him; she greets him naturally and hands him a glass. There is a complicity between Little Red Cap, her grandmother, and the wolf, who are united by their shared experience and the common understanding of their enlightened status.

Wie je droomt ben je zelf is a highly original retelling that uses the story of Little Red Riding Hood to discuss philosophical questions concerning life, death, identity, and fear. The three main characters have looked into the mirror of their souls and attained self-knowledge, while at the same time conquering their fear. Just as the fairy-tale characters in Biegel's story gain self-revelation through their dreams, readers are meant to learn about themselves through this modern fairy tale. Little Red Cap has recognized and accepted the wolf within. Biegel expects readers of all ages to look into the same mirror. As the jury remarked when the Dutch author won the 1973 State Prize for Literature for Children and Young Adults for his complete works, "young and old recognize themselves in the mirror that Paul Biegel holds up to them."[11]

The Wolf as Angst

In his short story "Fita verde no cabelo" (Green Ribbon in the Hair), the internationally renowned Brazilian author João Guimarães Rosa appropriated the story of Little Red Riding Hood to deal with important philosophical issues. The story was included in *Ave, palavra*, a posthumous collection of poems, tales, and meditations published for adults in 1970. In 1992, the story was extracted from the adult collection and issued as a picture book with illustrations by Roger Mello. The text had clearly not been written for children; it first appeared in the literary supplement of the newspaper *O Estado de S. Paulo* on 8 February 1964, just a few months prior to the author's death. The Brazilian scholar Gloria Pondé undertook its publication in an illustrated edition to mark the twenty-fifth anniversary of the death of this important Brazilian writer, who had never distinguished between young and adult audiences. The illustrator chosen to do the pictures believes that a good story should always interest adults as well as children.[12] Guimarães Rosa makes heavy demands on his adult audience, so young readers of *Fita verde no cabelo* are faced with an extremely difficult text, even with the assistance of Mello's visual interpretation.

The words "nova velha estória" (new old story), which appear in parentheses under the title of "Fita verde no cabelo" in *Ave, palavra*, are given the status of a subtitle in the picture book. They announce the intertextual play in this story of a little girl who is called Green Ribbon (Fita-Verde) because she wears a large, imaginary green ribbon in her hair. Familiar motifs from the classic tale are retained, but subtly subverted to convey new meanings that are often beyond the young reader's comprehension. However, even small children will decode the pre-text when the narrator describes Green Ribbon setting out to her grand-mother's, despite the fact that her pot contains a syrupy dessert, rather than but-ter, and her basket is empty so she can pick raspberries.

In this enigmatic retelling, which challenges even cultured adult readers, Guimarães Rosa approaches the story of Little Red Riding Hood from an exis-tentialist perspective. The Brazilian author was strongly influenced by the exis-tentialist philosophy of Jean-Paul Sartre, who published his important philo-sophical treatise *L'être et le néant* (*Being and Nothingness*) in 1943. For that reason, it is necessary to consider briefly the main ideas of existentialism. Existentialist philosophy views human existence as unexplainable or absurd, stresses the isola-tion of the individual experience in a hostile or indifferent universe, and empha-sizes freedom of choice and responsibility for the consequences of one's acts. The fundamental idea of all existential thought is that existence precedes essence. Human beings are totally free and entirely responsible for what they make of themselves by their constant choices. This terrifying freedom and responsibility are a source of angst. Conscious of the limits of mortality, human beings live with existential dread.[13] According to Sartre, those who attempt to flee angst through dreams and illusions are in "bad faith." Sartre's solution to the existen-tial dilemma is the dissolution of one's illusions. Paradoxically, Guimarães Rosa uses the genre of the fairy tale, which is closely associated with the world of dreams, to create a Brazilian-style existentialist retelling of the story of Little Red Riding Hood. Mello deliberately chose to highlight the existentialist inter-pretation in his illustrations for the 1992 edition, even though it was targeted at young readers.

The use of the familiar fairy tale underscores the universality of ontological questions concerning life and death. The protagonist of *Fita verde no cabelo* lives in a village, "neither big nor small," that could be anywhere, and her grand-mother lives in another similar village. Although the author paints a Brazilian decor, the local color accentuates the universal nature of the story. Likening the woods that Green Ribbon must cross to the Brazilian *sertão*, Pondé claims that Guimarães Rosa uses the local image of the *sertão* as a universal symbol of the world and the human adventure.[14] This imagery is developed in his celebrated novel *Grande sertão: Veredas* (*The Devil to Pay in the Backlands*), published in 1956. The Portuguese word *sertão* refers to a wilderness or forest area, remote from the more densely populated coastal area, so it constitutes a highly appropriate setting for an initiatory story. Like all of Guimarães Rosa's works, this one seems to be set in the state of Minas Gerais, where he was born and practiced medicine for several years. The local setting is played up by Mello's drawings of luxuriant vegetation, which bring to mind a tropical forest, perhaps the Amazonian rainforest. In the dense foliage, a small cat, an ocelot or a young jaguar, gazes intently at the heroine from a close distance, a rare sight indeed, as the cats avoid humans and are rarely seen, especially during the day. Its presence seems therefore to have a symbolic meaning. The jaguar is a solitary animal associated with bravery. More importantly perhaps, in Maya civilization, the jaguar served to communicate between the living and the dead, and was considered a companion in the spiritual world. The Amazonian cat is Green Ribbon's companion on a lonely spiritual journey that will require courage.

The description of the village in the first sentence immediately introduces the ontological theme of existence: "There was a village somewhere . . . with old men and old women who were getting old, men and women who waited, and boys and girls who were born and growing up." The voice of a collective narrator or storyteller, which is borrowed from the oral tradition, characterizes the works of Guimarães Rosa. In *Fita verde no cabelo,* the collective narrator tells the story of the human condition from an existentialist perspective. Even Little Red Riding Hood's naïveté is put into an existential context. The narrator's statement that Green Ribbon is the only one in the village who lacks good judgment is based on the fact that, for her, "everything was 'once upon a time.'" In Guimarães Rosa's retelling, the realm of fantasy is constructed as false consciousness and constitutes the illusion through which Green Ribbon escapes her angst. Unlike the other villagers, the young heroine has not yet learned to fully distinguish between fantasy and reality. In this sense, she reminds us of Biegel's Little Red Cap, who still sees the world in fairy-tale terms. But the manner in which Guimarães Rosa blurs the boundaries between reality and fantasy must be understood in an existential perspective. According to Sartre, consciousness can imagine what does not exist, as in the case of "that mill that people imagine seeing."

The substitution of a green ribbon for the traditional red hood, which prompts a name change and a new identity, is highly significant. The narrator tells readers that the girl who lacked common sense left the village with an "imaginary" green ribbon in her hair. Mello highlights the new attribute in his visual portrayal of the eponymous heroine. The first image of Green Ribbon is rendered entirely in black and white, except for the green ribbon. The ribbon appears as a rather abstract green squiggle that is not on her hair, but hovering unrealistically above her head, almost like a strange halo. By depicting only the green ribbon in color, Mello emphasizes its imaginary status and effectively illustrates, through his technique (a mixed media of pencil and Ecoline watercolor), the confusion of the real and the imaginary in the young girl's mind. According to Pondé, the substitution of an imaginary green ribbon for the red hood gives the girl the freedom to pursue her desires without guilt.[15] Within the existentialist context, however, the green ribbon symbolizes the fantasy and illusion that distort the young girl's sense of the real. It is only when she loses the ribbon that she acknowledges her freedom. Holding her hair back with a green ribbon appears to have been her mother's idea, but it is certain she did not intend it to be a useless, imaginary ribbon. The word "imaginary" is conspicuously absent in the lines that are repeated, like a refrain, as Green Ribbon explains that she has "the basket and the pot, and the green ribbon in [her] hair, as [her] mother sent [her]."

The loss of the green ribbon in the woods on the way to her grandmother's represents the dissolution of the girl's illusions. She is no longer the child whose view of reality was distorted by fantasy. Her fantasy-version of reality is completely shattered by her confrontation with death, in the form of the grandmother. A striking close-up of the girl, depicted so near to her grandmother that only the upper part of her head is visible, draws attention to the conspicuous absence of the green ribbon in her dark hair. The cover illustration is almost identical, except that Green Ribbon is portrayed outside against the blue sky, and a dragon fly, whose green wings have the distinct shape of a bow, seems to have just flown off her hair. By giving wings to the imaginary green ribbon, Mello indicates that the loss of the ribbon is equated with freedom. In the existentialist context, freedom is a source of dread, explaining the profound fear and sadness of the girl when she realizes that she has lost the green ribbon. Green Ribbon loses her childish innocence and her illusions on this trip to her grandmother's, while gaining a frightening new freedom. At her grandmother's, she is suddenly painfully conscious of the material reality of her body. Like the existentialist hero, she is aware only of her own feelings and physical needs in the immediacy of the present moment. While her dying grandmother tries to call her to her bedside, the young girl is preoccupied with her own fear, sadness, perspiration, and hunger.

Even the motif of the path receives an existentialist twist. Guimarães Rosa insists on the fact that the protagonist chooses the path she takes, symbolizing the in-

Daí, que, indo, no atravessar o
bosque, viu só os lenhadores, que
por lá lenhavam; mas o lobo nenhum,
desconhecido nem peludo. Pois os
lenhadores tinham exterminado o lobo.

Então, ela, mesma, era quem se dizia:
— Vou à vovó, com cesto e pote, e a fita
verde no cabelo, o tanto que a mamãe
me mandou.

Fita verde no cabelo, by João Guimarães Rosa, illustration by Roger Mello, illustrations © 1992 by Roger Mello. Used by permission of Roger Mello.

dividual's freedom of choice. Green Ribbon chooses the "crazy and long" path, rather than the shorter one, that is, the difficult path of the existentialist hero who acknowledges that human existence is absurd rather than the easy path of illusions and false consciousness. On the path through the dark woods, the girl is accompanied by her shadow, which Mello accentuates by its inordinate size. The enormous shadow almost supplants the heroine, as Green Ribbon is conspicuously absent from the illustration. Like the ribbon in the first illustration of the protagonist, her shadow is the only color in an otherwise black-and-white double spread. This is undoubtedly the moment at which the protagonist loses her green ribbon. It is replaced by the large green shadow, which seems to represent the sudden fear or angst that results from that loss. According to Sartre, our anguish is the shadow cast by our freedom. In this retelling, the wolf in the dark woods is an inner wolf, that of this Riding Hood's fear or, more specifically, her philosophical angst. According to the text, her shadow runs after her, evoking the image of a wolf trying to catch her. At her grandmother's she will meet the wolf face to face.

In *Fita verde no cabelo*, the only illustration of a "real" wolf appears on the title page, where Mello portrays a *loup-guará*, a species that still lives in the woods of Minas Gerais though it is in danger of extinction. Although the front half of the wolf is drawn realistically, the back half is a pale shape without fur, the lightly drawn pencil lines suggesting its gradual disappearance. Mello could be evoking the extinction of the *loup-guará*, but more likely he is suggesting that the wolf in the story is not a real wolf. The text tells us that there was no wolf in the woods because the woodcutters had killed him, but the qualification "not unknown nor hairy" suggests that there may be other forms of wolves. Mello's provocative illustration portrays two figures of muscular, shirtless woodcutters with wolves' heads. The illustrator thus introduces the theme of the man-wolf, which, in this case, is a hybrid creature that is part wolf, part man. This picture is an example of the illustrator's attempt to highlight Guimarães Rosa's distinctive blending of exterior reality and the inner world of the character. The illustrator suggests another possible interpretation, stating that the woodcutters may wear wolf heads "like a 'prize' for having captured the wolf." One woodcutter-wolf is looking directly at the viewer from blank, triangular eyes in an abstract or mythical wolf head, and the other is staring directly at Green Ribbon. She, in turn, is gazing seductively in their direction from the corner of her eye. While Mello admits that the two wolves recall the sexual connotation of the story, he adds that they are to be seen like any other "ordinary object of the landscape which might or might not be noticed by the girl." From her body language it is obvious that she is aware of the presence of the men-wolves. Their role in the story is nonetheless relatively minor. In Guimarães Rosa's recasting of the tale, as in Biegel's, the wolf to be feared is found within.

Even the motif of Little Red Riding Hood's pastimes in the woods is ingeniously reworked from an existential perspective. In the Grimms' version, the wolf accuses the little girl of ignoring the delights of the forest, the beautiful flowers and the lovely singing of the birds. Contrary to her German predecessor and so many people who pass by without noticing the existence of the things around them, Green Ribbon is "aware" as she walks along the path. It is only after the existential *prise de conscience* that life is lived in complete self-awareness. Green Ribbon is becoming truly conscious of the material universe. The details of the scene are borrowed, not from the Grimms', but from Perrault's description of Little Red Riding Hood's pastimes on the path, which include gathering hazelnuts and running after butterflies, as well as picking bouquets of flowers. In an obscure passage, Guimarães Rosa describes Green Ribbon's awareness of nature in rather absurd terms, which suggest that the girl now perceives the world differently, seeing the hazelnuts that don't fly (like butterflies), the butterflies that are never in bouquets (like flowers), and the flowers that are either plebeians or princesses. Mello develops the motif of the butterflies, which is not mentioned in the Grimms' version, to introduce the existential message into the illustration. As the heroine knocks on her grandmother's door, she is almost completely hidden from the reader by the large white shapes of a host of butterflies that flutter about her, as if they are trying to get the little girl's attention. Unlike the woodcutters, the butterflies are only white contours or dark shadows, because Green Ribbon has not noticed their existence.

The door scene respects the classic text fairly faithfully, although the grandmother adds a line that gives her character some local color, uttering the blessing "Deus te abençoe" (God bless you). Guimarães Rosa's style emphasizes a kind of archaic orality, which has its source in the popular tradition, by using the spoken language of Brazilians, revitalized terms from old Portuguese, words and expressions from different parts of the country, and the syntax retained by the peasants in remote areas.[16] As in Perrault's tale, the grandmother immediately tells the girl to place the items she has brought on the chest and come to her, but there is a new sense of urgency. She adds the highly significant words "while there is still time," referring, of course, to her pending death. Like the old lady in Biegel's retelling, Green Ribbon's grandmother is on her deathbed. The theme of time, which preoccupies Guimarães Rosa in all of his works, thus finds its way into his recasting of *Little Red Riding Hood*. This Riding Hood's late arrival at her grandmother's house takes on new significance, as the little girl's dallying becomes a question of life and death.

The crucial bed scene, in which Green Ribbon confronts death, is depicted in a striking double spread that constitutes the center page of the book. The illustration is rendered entirely in black and white to indicate that death has changed Green Ribbon's perception of the world, which appears now in all its stark reality. Her confrontation with death has shattered her fantasy version of reality. The grandmother is a dark, shadowy figure in the foreground, with her back to the viewer, and she looks toward the door on the verso, where her granddaughter is a tiny silhouette against the bright daylight. The figure of the girl appears to be unrealistically far away, as if her grandmother already sees her from the distant threshold of death. The grandmother's raised hand forms the shape of a wolf's

Fita verde no cabelo, by João Guimarães Rosa, illustration by Roger Mello, illustrations © 1992 by Roger Mello. Used by permission of Roger Mello.

head, as in the game adults often play with children, forming animal shapes on the wall with the shadow cast by their hands.[17] In this case, however, the grand-mother's hand forms the dark wolf shadow as it is held up against the light. The curious wolf/hand appears amid the huge, towering tropical trees that have in-vaded the bedroom to form a strange, interior forest.

The classic dialogue is retained, but it is cleverly adapted to reflect the shocked reaction of youth (and beauty) toward the infirm, decrepit body of the elderly. Significantly, Green Ribbon had deviated from the classic reply when she iden-tified herself at the door as the old lady's "beautiful granddaughter." The old woman's answers reflect her realization that she is seeing her beloved grand-daughter for the last time. In spite of her shock, Green Ribbon's affection for her grandmother is indicated by the fact that she addresses her as "vovozinha," a form of endearment indicated by the suffix -*zinha* and the prefix modification *vovo-* of the term for grandmother, *avó.* The text, image, and page layout work together to create a double spread of remarkable intensity and impact, despite its simplicity. Green Ribbon's comment is placed at the top of the verso and her grandmother's reply at the bottom of the recto, both contained within asymmet-rical white blocks outlined in black, which are not unlike speech bubbles. As if to underscore her granddaughter's words, the old lady's dark, hairy, skinny forearm and clawlike hand extend across the top half of the page from the right so that the girl's words appear to rest on the back of her hand. At the same time, Green Ribbon's smooth, white forearm and soft, delicate hand reaches out from the left so that her fingers extend into the block of text and point to her grandmother's reply. The profound meaning in the verbal exchange between the dying old lady and her beloved young granddaughter is thus rendered visually by the eloquent image of the two contrasting arms reaching out longingly toward each other, but not touching. Existential solitude and death have already separated them.

The illustrations make the presence of death tangible. The green shadow projected on the wall behind the grandmother's hand and forearm symbolizes the grandmother's angst in the face of death. While the young girl's arm and hand cast no shadow in this scene, they did when she was portrayed knocking on her grandmother's door, suggesting her sudden awareness of death. A strange, rather abstract line drawing of a wolf's muzzle protrudes onto the page to punctuate the grandmother's reply about her lips that are purple because she will no longer be able to kiss her granddaughter. The pale drawing that renders the muzzle unreal completes the process of transformation of the wolf, begun on the title page, into a nonexistent wolf, a symbol of angst and death. By simply changing the verb tense to the present in the grandmother's final reply, that her eyes are "so deep and lifeless" because she is no longer seeing Green Ribbon, the author effectively announces her death.

The wolf represents the menace of physical death in Perrault's tale. In Guimarães Rosa's recasting, readers do not witness the physical, but rather the symbolical death of the child. Although Green Ribbon is called "a little girl" in the text, she is portrayed as an adolescent or even a young woman in the illustrations. When she discovers the loss of the green ribbon, the protagonist is depicted as a mature-looking young woman, who has visibly aged on the way to her grandmother's. The fear that suddenly sweeps over Green Ribbon when her grandmother tells her to come closer marks the awakening of consciousness. The narrator tells readers that it is "as if she was coming to her senses for the first time." It is this *prise de conscience,* in the existential sense, that marks the coming of age of this particular Riding Hood. She experiences what could be called an existential initiation. Guimarães Rosa's story captures the vertiginous moment when the individual has the revelation of the inescapable reality of mortality and the nothingness of human existence.

The young girl's moment of *prise de conscience* is effectively evoked in Mello's illustration of a forlorn-looking Green Ribbon, whose face is completely hidden by her long dark hair after the loss of the ribbon that held it in place, just as her fantasies had held her world in place. The blank space on the opposite page symbolizes the emptiness that engulfs her after the death of her grandmother. The girl feels the angst that results from the sudden experience of death as the absurd human condition and the discovery that we are ultimately alone. Although angst or metaphysical anguish is not directed at any specific object, in *Fita verde no cabelo* it is symbolized by the wolf. Its overwhelming presence is indicated by the fact that the word "Wolf" is now written with a capital letter. The heroine screams: "Grandma, I'm afraid of the Wolf!" but there is no answer because her grandmother is no longer there, "except for her cold, sad, and sudden body." Guimarães Rosa's unusual choice of adjectives reflects the material reality of death from an existential perspective. The girl's terrified cry meets only with silence, the profound silence of the depths of the inner abyss into which the girl has been plunged. The girl will be devoured, not by the wolf, but by her own anguish. The conflict has been internalized in Green Ribbon, who has to come to grips with the wolf within, that is, the angst that is the result of her confrontation with death. Society can no longer protect this Riding Hood from death. The woodcutter, society's representative, will not come to Green Ribbon's rescue.

The last textless double spread, which depicts the protagonist standing on a hill staring off into a blank sky, as the buildings of a village are carried off into space, emphasizes the open ending. What was familiar in Green Ribbon's life becomes strange and hostile. A world that in childhood seemed so solid and so secure has become unstable and fluid. Green Ribbon has discovered that there is nothing to structure the world's existence. Mello's illustration is an attempt to render this dissolution of the world visible. In keeping with existentialist thought concerning the look, the illustrator wanted to suggest that "the way Green Ribbon looks at the scenery could subvert it." Mello insists that, unlike the classic heroine, Guimarães Rosa's protagonist is not "a passive Red Riding Hood."[18] She becomes, in fact, an existentialist heroine.

The prose text of *Fita verde no cabelo* is written in a dense, evocative, and poetic language that is extremely difficult to translate. The inventiveness, wordplay, alliterations, rhythm, and repetition of sounds and syllables can only be hinted at without sacrificing the meaning. To fully appreciate Guimarães Rosa's poetic power and playfulness, the work needs to be read in Portuguese. Like Biegel's retelling, it should preferably be read aloud to appreciate the rhythm and sounds of the language, which borrows heavily from the oral tradition. The innovative, experimental use of language that characterizes Guimarães Rosa's style is particularly effective in this "new old story." The innovative blending of the old and the new in this highly original retelling of *Little Red Riding Hood* sets up what Pondé describes as "a textual dialogue between the European sources and the emerging Brazilian culture, in search of a universal discourse."[19]

The serious and complex retellings examined in this chapter use the characters, imagery, and motifs of *Little Red Riding Hood* to address important psychological and metaphysical issues, notably fear/angst and death. Like the pretext, the retellings of writers like Cross, Biegel, and Guimarães Rosa explore the depths of our inner selves. During her trip through the dark woods and her encounter with the wolf, the heroine experiences the revelation of her true self. In these original crossover recastings, the wolf symbolizes the beast within that takes the form of Fear and/or Death. In *Wie je droomt ben je zelf*, commissioned for children, the tone is quite optimistic, as the main characters pass from the darkness into the light. Guimarães Rosa's existentialist retelling, intended for adults, is, in contrast, quite pessimistic, since Green Ribbon is plunged into the darkness of the frightening abyss of nothingness and metaphysical solitude. These retellings illustrate how complex themes can be communicated to readers of all ages through the story of Little Red Riding Hood. Their authors alter the reader's conceived ideas, investing the familiar story with philosophy, psychology, and metaphysics. Young readers will not understand all the levels of meaning in Biegel's and Guimarães Rosa's sophisticated retellings, which prove challenging even for adult readers, but they will sense the significance of Little Red Riding Hood's encounter with the wolf within.

5. Running With the Wolves

She suddenly knew frost and running and black stillness, and a platinum moon,
red feasts and wild hymnings, lovers with quicksilver eyes and the race of
the ice wind and stars smashed under the hard soles of her four feet.

—TANITH LEE, "Wolfland"

The oral tradition provides examples of resourceful and courageous Riding Hoods who outwit the wolf and escape, often by running *from* him.[1] Many contemporary versions prefer to have an audacious protagonist join the wolf and run *with* him. All the authors and artists discussed in this chapter present Riding Hoods who end up, to varying degrees, running with the wolves. A number of these protagonists have adopted the popular French proverb "One must howl with the wolves." Some of them even tame their wolves. In several cases, the classic roles are reversed, so that Riding Hoods are portrayed as wolves traveling in dangerous packs. According to the grandmother in Carol Lanigan's "All the Better to See You," from the feminist collection *Rapunzel's Revenge,* fifteen-year-old Rosa Hood, with her red leather jacket and punk hairdo, belongs to a "mean pack," whereas Billy Wolf is a nice, polite young lad (27).

In the preceding chapter, the wolf within was fear, which had to be confronted and overcome, or at least accepted, by Little Red Riding Hood. The chapter title may have elicited for some readers the image of Plato's "beast within," which Christianity subsequently connected with the wolf. For centuries this sinister image of the wolf as a symbol of bestiality prevailed, but as Sarah Greenleaf points out, we have now come full circle: "The beast within has been divorced from wolves and placed squarely where Plato left it twenty-four hundred years ago."[2] The wolf within is not only a symbol of fear, it also often represents the subconscious, instinctive impulses (especially in their darkest, most asocial and destructive form). This is acknowledged by the Chinese-born American author-illustrator Ed Young in the dedication to his picture book *Lon Po Po: A Red Riding Hood Story from China:* "To all the wolves of the world for lending their good name as a tangible symbol for our darkness."

The beast within is not found only in the male sex. Although the wolf has long been a metaphor of aggressive male sexuality, its carnal symbolism is now frequently applied to women as well. This fact is underscored in the 1994 film *The Company of Wolves*, based on Angela Carter's revisionings of the tale in *The Bloody Chamber*. In an attempt to reassure her daughter about sex, the mother tells her: "if there is a beast in man, it meets its match in women too." Modern Riding Hoods are often unconcerned with society's conventions and taboos. Many are portrayed as sensual beings who are sexually attracted to the wolf. The Riding Hoods in this chapter may still experience fear, but in most cases that is part of the powerful appeal of the wolf. Luisa Valenzuela's heroine suggests that both she and her mother share, and perhaps "like," the fear of the abyss associated with the wolf (105).

The wolf within can have positive as well as negative connotations. Giving oneself over to the inner wolf is presented in a favorable light in the 1992 bestseller *Women Who Run With the Wolves*, by the American author and psychoanalyst Clarissa Pinkola Estés. The first chapter is devoted to "*La Loba*, the Wolf Woman," the name the author gives to "the Wild Woman archetype." In the introduction to her book, Estés justifies her title by insisting on the affinity between women and wolves. She points to their positive psychic similarities, such as courage, devotion, endurance, strength, and intuitiveness, as well as to their trials: "both have been hounded, harassed, and falsely imputed to be devouring and devious." In her opinion, "the predation of wolves and women" by men is strikingly similar (2). Estés's successful book inspired a popular Web site, Wild Wolf Women of the Web (www.wildwolfwomen.com), but she is not affiliated with it. Furthermore, Annifrid (Frida) Lyngstad, formerly of the pop group ABBA, included the song "Kvinnor som springer" (Women who run), based on Estés's book, on her 1996 album *Djupa Andetag* (Deep breaths). The song is in praise of women who escape their trapped existence and run against the wind with the wolves. In many contemporary retellings of the tale, however, a little or not so little Red Riding Hood embraces a much darker bestial side. Some protagonists actually become werewolves or "women-wolves."

The Company of Wolves

Catherine Orenstein borrows the title of Carter's "The Company of Wolves" for a chapter in her insightful study *Little Red Riding Hood Uncloaked*. I use it in this section in a broader sense to refer to Riding Hoods who dare to keep company with wolves, but who do not necessarily have any wolfish instincts. In some cases, their relationship is just a matter of protecting common interests.

Estés concludes *Women Who Run With the Wolves* with an unusual retelling of *Little Red Riding Hood* titled "The Wolf's Eyelash." Obviously, from the title of the first volume in which the story appeared in 1970, *Rowing Songs for the Night Sea Journey, Contemporary Chants,* the psychoanalyst attributed a therapeutic purpose to her retelling. The stories included in her book were chosen from hundreds that she has worked with over decades and constitute those she feels most clearly express "the bounty of the Wild Woman archetype" (15). The final position in the book of her own story gives "The Wolf's Eyelash" special significance. Her reworking of *Little Red Riding Hood* means to offer women guidelines for living. Although the story is addressed to adults, especially women, it is quite suitable for the young adult audience that frequently consults the Web site.

The modern moral of Estés's poetic retelling, which she calls a "prose poem" (503), is transparent because the italicized lines appear first as a kind of epigraph and then again at the end of the tale: "*If you don't go out in the woods, nothing will ever happen and your life will never begin*" (499). The tale opens with a collective voice representing conventional society giving advice to the protagonist: "Don't go out in the woods." Reacting like any child told she can't do something, the protagonist wants to know why she shouldn't go into the woods. The answer she receives is based on the cultural construction of the wolf, as it is portrayed in fairy tales: "A big wolf lives there who eats humans such as you." The anonymous, collective warning is then repeated like a refrain that is somewhat reminiscent of the chorus in Greek tragedy. This collective voice assumes the cautionary role of the mother in the Grimms' version. Like her predecessor, the heroine disobeys. "Naturally, she went out," writes the narrator, who understands child psychology. However, the narrator also understands the psychology of the adult whose advice is ignored. When the girl meets the wolf, the collective voice "crows" a gloating "we told you." The protagonist defends her defiant disregard of their advice because, as she tells them bluntly: "This is my life, not a fairy tale, you dolts." The narrator's metafictive comment seems to contradict the protagonist and to suggest that this is indeed a fairy tale, because the wolf she meets is described as acting in the way of "wolves in tales of this kind."

Estés's self-reflexive story exposes its fictiveness in a very postmodern manner. When the girl asks the wolf in the trap how she is to know that he won't harm her if she helps him, the narrator informs readers that it is "her job to ask questions," alluding to the formulaic questions Little Red Riding Hood asks in the classic tale. The wolf is not referring to these questions, however, when he informs her that she has asked the "wrong question" (499). Even after the girl has freed the wolf's paw from the trap and bound it, she expects him to kill her. It turns out that she is also guilty of subscribing to the cultural construction of the wolf that comes from reading "too many of the wrong kind of tales." The wolf apparently knows the story of Little Red Riding Hood and the role the wolf plays in it, because he assures the girl: "I'm a wolf from another time and place" (500). His tone is not that of a sly seducer, but rather of a medieval knight, as he addresses her chivalrously as "fair maiden" or "kind maiden." True to his word, the wolf rewards the girl's kindness, giving her the gift of wisdom in the form of one of his eyelashes. The eyelash allows her to look through the wolf's eyes in order to weigh people for what they really are and to distinguish good from bad. Thus the wolf saves the girl from many misfortunes, including a good-for-nothing suitor.

Estés subverts the stereotype of the big bad wolf, turning him into a good, wise creature. She makes this the collective opinion of another anonymous group simply referred to as "they," undoubtedly the wise women of the community. The heroine learns that "it is true what they say, that the wolf is the wisest of all." If you listen closely to the wolf's haunting howling, according to the narrator/author, the wolf is always asking "the most important question," the only question worth asking. It is not a practical question concerning the whereabouts of his next meal, but a metaphysical question:

wooooooooor
aieeeee th'
sooooooooool?
Where is the soul? (502)

The story ends with a kind of refrain that repeats three times, in a pattern reminiscent of the tripartite structure so common in oral tales, the alternative advice in the italic chanting of the narrator/psychologist: "*Go out in the woods, go out*" (503). The story of the meeting with the wolf is recounted retrospectively, as the heroine has already defied the conventional advice and encountered the wolf in the woods. The words used to justify her actions to the cautionary chorus on the first page indicate that the protagonist has already learned the author's lesson:

"I have to go to the woods, and I have to meet the wolf, or else my life will never begin" (499). Women have much to learn from wolves, according to Estés, who provides her readers with "wolf rules for life" (498). Many Riding Hoods prefer to live their lives according to "wolf rules."

Picture books often present Little Red Riding Hood and the Wolf as friends or accomplices. This is particularly true in picture books for young readers, but it is also the case in a number of crossover picture books. The heroine of "Little Red Running Shorts," from *The Stinky Cheese Man and Other Fairly Stupid Tales* (1992), a popular American picture book that Jon Scieszka and Lane Smith specifically aimed at "Ages: All," has exchanged her traditional outfit for red track shorts and running shoes. This garb was intended to allow this modern Riding Hood to outrun the wolf, but she ends up running with him. This hugely successful postmodern picture book often appeals to adults even more than children because of the sophisticated metafictive play. Throughout "Little Red Running Shorts," playful attention is brought to the title of this particular "stupid tale." Although the title is self-explanatory, Jack the Narrator (of *Jack and the Beanstalk* fame) begins by telling readers the obvious: "See, it's about this girl who runs very fast and always wears red running shorts." This narrator leaves absolutely nothing to the reader's imagination: "That's where her name comes from, get it?" Scieszka plays with the tag "the end" by having Jack punctuate his brief preliminary summary of the plot with the words: "*The End*," before inviting readers to "sit back, relax, and enjoy—'Little Red Running Shorts.'"

When Jack gives the characters their cue, Little Red Running Shorts and the Wolf refuse to tell the story, claiming that the narrator has appropriated their narrative and already told all in his introduction. Tex Avery used a similar self-reflexive gag in his 1937 cartoon *Little Red Walking Hood*, in which the Wolf interrupts the narrator and refuses to continue, although it is for a different reason: "I'm fed up with that sissy stuff. . . . Every Hollywood studio has done it this way!"[3] In Avery's cartoon, both Red and Granny join the revolt, but the shocked narrator is given a second chance. That is how the fairy-tale heroine is reborn as a Red Hot Riding Hood. Scieszka's panic-stricken narrator protests and pleads with the characters of his next story, but they remain unmoved because Jack has, as the Wolf puts it, "blown it." The two characters take off together in a huff, leaving the following page completely blank.

Smith's witty pictures depict the two main characters, a well-dressed wolf in a suit and bow tie and wearing glasses, and a punk heroine with spiked hair, a most unlikely couple, abandoning Jack and making tracks toward the left side of the page to leave the book (plate 22). Their footprints lead back to the opposite full-page illustration where white cutouts of the Wolf and Little Red Running Shorts indicate their absence from what Rod McGillis calls the "nonstory" that ends before it begins (plate 23).[4] Readers are left with the image of Little Red Running Shorts and the Wolf leaving the book together. Little Red Riding Hood and the Wolf have become unlikely accomplices, two characters pitted against an incompetent narrator.

Although the Little Red Riding Hoods and wolves in F'Murr's *Au loup!* are generally engaged in open warfare, they do hang out peaceably in a few comics. One particularly funny comic portrays a very old Riding Hood and an equally old wolf, whose running days are obviously over since they are both hobbling about on canes. The senior citizens' happy reunion is interrupted by the sudden appearance of their offspring, a young Little Red Riding Hood being chased by a young wolf. From the sidelines, the proud elders shout encouragement and advice. Then the old wolf takes the old lady by the hand and leads her to a bench, where they can watch the goings-on of their descendants more comfortably (39). It is not only in their golden years, however, that Little Red Riding Hood and the wolf keep company in F'Murr's comics. When a shady developer manages to build a skyscraper right in the middle of Little Red Riding Hood's forest, an angry wolf and an enraged Little Red Riding Hood, in agreement for once, confront him with the fact that the forest is now a classified site with its own reference number, which they are able to cite as 47777a (49).

Politically correct versions of the tale also provide opportunities for Riding Hoods and wolves to join forces. In a similarly comic vein, Red Riding Hood, the wolf, and Grandma band together against the "woodchopper-person (or log-fuel technician, as he preferred to be called)" in James Finn Garner's politically correct "Little Red Riding Hood." The heroine accuses the woodchopper-person of being "sexist" and "speciesist" for thinking that "womyn" and wolves can't solve their own problems without male intervention, and the grandmother chops his head off with his own ax. The "commonality of purpose" the three characters feel after this ordeal leads them to set up "an alternative household based on mutual respect and cooperation." The narrator's assurance that "they lived together in the woods happily ever after" indicates the success of their enterprise (4). Garner's particular brand of tongue-in-cheek humor, which pokes fun at the phenomenon of political correctness, was intended for adults, but is also appreciated by young readers, as customer reviews on Amazon.com indicate.

The collection of "more or less politically correct" tales, *Le mariage politiquement correct du petit Chaperon rouge* (The politically correct marriage of Little Red Riding Hood, 1996), by the French-born author Pierre Léon, contains three tales devoted to the story of Little Red Riding Hood. The title page indicates that these tales are "for nostalgic, liberated adults," although Léon's introduction mentions both adult and child readers (xii). In the first tale, "La grand-mère économiquement défavorisée de la petite Chaperonne rouge" (Little Red Riding Hood's economically underprivileged grandmother), the old lady reminisces about the handsome wolf she had known (in a sexual sense) in her youth and wonders what has become of him. Léon integrates original events within the framework of Perrault's tale. The scene then shifts to the wolf, who has just learned from Little Red Riding Hood in the woods that the grandmother is still alive. It is then his turn to recall his memories of the young shepherdess with whom he had played so many years ago. What began as a game of "Loup y es-tu?" always ended with them making love. In Léon's retelling, intended principally for adults, the games that Little Red Riding Hood and the wolf play together have an explicit sexual connotation.

The formula about the *chevillette* and the *bobinette* is humorously reworked and incorporated into a sentence that ends with the two senior citizens in each other's arms full of the happy memories of their youth. The former lovers exchange a parodic version of the familiar dialogue; they compliment each other on various body parts that have remained attractive, even beautiful. A humorous black-and-white drawing by the author depicts the elderly grandmother and the old wolf in bed, while a thought bubble above the bed portrays the couple as they used to look in the good old days when they were lovers. The grandmother goads the wolf, who is against euthanasia, into admitting that she is pretty enough to eat (a play on the French expression *mignonne à croquer*). When the wolf is once again provoked into devouring her in a single bite, he tries to justify his action by reminding himself that she wanted it and that psychoanalysts call it the ultimate proof of love. Vowing never to eat anyone else, he leaves Little Red Riding Hood for his grandson, assuring the young wolf that the girl will not be sorry to meet him. The implication is that their encounter will also be a sexual one.

As the old wolf heads into the woods, he is thinking about "the sequel" that readers believe they know. Léon not only turns Perrault's classic tale into a sequel but also proposes to tell us the "true story" of Little Red Riding Hood (23). While the first tale relates the story of Little Red Riding Hood's grandmother and the grandfather wolf, the longer work is devoted to the "culturally, intellectually, and sexually liberated" granddaughter and the wolf's timid young grandson, Lulu, who also become lovers (27).[5] When the emancipated girl realizes it is Lulu, the Wolf, in the bed, she deliberately starts a provocative striptease. This Riding Hood takes complete charge of the situation, both asking and answering the questions of the ritualistic dialogue before planting a kiss on the end of the wolf's nose. The narrator's feigned modesty is not out of consideration for young readers. When he pronounces what happened next "not very relatable" (31), he is really inciting readers to imagine their sexual games.

Despite his shyness, Lulu lives up to his grandfather's reputation. In a moment of "supreme ecstasy," the young wolf ends up devouring the beautiful girl. Like his grandfather, Lulu assures himself that he devoured her "out of love" (38), and Little Red Riding Hood uses the same Freudian explanation to justify his behavior to her parents, after her father, a tree-cutting technician, rescues her. On more than one occasion, hereditary instincts come to the fore. While the Wolf is having dinner with Little Red Riding Hood's family, he is overcome by a "familial reflex" and tells her she is "sweet enough to eat" (35). This Riding Hood and Wolf seem destined to marry and live happily ever after. In a humorous exaggeration of the common theme of the wolf's repentance, Léon's Wolf undertakes a pilgrimage to a convent in Quebec, after secretly promising to come back and marry Little Red Riding Hood. While the lovesick girl pines away for her beloved Wolf, he betrays her with one of the schoolgirls at the convent. Léon provides a highly original ending by borrowing a page out of *Sleeping Beauty*. A prince, who thinks that Little Red Riding Hood would make a charming princess, waits by her side while she sleeps for a hundred years. When she awakens, Little Red Riding Hood mistakes him for her Wolf, as the prince has undergone a hairy metamorphosis during the one-hundred-year wait. The title of Léon's sequel indicates that Little Red Riding Hood's marriage to a hairy prince is more politically correct than would have been her marriage to the Wolf, a union her parents opposed. As we have already seen, however, some Riding Hoods do end up marrying their wolf.

When Riding Hoods keep company with wolves, they do so for a variety of reasons. For the heroine of Estés's story, the wolf is a wise mentor. Paradoxically, Little Red Riding Hood often finds in the wolf an accomplice or an ally, whether it be against an incompetent narrator, as in "Little Red Running Shorts"; against a dishonest land developer, as in F'Murr's comic; or against the wood-cutter, as in Garner's tale. Riding Hoods may also seek out the company of wolves because they are such good lovers, as in Léon's humorous tales, which demonstrate the wolf's prowess as a lover at any age.

Taming the Wolf

A number of Riding Hoods dream of taming the wolf. The heroine of Luisa Valenzuela's retelling thinks to herself: "The wolf doesn't seem so bad. He seems like he could be domesticated, sometimes" (110). The protagonists of some versions actually succeed in domesticating the wolf. The final plate in the Norwegian picture book *Rødhatten og Ulven,* by the author-illustrator Fam Ekman, portrays the male protagonist leading the wolf home on a leash. The resurrected wolf's shrunken size is humorously explained by the loss in the seams when the grandmother stitched up the wolf's belly on her sewing machine. The animal no longer bears any resemblance whatsoever to the tall, sexy she-wolf, in the red dress and heels, who had turned her seductive charms on the boy. The wolf now looks like a small, docile dog. Thus the little country boy returns from the city with a new pet, a "small good wolf" on a ribbon leash.

In some cases, Red Riding Hood breaks, rather than tames, a dangerous wild animal that poses a threat to society. The wolf that Anne Sharpe's "Not So Little Red Riding Hood" encounters in the woods is a well-groomed, two-legged predator, whose after shave of choice is Brut. We have already seen the perverted thinking of this aggressive male, for whom all women, at least those dressed in red, are provocative temptresses. Initially, Scarlet runs from her stalker, who is soon running on all fours, having undergone a monstrous transformation not unlike that of the dangerous man-wolf in Bruno de La Salle's retelling. In the end, however, the aspiring rapist is left "whimpering for mercy" at the hands of the black belt karate expert in the scarlet cape, who disdainfully flicks him aside with her boot (49). This broken wolf may be less tempted to stalk Riding Hoods in the future. Not all Riding Hoods wish to domesticate or break the wolf, however. Some prefer to run wild and free with the wolves. It is doubtful that Valenzuela's sultry heroine really wants to domesticate her Big Bad Wolf.

The French author Pierrette Fleutiaux published a feminist retelling of *Little Red Riding Hood,* titled "Petit Pantalon Rouge, Barbe-Bleue et Notules" ("Little Red Pants, Bluebeard, and Notules"), in her 1984 collection *Métamorphoses de la reine* (Metamorphoses of the queen). The innovative collection won the prestigious Prix Goncourt for short stories, a major prize for adult fiction, although young adults also read the collection.[6] As the title suggests, "Petit Pantalon Rouge, Barbe-Bleue et Notules" is a bricolage of two fairy tales, in which Little Red Pants, after learning to tame wolves from her mother and grandmother, marries Bluebeard and saves his seven wives. Fleutiaux's feminist take on Perrault's tales, in which a fearless Little Red Riding Hood encounters Bluebeard, is reminiscent of Gotlib's 1971 comic, mentioned in chapter 3. Gotlib's Little Red Riding Hood has no intention of taming Bluebeard when she marries him, however. She is more apt to whip him into a frenzy. In both cases, Bluebeard seems to have met his match in the little girl in red.

Fleutiaux's lengthy tale, which is included in its entirety at the end of this chapter, plays with its pre-texts in a sophisticated manner. Readers will immediately be struck by the author's distinctive style, which pastiches the classic language of the original tales. Perrault's *Contes* are ingrained in French childhood; it is the one text that "every French child knows by heart before going to school."[7] Comparing the tales' seventeenth-century language, which is introduced in childhood, to "a period costume," Fleutiaux explains that rereading them was similar to entering into "a costume ball." In order to get over the depression she experienced in adulthood, it was necessary to rediscover the dress-up clothes of childhood play.[8] Certain familiar lines, which are etched in the memory of French readers, are taken word for word from Perrault, for example, the memorable description of the heroine's precipitous descent of the stairs leading to Bluebeard's forbidden chamber. In rewriting Perrault's tales her way, however, the author found that she needed "to play with this language, to make its starched side rip with street expressions, to introduce anachronisms, to curtsey so low sometimes that the seams burst!" The witty and sophisticated language play in this unusual retelling is largely responsible for its acclaim by readers and the literary establishment.

The foreign element in the title illustrates the tongue-in-cheek parody that appeals so strongly to Fleutiaux's readers. Although "Notules" seems to have the same status as Little Red Pants and Bluebeard, it is not an obscure fairy-tale character, but merely an embellished name given to the notes at the end of the text. In a pseudo-scientific fashion, witty notes explore the various interpretations researchers have attributed to the enigmatic locutions of the wolf with the glued jaws. Fleutiaux pokes fun at scholarly folk and fairy-tale research, where an obscure detail can result in the flow of a great deal of ink or even provoke a major literary quarrel. The long list of eminent experts involved in the absurd debate over the meaning of the wolf's utterances accurately reflects the wide range of researchers drawn to the field, with the humorous exception of "stomatologists" (137).

Fleutiaux's retold tales are full of witty metafictional play. When the narrator justifies treating the famous tower scene expeditiously, because these facts are well known, the implication is that they found their way into Perrault's version of *Bluebeard*. However, Fleutiaux has even radically transformed these famous facts. For that matter, even the key motif of the forbidden room undergoes a major makeover. Fleutiaux portrays it as a tiny, cramped cupboard containing not only Bluebeard's seven wives but also his two brothers, none of whom are quite dead yet. The narrator also states that the events that follow the tower scene require dwelling upon in order to rectify the numerous errors that have slipped in over time. Tongue in cheek, Fleutiaux thus claims to reestablish the "true" story that Perrault's classic tale of *Bluebeard* has corrupted. At one point, both of Perrault's tales are humorously demoted to the status of mere variants. A humorous note mentions variants of the tale in which the firebrand doesn't talk, and the adventure gets lost in the subterranean passages or "divides into two, sending LRP into a wolf's intestines and Bluebeard to the blade that split his" (138).

Fleutiaux includes ingenious intertextual allusions to other fairy tales, as well to other genres, many of which younger readers can recognize. The strange image of Bluebeard's beard, as a bush of brambles and thorns that completely cuts him off from the world around him, cannot help but evoke the impenetrable thorny bush that grows up around Sleeping Beauty's enchanted castle. There is even an unlikely reference to Perrault's *Les Fées* (*The Fairies*): when Bluebeard's beard begins to grow "black thoughts like toads came out of [his] mouth" (129). The lost heroine's laments in the underground passages are a series of clever intertextual references to fairy tale and myth, as she asks herself why she didn't leave "little stones" or "a long thread" (123). General allusions to stereotypical fairy-tale characters abound. The curious, jealous women who accompany her mother and grandmother to the castle after Bluebeard's departure imagine Little Red Pants as an "ogress" (119). The scene provides Fleutiaux, as it did Perrault, with a wonderful excuse for some mild social satire. Instead of an ogress, they find a little village girl in modest red pants, who, in their minds, does not know how to dress or behave in accordance with her new status, but who, in fact, has simply remained spoiled by her marriage to a fine gentleman. Fleutiaux paints the envy of the women from all social levels, including the peasants who feel that television deceived them with regard to "the appearance of prince charmings" (120).

In the preface to her collection, Fleutiaux explains that when she began rereading Perrault's *Contes* as an adult, it occurred to her that "these tales were children's tales and that [she] wasn't a child, more specifically that these were tales for little girls and that [she] was a woman" (10). As such, she was suddenly struck by the fact that "on the horizon of [her] adult life," she had been offered an image of "adult women [as] shrews, bad mothers, witches, cruel stepmothers." Rereading Perrault's tales provoked a sudden awareness the author had not even gained during her participation in consciousness-raising groups for women in the United States during the late 1960s and early 1970s. A desire to rewrite the tales followed the author's initial reaction of anger and rejection. She stresses, however, that the feminism in her revisionist tales is not presented as a message, as it is in some feminist retellings. Fleutiaux enhances, enriches, and develops the roles of adult women in her reworkings of the classic tales. Her retelling of *Le Petit Poucet,* for example, casts the ogre's wife in the eponymous role. "The Ogre's Wife" is the only tale from Fleutiaux's collection that has previously been published in English. In "Petit Pantalon, Barbe-Bleue et Notules," Bluebeard's wives also become individuals, who have a heated discussion of his past treatment of them while he lies unconscious at their feet.

Fleutiaux cleverly reworks the familiar incipit of *Le Petit Chaperon Rouge* to set the stage for a highly unconventional heroine who is more than a match for the wolf. Familiar words and entire sentences from Perrault's tales are cleverly woven into a narrative about a heroine who is quite the opposite of her naive precursor. The first lines are faithful to the classic tale, with the exception of several highly significant substitutions and additions. Rather than being the "prettiest," this heroine is the "liveliest" ever seen (105). Perhaps this lively little girl bears a slight resemblance to the young author, who admits that she spent much of her childhood in a small town in central France "running around the countryside."[9] The addition of two relative clauses to qualify the mother and the grandmother turn them into emancipated women. Readers are told that the mother had never had a husband, whereas the grandmother had had several. The author's feminist intentions are already manifest in the genealogy of this Riding

Hood. The item of clothing that characterizes the heroine undergoes a symbolic change as well. Instead of a red hood, it is red pants that suit her so well that she is called "Little Red Pants." The new outfit is all the better to tame wolves in!

In her revisioning of *Le Petit Chaperon Rouge*, Fleutiaux presents three generations of women who turn the classic stereotypes upside down. The traits that are privileged are not the feminine qualities with which Perrault endows his fairy-tale heroines (beauty, innocence, passivity). In addition to emphasizing the heroine's liveliness and courage, the narrator informs readers that Little Red Pants "grew in strength and in wisdom" (105). As in *Bye Bye Chaperon Rouge*, Fleutiaux stresses the role played by older generations of women in the young girl's education. While the mother teaches Little Red Pants bravery and practical skills (repairing roofs, plowing the fields, and building walls), her globe-trotting grandmother uses her books and memories to provide the girl with a more worldly knowledge that, according to the narrator, would have amazed the village women. As their reward at the end of the story, the mother and grandmother each ask for the hand of one of Bluebeard's brothers, and the old lady requests the younger of the two. The women certainly wear the pants in this tale!

When Little Red Pants' mother sends her out one day to play with the wolves around the cottage, it is really the beginning of her wolf-taming lessons. The wolf-taming scene is repeated three times, with variations, on three consecutive days, creating the familiar tripartite structure. The rhythms and patterns of the oral tradition are used with consummate skill in this retelling that subverts the traditional tale while maintaining its mythic content. During each of the three trials of this initiation, Little Red Pants' mother gives her a magical object: the gum-that-sticks everything, a whip, and a firebrand. The young girl finds wolves vastly superior to the other mounts she had experienced in the past, that is, domesticated dogs, donkeys, and piglets. The image of Little Red Pants riding a piglet calls forth that of the unruly Riding Hood that Philippe Corentin depicts terrorizing an assortment of domestic and wild animals from the back of a squealing, panic-stricken pig in *Mademoiselle Sauve-qui-peut* (Miss Run-for-Your-Life, 1996). The mischievous little girl whipping the pig with a croplike stick seems to be in training for taming wolves. These Riding Hoods are a different breed of female from the stereotypical women portrayed in fairy tales. When Little Red Pants generously offers to give Bluebeard's terrified seventh wife her gum, whip, and firebrand at the end of the tale, the fearful woman admits that she would even be afraid to practice on dogs or cats.

Each of Little Red Pants' trials is more difficult and each ride more exhilarating than the previous one. The third wolf does not merely go obediently in circles around the house, but cunningly heads back toward the forest in order that the girl must confront the entire pack. Fleutiaux paints a spellbinding image of the little girl gripping the wolf's flanks with her legs and whipping his croup, as she twirls her blazing firebrand high above her head and leads a cavalcade of fiery-eyed wolves through the forest until dawn. With the magical words of her evocative prose, the author depicts these striking scenes in powerful images for her readers. The author admits her predilection for these "almost visual" scenes that she saw "almost like picture-book illustrations," a comparison that suggests young readers are never far from her mind. Several wolves in the pack are humanized by means of humorous dialogue that echoes the wolves' bantering in Paul Biegel's retelling. To try to save face in front of his peers, Little Red Pants' first victim denies that the girl was riding them and claims that she was actually running after them, because they wanted nothing to do with her. This little girl, who has confidently assumed the dominant role, has injured their masculine pride.

In keeping with the ritual separation from the family that characterizes adolescent initiations, Little Red Pants is warned before the final trial that she will be locked out of the house until daylight. This Riding Hood knows no fear; on the contrary, she passionately enjoys playing with the wolves. The sexual connotations of the games that mark her coming of age are transparent. The narrator recalls, for example, the potent effect of the strong, animal odor of the wolf on Little Red Pants. It is evident that the heroine of Fleutiaux's retelling relishes "riding the red." Having successfully completed the rite of passage, Little Red Pants' mother and grandmother welcome her home and give her a ritual bath before putting her to bed, where she sleeps for three days and three nights, a symbolic initiatory death that precedes her rebirth.

After Little Red Pants' initiation, the scene shifts suddenly to Bluebeard. Once again the incipit contains strong echoes of Perrault's version of the tale. The seventeenth-century images of dinner services of gold and silver and fine coaches (although Fleutiaux's are chromium plated rather than gilded) contrast humorously with anachronistic references to various aspects of contemporary life. A striking contrast is set up between Bluebeard's hairy face, which cannot be cured by lasers and hormones since they have not yet been invented, and the smooth, clean-shaven cheeks of the handsome television announcers who constitute the current prince charmings. Although the reader is well ensconced in the familiar story of Bluebeard before Little Red Pants is suddenly mentioned again, the two stories are smoothly linked. Little Red Pants is reintroduced at the point where Bluebeard has had to resort to searching for a bride among the country's peasant women. It is suggested humorously that Little Red Pants' well-traveled grandmother might be the only woman open-minded enough to consider this match, but she is once again off traipsing around the world and has not heard about this latest eligible male who is scouring the countryside for a bride. As to the other two eligible women in the family, they are both otherwise occupied, the mother with her daughter, and Little Red Pants with the wolves. Although Bluebeard is also billed in the title of Fleutiaux's tale, he does not share equal status with the eponymous heroine, as is suggested by his absence from the opening pages as well as the final scene.

The scene in which Little Red Riding Hood is sent to her grandmother's is subverted in order to adapt it to the new circumstances: Little Red Pants' mother gives her the traditional cake and little pot of butter, but she is told to take them to the village inn to try to get news of her globe-trotting grandmother. The mother's cautionary role is limited to a reminder to take with her the gum, whip, and firebrand, which constitute the new attributes of this self-sufficient heroine. On the way, she encounters, not a wolf, but Bluebeard, who appropriates a modified version of the wolf's line to ask the girl, mounted on a wolf, where she is going "on this dangerous equipage" (114). Although she obligingly answers his question and imprudently accepts his offer of a ride in his carriage, it does not seem to be due to naïveté, but rather to the fearless little heroine's desire for new experiences. A detail the narrator provides suggests that Little Red Pants is not as naive as she may appear. Although it may be a subconscious gesture, as she sits down beside Bluebeard, the girl tightly holds the pockets containing her wolf-taming tools.

Very different from the other women Bluebeard has encountered, the lively little girl proves her fearlessness and unconventionality by agreeing that a blue beard is quite amusing and that going cross-country on unknown paths is more fun than taking beaten paths. Their conversation is nonetheless punctuated by the expression "By my mother and my grandmama," which Little Red Pants uses repeatedly to indicate her surprise concerning the color of his beard, the carriage recklessly leaving the road, and the unknown path through the woods. The spontaneous reference to the older women indicates that subconsciously Little Red

Pants is aware of the danger these things represent, but at the same time the adventuresome girl is attracted by that danger. Bluebeard's annoyance at the constant mention of "this mother and this grandmama" seems to turn them into invisible chaperones (116), but they are soon completely forgotten by Little Red Pants, who does not seem in the least troubled by the fact that the man with the strange blue beard has kidnapped her.

In Fleutiaux's variation on the bed scene, Little Red Pants takes the initiative. A new stage in the heroine's life is marked by a name change: from this point on the author humorously abbreviates her name to PPR (in English LRP). Little Red Pants is about to become a woman. If there was any doubt previously as to the symbolism of Little Red Pants' firebrand, the sexual connotation is now unmistakable. A blushing Bluebeard tells the cheeky little girl in red that she must marry him before she can see his firebrand. Like a small child eager to try out a new toy, LRP is willing to do anything to get her way. Henceforth LRP and Bluebeard (referred to on this one occasion only by the abbreviation BB that suggests a well-matched couple) spend their nights "exchanging their firebrands" (117) or, as Nalo Hopkinson would put it, "riding the red." "Petit Pantalon, Barbe Bleue et Notules" restores some of the explicit sexual content of what, in the oral tradition, was a rather bawdy tale, but the violent sensuality has a modern erotic overtone that elevates female sexuality.

The versatile firebrand constitutes a magical agent, according to Propp's terminology, but Fleutiaux elevates it to the status of a character with a major role and a distinctive personality. In some ways, it seems to be a parody of the animated objects in Disney films. When she cites this passage as one of the visual scenes she envisaged like "a cartoon," the author describes the firebrand as a "chevalier servant" (attentive escort) to Little Red Pants, referring to the *chevalier servant* of the court ladies in seventeenth-century France. Fleutiaux sees the firebrand as "the eternal suitor who will never be the true Lover," and who must content himself with the role of a faithful servant.[10] With metafictional self-consciousness, the firebrand is aware of its great destiny and impatient "to play its major role" in the story (126). Having led the heroine to the secret room, but fearing that the action is getting mired down when she prepares to abandon the "lying phantoms" to their fate, the firebrand takes charge (124). Fleutiaux's appropriation of the discourse of epic literature to talk about the firebrand creates a very funny parody of the genre. On numerous occasions, the narrator interrupts the narrative to extol the valor of the firebrand. At the most dramatic point in the story (LRP has already used her first two magical objects against Bluebeard and is forcing him to retreat with the firebrand), the narrator suddenly interrupts the narration of their formidable confrontation "to render praise to the firebrand" for the prodigious exploit that incited him to relate this tale. The heroic feat, which consists of attacking and consuming Bluebeard's hair, seems absurdly simple for a firebrand, but the effort leaves him in a state near death. According to the narrator, the firebrand sinks "back into oblivion" after his moment of glory (127), but, in actual fact, his role in the narrative is not yet over. Like an injured knight, he will revive long enough to offer his service and intervene heroically in the story on two more occasions. The last breath of the dying firebrand is used to try to keep Bluebeard and Little Red Pants together, but the futility of his efforts is suggested comically by the fact that his words are indecipherable and have to be explained in a note. Here the discourse slips into that of romance literature, as the narrator informs readers that even the firebrand is incapable of fanning the "smoke and ashes" of their love back into flame (133). In Fleutiaux's tale, which establishes itself as the "true" version, the firebrand is the magical agent that allows the heroine to tame the wolf.

This little Riding Hood does a great deal of running as she awaits the return of her wolf. The dramatic scene between the heroine and her sister, Anne, in Perrault's *Barbe Bleue* is reworked into an amusing scene in which LRP runs between the underground passages, where she asks the wives and brothers if they are still alive, and the tower, where she asks her mother and grandmother it they have seen anyone yet. As LRP ascends and descends, the "yes" becomes weaker and the "no" more weary. Fleutiaux humorously exaggerates the toing and froing. Although it continues throughout a very long day, the narrator informs readers of the need to condense the scene into a few minutes, so that it is repeated only three times, as are so many events in fairy tales. The drama in this scene is heightened in Fleutiaux's re-version because nine other people's lives depend on this brave Riding Hood. Little Red Pants joins the ranks of the fairy-tale protagonists whose small size is no indication of their valor. Bluebeard admits later that it was quite fortunate that he had never been told he could only be delivered from the spell by a fearless woman, because, in that case, he would never have considered "such a Little Red Pants."

Fleutiaux cleverly transforms Bluebeard into a wolf. The Bluebeard who returns from his journey is no longer the "loving husband" with the blue beard, but a merciless "monster" covered in long, black hair from head to toe. The fact that

Bluebeard plays the role of the wolf in "Petit Pantalon Rouge, Barbe Bleue et Notules" is clearly indicated on his return to the castle. As Bluebeard leaps at LRP, his transformation seems to become more complete with each detail added to his description: long bristling hair, eyes that shine like "bloody glowing coals," ferocious howling, and large open mouth (the word *gueule* suggests an animal's mouth). The wolflike characteristics are multiplied until it is impossible not to associate the two villainous fairy-tale characters: shiny teeth, fangs, snapping jaws, paws, and the term "fauve" (wild animal). Finally, Bluebeard is referred to explicitly as "the wolf" (126–27). The heroine makes the connection almost immediately, as the memory of the dark forest and the violent wolves that she had ridden suddenly surfaces. Now the girl uses the gum, whip, and firebrand, still in the pockets of her red pants, to tame the ferocious Bluebeard. He later expresses his gratitude toward the mother and grandmother for raising Little Red Pants without fears or constraints and accustoming her to wolves from her childhood, thus saving him from his horrible destiny.

Fleutiaux's Bluebeard is portrayed in a much more sympathetic light than Perrault's. The metamorphosis accomplished by the firebrand reveals a handsome man who combines both feminine and masculine qualities. The narrator describes him as "full of virile grace and firm gentleness" (127). The author turns gender stereotypes upside down. The new Bluebeard is overcome by emotion and faints on more than one occasion. Bluebeard's amazing transformation into a handsome gentleman reverberates of *Beauty and the Beast*. This is reinforced when readers learn that Bluebeard has been the victim of a curse. The source of the spell, as well as the reasons for it, remains a mystery. Fleutiaux parodies the final wrap-up scene in murder mysteries when Bluebeard gathers everyone in the castle's great room to explain how he had come to commit such crimes. They are mitigated by the fact that this Bluebeard had imprisoned each of his unfortunate victims in the secret cupboard with bread and water, instead of "eating her alive," as the curse dictated (129). This variation on the fate of Bluebeard's wives serves to further link his story to that of Little Red Riding Hood, who was eaten alive by the wolf.

The dizzying vision of his eight wives forming a moving flower provokes one of Bluebeard's fainting spells. Fleutiaux's striking flower metaphor describes Bluebeard's wives in a very evocative manner. As the red pistil full of life at the center of the strange flower, Little Red Pants supports the seven wilted petals that represent the other wives. The author cleverly develops the flower metaphor,

UNIVERSITY OF MINNESOTA
LIBRARY

first to describe this polygamous Bluebeard's problematic domestic situation, and then to provide an original solution. The singular flower is attractive but also poisonous, because the love of eight women is too much for a single man. Before Bluebeard's eyes, the flower changes shape, as the petals arrange themselves in couples, leaving three large petals (which take on new life) and a single small petal encircling the red pistil. The forbidden room takes on new meaning when Bluebeard is forced to recognize that six of his wives have become lesbians while in the closet.

Fleutiaux takes great delight in parodying the fairy-tale happy ending. The narrator claims to skip the joy of the reunion in the interests of authenticity, since the confusion makes it impossible to say with certainty who was kissing whom. Everyone's tears are described; even the "virile" Bluebeard can scarcely hold back his tears. Bluebeard's emotional state is attributed humorously both to the past, because memories come flooding back "multiplied by seven" (129), and to the future, because he already foresees all the terrible complications, rifts, and possible lawsuits he may have to face as a polygamist with eight wives. The happy reunion is followed immediately by an unexpected farewell scene. Little Red Pants and Bluebeard are not destined to live happily ever after. The tangled relationships are humorously highlighted in a complicated farewell. Little Red Pants takes leave of Bluebeard, assuring him of the friendship she owes "a great-uncle, uncle, ex-husband, and almost brother-in-law," and bidding him take care of his "two sisters-in-law, [her] mother and grandmother, as well as [his] brothers, [his] six ex-wives, and [his] wife" (134).

After his final transformation, Bluebeard is portrayed as a passive and docile man, hardly a good match for Little Red Pants. Even after the first six wives decide they don't need a man to make them happy, Bluebeard is still unable or unwilling to choose between wives seven and eight. If he leans slightly toward Little Red Pants, it perhaps is largely out of gratitude and self-interest (she would be in a better position to cure him again if he should have a recurrence) rather than passion. Bluebeard does nothing to try to dissuade Little Red Pants from leaving, no doubt relieved not to have to make a decision. This clean-shaven, mild-mannered Bluebeard is obviously far too tame for a wild young woman used to riding wolves. The open ending leaves readers to imagine the future of this fearless Riding Hood, who sets out on the main road with her basket in lieu of the hobo's stick. The seventh wife's appropriation of the wolf's familiar question about Little Red Riding Hood's destination emphasizes the open ending. This time the question is left unanswered because, as the narrator asks: "who can answer such a question?" Certainly not this adventurous Little Red Pants, who will no doubt find other wolves to tame!

The innovative retelling "Si esto es la vida, yo soy Caperucita Roja" ("If this is life, I'm Red Riding Hood") by the Argentinean author Luisa Valenzuela was published for adults in 1993 in her short story collection *Simetrías,* which appeared in English in 1998 under the title *Symmetries.* Valenzuela's re-version of the story of Little Red Riding Hood, like all of her writing, makes heavy demands on the reader. She presents a Riding Hood who has grown up, as the elimination of the epithet "Little" in the English translation of the title emphasizes. In a story with erotic overtones, Red Riding Hood encounters a wolf who "makes obscene gestures" at her from the woods, gestures that she does not really understand (105). Valenzuela's original take on the story of Little Red Riding Hood is the first tale in a section of her collection titled "Cuentos de Hades." The title is a clever play on words that substitutes the underworld of Greek mythology for the Spanish word *hadas* (fairies), turning "fairy tales" into "tales from Hades." In the English edition, the translator has rendered the play on words by titling the section "Firytales." Although perhaps not as "red hot" as Tex Avery's Riding Hood, Valenzuela's heroine is a fiery, sultry, Latin American woman. Valenzuela's provocative retellings of traditional tales are intended to force readers to reevaluate their comfortable yet often unsound assumptions and beliefs.

"Si esto es la vida, yo soy Caperucita Roja" demonstrates the bold experiments with narrative structure that characterize all of Valenzuela's works. A constantly shifting point of view creates an atmosphere of ambiguity and uncertainty. The story is focalized sometimes through Red Riding Hood, at other times through the mother. The cautionary scene is recounted in interior monologue that shifts from one to the other in a rather confusing manner:

> I warned her about the other thing too. I'm always warning her and she doesn't listen.
>
> I don't listen to her, or hardly at all. . . .
>
> No, dear, says mama.
>
> I listen to mama but I don't hear her. I mean, I hear mama but I don't listen to her. (104)

The characters contradict themselves and each other, further heightening the ambiguity of the narrative. According to the mother, she didn't tell her daughter to put on the "the little red cape that [her] grandmother knitted for [her]," because "her grandmother doesn't knit yet" (103). However, the girl describes her grandmother as a nice little old lady who "knits and knits." She even explains the meaning of this pastime: "She's knitting out her yearning for red, she's knitting the hood for me" (105–6). The sexual connotation of the old lady's yearning is obvious. She reminds us of Hopkinson's grandmother, who dreams of "riding the red" just one more time. However, it is now Little Red Riding Hood's turn. The mention of the word *wolf*, first pronounced by the mother, provokes a string of contradictory remarks on the part of the daughter. The girl denies saying the word *wolf*, then admits that she says it but insists that it doesn't help. Almost in the same breath, she concedes that it may help because she avoids certain sections of the path that might "hurl [her] into the abyss." Even this statement seems uncertain because the protagonist immediately confesses, at first hesitantly and then decisively: "I might—I'm afraid—rather like abysses. I do like them." Red Riding Hood not only contradicts herself but also her mother, who refuses to admit that her daughter likes abysses:

But you like them too, mama.
    Well, I both like them and fear them. (105)

The girl's thoughts are interwoven with her mother's, so that it is impossible to know through whose consciousness they are being processed. Sometimes the narrator feels the need to identify which of them is speaking. Readers are told at one point that the voices of the mother and daughter "become superimposed" (105). Not only is it often difficult to identify the voice speaking, but that voice also may present alternative possibilities. With regard to the wolf the grandmother lets into the house, the narrator speculates: "Perhaps it's the same wolf, perhaps the grandmother likes him, or has taken a shine to him already, or will end up accepting him" (106–7). The subjectiveness of the story is highlighted when Red Riding Hood qualifies her statements with phrases such as "or so I hope" (104) and "or so I believe" (114).

Using self-conscious language, the author plays with the conventions of the fairy tale. The protagonist refers to her red cape with the hood as the "so-called riding hood" (104). Four pages into the story, an anonymous narrator, who uses the first person plural, calls the protagonist "Red Riding Hood" for the first time, adding "as we will call her from now on" (106). Toward the end of the tale, Red Riding Hood admits that "no one remembers [her] name now" (114). The parodic intention of Valenzuela's metafictional retelling is clearly indicated when she relates it to the fairy tale *The Frog Prince*. The protagonist draws a comparison between fairy-tale frogs and fairy-tale wolves: "How many frogs does one have to kiss before finding the prince? How many wolves, I ask, will we meet in a lifetime?" (108) This Riding Hood seems to despair of ever finding the right wolf.

Valenzuela manages to draw the reader into the woods to walk alongside her Riding Hood. It is unclear whether Red Riding Hood is telling herself or the reader or both that there is no turning back. The protagonist's journey seems to become the reader's through a simple, yet clever, word substitution. "Page" and "path" are used synonymously when Red Riding Hood warns: "There's no going back. You'll find that out at the end of the page, at the end of the path" (105). Sometimes the protagonist shifts from the first-person singular to the plural, leaving us uncertain whether she is including readers or other Riding Hoods en route to grandmother's. Toward the end of the tale, she evokes the "other riding hoods" who will also have set off into the wood, one of whom may even be her own daughter (114).

Familiar events and dialogue are appropriated from the pre-text, but they are subverted to convey new meanings. When the wolf puts the traditional question about her destination to the heroine, whom he addresses as "Little" Red Riding Hood, the protagonist replies in unladylike language: "Piss off, I say, because I feel big and brave" (108). As in *Bye Bye Chaperon Rouge*, Valenzuela superposes multiple encounters with the wolf, but in this complex tale, they seem to blur together to form one never-ending trip along a very "long, long path" that represents the journey through life (104). The same question is asked over and over, although the reply is not always the same: "The wolf keeps asking me where I'm going and I usually tell him the truth, but I don't say which path I'm taking or what I'll be doing on that path or how long it will take me." If the protagonist doesn't always tell the truth about her path, it is partly because she is unsure: "I don't really know, I only know—and I don't tell him this—that I don't mind the twists and turns or the shady grottos if I find a bit of company there and a few fruits to gather along the way . . ." (109). This Riding Hood is not in any hurry to get to her grandmother's.

Conventional motifs are also used in an innovative manner. In her basket, this Riding Hood gathers fruit, which is an increasingly transparent metaphor for men. A vague reference to the "tempting fruits in these latitudes" is followed by an explicit comparison: "There are men who are like fruit: they are sweet, tasty, juicy, irritating." Valenzuela's protagonist is perhaps a connoisseur: "It's a question of tasting them one by one" (108). After Red Riding Hood takes a bite, she carefully places the fruit in the basket for her grandmother. She compares her basket to "a bottomless barrel" (112), yet it is "full" when she finally reaches her grandmother's (115). In spite of the basket's increasing weight, the protagonist keeps adding to it anything she thinks might "give pleasure" to her grandma, although she admits that "the pleasure is, above all, [hers]" (109). The striking metaphor is developed throughout the tale, as Red Riding Hood describes the men she has known as tasty-looking fruit that turns out to be "bitter and indigestible," that leaves her "feeling hungry," or that eventually seems to lose its flavor (112).

In this erotic retelling, the sexual symbolism of the red cape is played up, but the heroine herself associates it with her sensual desire. As the heat increases symbolically in the now "tropical" wood, "she feels like tearing off her cape, or, rather, tearing off the rest of her clothes and then rolling about on the cool moss, wrapped only in the cape . . ." (108). The red cape is also used to express the passage of time, as this Riding Hood makes her unending journey through the woods. After only a few pages, readers are told that the cape is "becoming shiny with wear" (108), and when a thread of her cape hooks on a tree on the following page, the garment is described as "ragged" (109). Yet her red cape "gleams in the midday sun" of her prime (110) and, a little later, her "beautiful cape" takes on "a new elegance" and "clings to [her] body," reflecting the heroine's newfound maturity, as she becomes the mother who sends her daughter into the wood, while at the same time continuing her own journey (111). Farther along the path, she wonders if her grandmother will be able "to darn [her] cape" (113), but toward the end of the tale, she stops "to mend [her] now rather threadbare cape," using the spines that have ripped it "as pins to hold the torn pieces together" (114). The cloth of her mended cape has entirely lost its red color, faded with wear and time. Past, present, and future seem strangely to fuse into timelessness.

"Si esto es la vida, yo soy Caperucita Roja" demonstrates brilliantly how an author can use the traditional imagery and motifs of the tale without necessarily ascribing to the ideology of the original. Like all of the author's work, this tale has a feminist slant. Valenzuela portrays a mother who "grows bored" at home with her door locked against the wolf, a Riding Hood who "has little chance of growing bored and plenty of opportunity for becoming disenchanted" in the wood where "there is always a wolf," and a grandmother who "is also going to be daring" by opening her door to the wolf (106). Eventually the three characters become one, as Red Riding Hood continues along the path of life: "I am Red Riding Hood. I am my own mother, I am walking towards my grandmother" (112).

Sometimes this Red Riding Hood puts on a sheepskin "to tempt" the wolf, or she goes right up to him and "egg[s] him on." Although she is afraid of the wolf, she is sorry he ignores her. He is the object of her sexual fantasies: "Sometimes, when I'm sleeping alone in the middle of the wood, I feel him very close, almost on top of me, and I experience a not wholly unpleasant tingling sensation." Her desire for the wolf is apparently to blame for her promiscuous behavior: "Sometimes, so as not to feel him there, I sleep with the first man I meet, any tasty-looking stranger will do." But the remedy backfires because it only makes her "more aware of the wolf than ever" (110). This Riding Hood misses the wolf who has distanced himself from her, *her* wolf, the one she affectionately calls Pirincho. Her plaintive cries subvert the wolf's question: "Oh, wolf, wolf, where have you got to?" (113).

The protagonist confesses that she is not in a hurry to arrive at her destination. The "old woman" that she prefers to keep waiting is not only the grandmother but also her elderly self. The heroine asks her mother's forgiveness, assuring her that she is carrying out her mission "but at [her] own pace" (113). As she nears the end of her journey, however, this Red Riding Hood is no longer content to walk through the woods, she wants "to run and be free" (114). As she runs through the woods with her cape "flapping" behind her, she imagines the "other red riding hoods" who have set out after being warned to watch out for "the Big Bad Wolf." She ridicules the idea that the wolves encountered by "red riding hoods nowadays" are "bad," claiming they are, in fact, "kindly, incompetent [and] inept." This may be a comment on the many sympathetic, good wolves that Riding Hoods meet in contemporary retellings. In any case, they compare unfavorably with the wolf from her past: "*My* wolf, the one who got away, now he really was bad." That thought induces her to run through the wood: "I believe I can remember the end of the story. That's why I hurry on" (114). This Riding Hood prefers a Big Bad Wolf.

The magic realism that characterizes Valenzuela's works is particularly effective in the recasting of a fairy tale. When Red Riding Hood finally arrives at the door of her grandmother's log cabin, she has undergone a transformation. The heroine who stops on the threshold to catch her breath describes herself in terms befitting a wolf: "I don't want her to see me with my tongue hanging out, red as my cape once was, I don't want her to see me with my teeth bared, and my mouth drooling" (114–15). Her "hair is rough and bristling" and she must "smooth [her] fur." Aware of her wolfishness, Red Riding Hood is afraid that her grandmother will "mistake [her] for someone else" and be frightened. Not only does Red Riding Hood resemble a wolf, she also behaves like one as she tries to compose herself at her grandmother's door: "I lick my wounds, I howl quietly" (115). She even stretches out at the old lady's door for a while, before the cold prompts her to knock. Red Riding Hood has been transformed into a wolf, but the grandmother who awaits her is also a wolf.

The archetypal situation inspires a voice within the protagonist to repeat the ancient formulaic words. The familiar, final climactic line deviates from the original dialogue, becoming the source of a startling ending. Before the girl-wolf can "open [her] mouth" to mention the grandmother-wolf's "mouth which is, in turn, opening," there is a surprising recognition scene: "I recognise her, I recognise him, I recognise me." Red Riding Hood, the wolf, and the grandmother are one and the same. This revelation casts the dramatic devouring scene of the classic tale in an entirely new light. The tragic conclusion of Perrault's version becomes a happy ending: "And the mouth swallows and at last we are one. All nice and warm" (115). This fusion of the three figures at the end of Valenzuela's tale evokes the popular doll that unites the three characters in a single entity. The wolf this Riding Hood has been running toward for what seems like an eternity has been within her all along.

The sensual atmosphere that permeates "Ulven og Rødhette" (The Wolf and Little Red Riding Hood, 1986), by the Norwegian author Annie Riis, is surprisingly similar to that of the Argentinean retelling. Riis's tale was published in a short story collection titled *Kom inn i min natt! Kom inn i min drøm (Come into my night! Come into my dream!)*, which was edited by Solveig Bøhle and based on a radio program she aired after midnight. Although the collection was addressed to adults, the stories initially had an audience largely composed of young adults due to the late hour at which they aired. The authors who contributed to the collection had been asked to describe, in the form of a short story or a fairy tale, feelings that can invade our dreams. Convinced that many fairy tales contain a bit of the same "stuff that dreams are made of," Riis naturally chose to do a retelling in this genre. The selection of this tale was due in part, she feels, to the fact that she had just read the Swedish translation of Bettelheim's *The Uses of Enchantment* and had been particularly impressed with his interpretation of *Little Red Riding Hood*. Although Bettelheim's influence is undeniable, Riis's "dream-story" turned out to be "a feminist version" of the classic tale.[11]

A short poem introduces the tale, which is written in poetic prose. The preliminary poem establishes the sensual atmosphere of colors, feelings, and desire that pervades the entire text. It also suggests the possibility that the entire story is nothing but a dream. The first-person voice of the poet-protagonist evokes the troubling temptation that draws her toward something warm and soft that is described as "Wolf-nearness." In an intimate first person, a young girl "between childhood and puberty," continues the story. The heroine claims not to be afraid because she is "a big girl now," but she admits that she no longer knows exactly who she is (28). This Riding Hood is experiencing pubescent identity problems. The young girl's awakening sexuality makes her a stranger to herself. Her new-found sexuality is symbolized by the ruby-colored velvet cloak, which shines bright red in the colorless landscape of gray hues into which she sets out for her grandmother's. She pulls the cloak's hood up over her head to protect herself, not against inclement weather, but against an unknown, invisible presence. That unfamiliar, disturbing presence is the wolf and all that he symbolizes. In the gray landscape, her red hood shines like a beacon, attracting the wolf, rather than protecting her from him.

The author describes the young girl's mixed reactions during her encounter with the wolf in the woods in the following terms: she is simultaneously "frightened by and attracted to this Don Juan in the shape of a Wolf." This Wolf is not described in the customary manner. No mention is made of his mouth or teeth. His peculiar eyes, two yellowish-green points of light, yield to the girl's returned stare. She notes his resilient body and long wagging tail. His voice is as sweet as the honey in her basket, his muscles are strong, and his hair is a golden gray. He is indeed portrayed as an attractive Don Juan figure. The girl cannot resist sinking down on the grass beside the Wolf, whose presence, like her red cloak, colors the dull landscape. The contradictory softness and strength of the forepaw he lays in her lap is new to her. The protagonist describes an erotic scene rather naively: her hood has fallen off her shoulders and her "red cloak embraces [them] in the grass" (29). She seems to have succumbed to the dizzying odor of lilies of the valley and the sensuous feel of the Wolf's long, warm tongue licking her throat and cheeks, seeking her mouth. Fam Ekman's illustration on the title page of the tale portrays an anthropomorphic wolf, with human-looking limbs, holding Little Red Riding Hood in his arms and licking her cheek. Gazing at him out of the corner of her eyes, with a slight smile on her lips, the girl shows no sign of protest. "Ulven og Rødhette" is a tale of sexual awakening.

As in Perrault's version, the presence of woodcutters temporarily saves the girl. The Wolf is sent on "to a more experienced woman, her grandmother," writes the author, who has adopted Bettelheim's interpretation. The heroine is certain that at her age, her grandmother "has met all the wolves there are in the world" and will know how to deal with them (30). When the girl realizes, after the ritual dialogue, that it is really the Wolf, she seems at first to surrender to him, spontaneously undressing and joining him in the bed, where she covers them both with her red cloak. The scene is reminiscent of Carter's "The Company of Wolves," because the girl appears to embrace her erotic identity and offer her flesh to the wolf. At "the crucial moment," however, she "suddenly takes charge," explains the author. This time, as the big, warm, wet tongue approaches her, the girl devours first the tongue and then the entire Wolf, in a single bite. The sensuality of the text makes this unexpected twist all the more surprising. Riding Hoods usually only eat the wolf in humorous retellings. Of her own accord, Little Red Riding Hood throws grandmother's red cloak on the fire before falling asleep in the bed. The girl realizes she won't need the garment anymore. Her sexual initiation is complete.

In an unusual reversal of the Grimms' rescue scene, the hunter cuts Little Red Riding Hood's belly open to release the Wolf, who slinks away with his tail between his legs and the grandmother still in his belly. The celebration that often ends the tale is transformed into an intimate tête-à-tête between Little Red Riding Hood and the hunter, who drink a toast, apparently to their future happiness, with the sweet wine from the basket. According to the author, Little Red Riding Hood's encounter with the Wolf has prepared her "for an adult life with the Hunter." The heroine and the hunter are united in a happy ending, which, says the author rather ambiguously, "we can hope will last as long as the fairy tale–dream!" In Riis's retelling, Little Red Riding Hood only runs with the wolf in order catch the hunter.

Not surprisingly, the majority of retellings examined in this section are feminist revisionings of the tale that subvert conventional gender roles. Although all

"Ulven og Rødhette," by Annie Riis, illustration by Fam
Ekman, illustrations © Gyldendal Norsk Forlag. Used by
permission of Gyldendal and Fam Ekman.

of these Riding Hoods tame or master the wolf, how and why they do so varies
greatly from one re-version to the next. The wolf may be domesticated and
turned into a harmless pet or a docile husband. Sometimes he is broken completely so that he is no longer a danger to any female. In a number of retellings,
the wolf must be caught and internalized in order for Little Red Riding Hood to
become a mature woman.

From Wolf Tamer to Girl-Wolf

One of the most intriguing and provocative picture books inspired by the famous
tale is Anne Ikhlef and Alain Gauthier's *Mon Chaperon Rouge* (My Red Riding
Hood, 1998), which casts Little Red Riding Hood in a variety of roles ranging

from wolf tamer to girl-wolf. Their picture-book retelling is an erotic, nocturnal version of the tale that makes high demands on the reader. The children's department of the French firm Seuil published it for ages six years and up, but some
critics consider it to be a sophisticated picture book primarily for adults. The sensuality and eroticism of both the text and the illustrations are not unusual in contemporary European children's books, but the complexity of the images and the
sophistication of the textual layering make this a picture book for adults and
adolescents, as well as children. Ikhlef had already reworked the same tale in a
short film, *La véritable histoire du Chaperon rouge* (The true story of Red Riding
Hood), that was presented at the Cannes Film Festival in 1985. Many resonances
of the equally provocative film are to be found in the picture book that was published thirteen years later.

Whereas Claude Clément and Isabelle Forestier's *Un petit chaperon rouge*
adopts the impersonal, general indefinite article *un* two years later to tell the story
of a kind of "Everychild," Ikhlef's title uses the personal, possessive adjective
mon to give a highly personal interpretation of a tale that has a very universal
quality. The author of *Mon Chaperon Rouge* explores the psychological and sexual implications of the tale in a poetic and sensual text about a Riding Hood who
plays with fire, apparently without getting burned. The tale is set in a dark and
disturbing nocturnal setting, against which the vivid, blood red worn by the protagonist appears almost to blaze. Like Riis's protagonist, this Riding Hood stands
out strikingly against the dark landscape.

This picture book examines the complex and equivocal relationship between
Little Red Riding Hood and the wolf, a couple that seems joined for eternity, as
Gauthier's evocative cover illustration suggests. He depicts the young girl's red
dress as an elegant, swirling extension of the lascivious wolf's red tongue. Although inseparable, the two figures appear as complete opposites, the dark, an-
gular, pointed shapes of the wolf contrasting markedly with the bright, rounded,
soft shapes of the girl. In this intimate tête-à-tête, the secondary characters are
virtually eliminated, with the exception of the mother. The hunter is completely
absent. We are reminded of the protagonist's words in Valenzuela's retelling:
". . . if anyone tries to tell you that there was a woodman involved, don't believe them. The presence of the woodman is a purely modern interpretation"
(107–8). Even the grandmother is physically absent from *Mon Chaperon Rouge,*
where on one occasion the rather surrealistic profile of a melting white face on
a burning candle symbolically represents the old lady.

The countless retellings bear witness to the fact that the story of Little Red Riding Hood cannot be confined within the classic script. Ikhlef engages in a sophisticated dialogue with folkloric and literary voices within the *Little Red Riding Hood* tradition, and her retelling needs to be read intertextually within that heritage. In a manner not unlike Carter's stories in *The Bloody Chamber* and her film *The Company of Wolves*, Ikhlef's picture book and film are metanarratives that comment on the ancient tale while reworking it. The voice of a new generation of storytellers is added to the voices of centuries past. The rich, multilayered text of *Mon Chaperon Rouge* is inspired by different versions of the tale from both the literary and oral traditions, fragments of which are woven throughout the poetic narrative. Also embedded in the text, which is largely composed of dialogue, are other popular forms, such as nursery rhymes, counting rhymes, riddles, and songs. They serve to evoke and preserve the timeless atmosphere of popular folklore and provide a constant reminder of the tale's origins in that tradition.

We have seen that many contemporary retellings, especially by women authors, insist on the oral folk tradition and women's role as storyteller. Ikhlef retains the figure of Little Red Riding Hood's mother, but gives her a different part to play in her revisioning of the tale. A striking double spread depicts a curvaceous, full-figured mother with moon breasts, one a full moon, the other a crescent, set against a symbolic Milky Way. In arms folded as if to rock a baby, the mother holds the tiny figure of a prepubescent, flat-chested Red Riding Hood and prepares to tell her a bedtime story. Ikhlef insists on the ancient origins of the tale that is about to be told, by having the mother preface her story with the words: "A tale is more than a thousand years old." Through the storyteller's words to her daughter, the author reminds the reader of her own crossover tale that "Everything you hear / Is not only for children." Like the oral versions of the tale told around the hearth, this tale is meant for adults as well as children. Gauthier's evocative and thought-provoking illustration of the moon-breasted mother confirms that this picture book is not intended only for children. Gauthier is an artist who turned to illustration later in his career, and his sophisticated illustrations therefore tend to appeal more to adults than to young readers.

The tale the mother tells her daughter is the literary version penned by Perrault. Excerpts of the classic tale are embedded in quotation marks in Ikhlef's text, and they are written horizontally on the verso of a large book within the book. The bedtime story is cleverly transformed into a cradle in the illustration (plate 24). It is not clear whether the mother's hand resting on the side of the book/cradle is preparing to turn a page or to rock her daughter. The little girl in red, who falls asleep in the middle of her mother's story and dreams with a contented smile that she is Little Red Riding Hood, is depicted sleeping inside the pages of the large book. This Red Riding Hood holding a toy wolf as she dreams educes strong reminiscences of Clara asleep with the Nutcracker in her arms in E. T. A. Hoffmann's famous tale, "The Nutcracker and the Mouse King." The toy wolf is a miniature replica of the multiple anthropomorphized wolves that lurk in the tubular, stylized trees of the dark forest in the background, like the obsessive images of a dream.

Ikhlef also embeds numerous excerpts from earlier and lesser-known oral versions. Her sources include the now somewhat celebrated tale from the Nivernais, "The Story of Grandmother," but also a number of more obscure versions collected in the Loire basin, the Forez, the Velay, the Morvan, and the Alps.[12] Among the elements borrowed from oral variants collected in France are the wolf's question about the path of needles and that of pins, the cruel cannibalistic scene in which the wolf offers the little girl the flesh and blood of her grandmother, the ritualistic striptease, and the scatological happy ending in which the girl escapes by pretending she has to relieve herself. The marked contrast between the lines of traditional versions embedded in the text and the modern details in Gauthier's rather abstract illustrations underscores the timeless quality of a tale that has fascinated audiences over the centuries. The wolf who initiates the dialogue about the pins and needles in the encounter scene is portrayed wearing a gray business suit and standing beside an enormous, black automobile that symbolizes power. In stark contrast, the protagonist is a village girl whose red cap, long red gown, and wooden clogs give her a decidedly medieval look. Like her predecessor in an oral version from the Forez, Red Riding Hood tells the wolf that she prefers the path of pins, with which you can adorn yourself, to the path of needles, with which you must work. She nonetheless takes the latter because readers are immediately told that she lingers picking up needles. In keeping with another version from the Morvan, the needles she gathers for her grandmother have large holes, which will be easier to thread for an old lady whose eyesight isn't what it used to be. Threading the eye of a needle was a sexual symbol in the folklore of seamstresses. As we saw in chapter 2, the path of needles symbolizes sexual maturity, whereas the path of pins marks a girl's coming of age. Like her predecessors who choose the path of needles, Ihklef's heroine appears to be assuming prematurely the sexuality of an older woman.

Ikhlef reworks a popular counting rhyme to retell the story of the cannibal repast found in "The Story of Grandmother" and its variants. The heroine is reciting the rhyme on her fingers in the dark wood to set her mind at ease as night falls, at the very same time the wolf is devouring the rest of the old lady and setting aside some of her flesh and blood for the little girl. The last line about the little finger eating everything is ironically timed to coincide with the wolf swallowing the last of the grandmother. The words of the rhyme relating the demise of the grandmother appear on the back of a burning white candle. Decorated with the melting face of the old lady, the candle evocatively portraying her gradual disappearance. This page offers an excellent example of the intimate relationship between text and image in this remarkable book.

As in most oral versions, the voice of an animal points out Little Red Riding Hood's cannibalistic act to her. Ikhlef superposes fragments of the warning scene from a number of variants. The girl is warned not only by a cat, as in the version from the Nivernais, but also by birds, which is the case in a number of versions.[13] Whereas the wolf always eats the grandmother raw, Little Red Riding Hood generally eats her cooked, as she does here. The cat's warning, which is given by a crow in the version from the Hautes-Alpes, suggests the culinary technique being used. The French verb *fricasser* means to cut up and cook in sauce. Sometimes the girl drinks the blood as wine, but often it is added to the dish, as Red Riding Hood does here. The result is a grandmother fricassee. The caged birds' warning will be more comprehensible to young readers, as it does not contain any archaic terms, although the young heroine does not understand even this straightforward warning.

The girl's arrival at her grandmother's house and the cannibalistic scene that follows are combined in a single full plate. In a very abstract manner, Gauthier portrays a decapitated Red Riding Hood pushing back the pages of a large book like a stage curtain. The symbolic, dreamlike vision seems to depict the punishment of the little girl for her unwitting crime against her grandmother. A brightly colored bird replaces her decapitated head, which lies at her feet, and the girl's right hand holds a large balloon that takes the form of a gigantic eye, symbolizing the cat that watches her accusingly as she eats and drinks. The yellow eyes of the wolf stare fixedly from the verso, where he sits sedately, hands folded in his lap, in a large armchair, looking very much like a spectator enjoying a play from a plush seat in a private theater box.

Although Perrault's bed scene retains the sexual innuendo of the wolf's invitation to join him in the bed and the instruction to undress, it does not contain the lengthy striptease of earlier oral versions. Like Carter, Ikhlef uses "the latent content of those traditional stories," a content that is "violently sexual."[14] The wolf's invitation to lie down with him is repeated in an even more evocative manner, as she is to warm his cold feet (the reference to a body part links the invitation to the ritualistic dialogue). Moreover, Red Riding Hood replies with apparent eagerness: "I'm coming! I'm coming!" Gauthier's sensuous illustrations highlight the erotic elements of the tale. The double spread accompanying the striptease scene is one of several that are composed around the power of the gaze. The artist takes his cue from the text, where the narrator introduces the formulaic dialogue by commenting that the wolf doesn't take his eyes off Red Riding Hood. This time the man-wolf's gaze is hidden from the view of readers, who have been positioned directly behind his shoulder so that they share his perspective. However, the cat that he pets on his lap gazes directly at the reader with the same yellow eyes as the wolf-man in the previous illustration. It is surprising that the grandmother's cat, who had tried to warn the girl and at whom the wolf had suggested she throw her clog,[15] should willingly curl up in the man-wolf's lap and allow itself to be petted. Gauthier offers an explanation by depicting the cat as the stereotypical witch's familiar and giving it the same yellow devil's eyes as the wolf.

The traditional striptease is turned into an erotic spectacle. Ikhlef retains the elaborate ritual dialogue in its entirety, drawing out the striptease, as the little girl asks in turn what to do with her apron, bodice, stockings, and skirt, and the wolf tells her each time to throw the article in the fire, as she won't need it anymore. Gauthier has skillfully turned readers into complicit spectators, who peer voyeuristically over the man-wolf's shoulder at the erotic performance that is just beginning behind a large, red curtain, pulled back to reveal the little girl. As she shrugs one shoulder out of her red dress, she gazes directly at the man-wolf, as well as readers, with an enigmatic smile on her lips.

Ambiguities in both the textual and visual narratives of this sophisticated picture book present challenges even for older readers. The manner in which the naked little girl "jumps" onto the bed suggests a certain alacrity. Yet the choice of the verb *frémir* to describe her reaction when she stares at the black mouth of the wolf, once she is on the bed, is highly ambiguous, as it could indicate that she shudders with horror or quivers with pleasure or anticipation. This emotional response introduces the dramatic dialogue about the grandmother-wolf's physical features, in its longer, more risqué version from the popular tradition that begins with her/his hairy body. Ikhlef seems to highlight this particular line, as it is the only one introduced by the girl's surprised "Oh, Granny," which precedes each of the questions in "The Story of Grandmother." The wolf-grandmother's reply deviates slightly from the more familiar "the better to . . ." pattern, which is used throughout the rest of the dialogue. "It's from old age, my child!" she answers, in keeping with an oral version from the Loire. Only an elite of cultured adult readers, for the most part folklorists, will recognize the wealth of allusions to the rich oral tradition of the tale.

By explaining the grandmother's hairiness in terms of her age, "the post-menopausal woman is . . . masculinized."[16] This physical feature, more than any other, would allow the possibility of confusing granny with the wolf. Perrault's retelling continues this "crucial collapse of roles," as Marina Warner reminds us in *From the Beast to the Blonde*.[17] A number of contemporary women authors go much further. Carter, for example, explores this analogy in a highly original manner in her short story "The Werewolf." The werewolf who attacks the little girl on the way to her grandmother's and whose hairy paw the child chops off with her father's knife turns out to be her grandmother. In Carter's tale, the old lady runs with the wolves, but the superstitious locals take the poor old woman for a witch and stone her to death.

The formulaic dialogue in Ikhlef's tale is interspersed with the narrator's suggestive description of the girl's body movements as she slides onto the wolf's dark body and eventually puts her hand into the wolf's jaws. The words are charged with all the figurative meaning of the French expression *se mettre dans la gueule du loup* (to throw oneself into the lion's jaws). Gauthier's provocative illustration of the intimate scene portrays the naked, prepubescent body of Little Red Riding Hood lying on top of the wolf, with her long, thick hair hanging down seductively (plate 25). Their heads are close together and their eyes are locked in a powerful gaze. The red bed curtains frame the double spread like theater curtains pulled back to reveal a stage on which a love scene is being enacted. The wolf's hairiness is depicted in a somewhat surreal manner. From a green body that seems to equate the wolf with Mother Earth, grow, not coarse body hairs, but blades of grass, as well as a large red flower that appears to have blossomed from his heart as an offering to Little Red Riding Hood. The little girl's hand is stretched out as if to pluck the flower, or perhaps to caress the wolf's green hair. In this scene, Red Riding Hood seems to obey her awakening sexual desires and offer her flesh to the wolf. It is difficult to determine if Little Red

Riding Hood is a rape victim or a rustic seductress in this recasting of the tale. Although the image of the child portrayed in the more sensual scenes may shock some readers, the picture book is much less disturbing than the film, since the heroine of *Mon Chaperon Rouge* appears much older than Justine Bayard, the five-year-old actress who played the lead role in *La véritable histoire du Chaperon Rouge*. After obligingly doing the striptease and climbing into the bed, the girl lovingly caresses the wolf, played by the actor Didier Sandre.

In spite of the girl's compliance with the wolf's demands and her apparent serenity as she lies staring into his eyes, the narrator tells us at the end of the lengthy dialogue that the child is frightened. As in Viviane Julien's novel and Márta Mészáros's film, Ikhlef's picture book and film show the mixed feelings of attraction and fear that an adolescent girl feels with regard to sex and its metaphor the wolf. Like many of her predecessors in oral versions, Ikhlef's Red Riding Hood tricks the wolf into letting her go outside to relieve herself. There are numerous variations of this scatological scene. As in "The Story of Grandmother," this wolf ties a woolen thread to the girl's foot before he lets her go. Ikhlef retains the bawdy tone and coarse language of the oral tradition. When the girl doesn't return, the impatient wolf asks her repeatedly if she is "making a load." Whereas most of her early predecessors run away, Ikhlef's protagonist stays and courageously confronts the wolf. The girl seizes a large stake and drives it into the wolf's mouth, as if to impale him. The wording seems deliberately chosen to recall the method used to destroy vampires, although in that case, of course, the stake had to be driven through the heart.

On the very first page of text, Ikhlef introduces the theme of the werewolf, evoking popular beliefs and oral versions of *Little Red Riding Hood*, such as "The Story of Grandmother," in which the little girl meets a werewolf rather than a wolf. Ikhlef's narrative presents a "man wolf" howling at the moon as he turns into a werewolf. Gauthier's image of the werewolf on the first page reminds us that werewolves were not only devilish creatures but also tormented beings. In medieval narratives like Marie de France's *Lais*, the werewolf evokes pity and sympathy, because the condition was considered a curse and resulted in banishment from society. The pan pipes the werewolf plays beneath the full moon associate the wolf with the Greek rural god Pan. Gauthier introduces the theme of the werewolf in a very different manner on the title page. A sequence of five pictures depicts the wolf gradually being transformed into an elegant gentleman. In the intermediary stages of the metamorphosis, the creature is wearing a dark mask, which becomes a leitmotiv throughout the book. In one intriguing illustration, Red Riding Hood wears the wolf mask and is thus transformed into the wolf or an enigmatic creature who, like Patricia Joiret's Mina, embodies both roles (plate 26). The tiny figure in the dark woods stares menacingly up at the reader with her yellow wolf eyes. The wolf sometimes appears as an animal, but more often as an anthropomorphized wolf, whose mask may or may not hide a man, and at other times as a man, with or without a mask.

The characters in classic fairy tales are portrayed as good or bad, black or white. Ikhlef's Red Riding Hood and the wolf are decidedly gray in color, or sometimes alternately black and white. Images of light and darkness, heaven and hell are present throughout the text and illustrations of *Mon Chaperon Rouge*. The protagonist's fall from innocence is suggested already on the cover, where a large green apple in Red Riding Hood's basket hints at her association with Eve. In two illustrations, Red Riding Hood is depicted with a braid that ends in the head of a serpent, whose fangs extend menacingly. On the first occasion, she is sitting in front of the hearth, while the head of a huge wolf-devil emerges from the flames in the fireplace. The scene certainly manifests the temptation of Eve by the devil, but it is not clear if the serpent is the devil's accomplice or if, as an extension of her braid, it symbolizes the potential for evil within the girl. Embedded in the narrative is a nursery rhyme the girl recites about going to heaven, hell, or purgatory, depending on the color of your eyes. Although the wolf is generally depicted with yellow eyes, the mesmerizing eyes of the wolf-devil that stare out of the fireplace, as if to hypnotize the protagonist and/or the reader, are now decidedly green. The girl with the serpent braid returns the gaze with what appear to be gray eyes, which, according to the nursery rhyme, "go to paradise." As she fixes the wolf-devil with her unblinking, gray eyes, she repeats the line: "Green eyes will go to hell."

This retelling of *Little Red Riding Hood* emphasizes the age-old struggle between good and evil, light and darkness, God and the devil, a struggle that is expressed in the popular terms of children's games. Hopping along the path in her wooden clogs, Red Riding Hood's feet become, in turn, "God's feet! / devil's feet!"; the rhythm picks up as the little girl shouts: "god! devil! god! devil!" Ikhlef and Gauthier skillfully portray the inner conflict of the forces of good and evil within characters that are generally depicted as either one or the other. One particularly evocative double spread illustrates the dualistic nature of the heroine, whose small figure is shown as a black contour against the sun, so that she casts a huge, dark shadow across both pages. Rather than reflecting the little girl accurately, the troubling shadow has devil's horns and picks a flower whose petals are doubled by flames of a similar shape and color. Contrasting with the large sun in the left-hand corner is a sliver of moon in the right-hand corner, under which the small figure of a wolf in his natural form peers out of the night. True to conventional imagery, the wolf is associated with darkness and Red Riding Hood with light, but it is an eerie, ominous, somber light, and in it she casts the shadow of a devil. While the protagonist yields to the devil in certain scenes, Ikhlef's variation on the ending of oral versions presents an innocent-looking Red Riding Hood engaged in combat against the forces of evil, symbolized by the huge, menacing jaws of the wolf. The author adds an original touch by having the little girl stare the wolf in the eyes and urge him repeatedly to "deliver" himself from what can only be the clutches of the devil. Wondering if a wounded wolf can be reborn, Red Riding Hood seems to hope for the wolf's redemption in this scene.

At night, the frightened girl plunges into the dark, powerful gaze of the wolf. The accompanying illustration portrays the little girl sleeping peacefully, stretched out on the back of an enormous, docile wolf who now stands on all fours. Like the wolf with whom the protagonist of Carter's "The Company of Wolves" sleeps "sweet and sound," the wolf that Gauthier portrays in this scene is a "tender wolf" (118). As if he does not want to disturb the girl's sleep, he stands still, serenely staring at the viewer with eyes that are no longer terrifyingly dark, but as bright as the stars in the night sky above them. The large circle that encloses Red Riding Hood, the wolf, and the starry firmament, sheltering the sleeping girl from the inclement weather beyond, where lightning bolts flash in a dark, starless sky, is actually the wolf's eye. Within the wolf's dark eye, the couple inhabit their own intimate, nocturnal world. The following double spread confirms this interpretation, as a tiny figure of Red Riding Hood stands on a large leaf staring into the wolf's huge eye. Another large leaf that almost seems to form his eyelid hides the wolf's other eye, and the raindrops on the leaf resemble teardrops shed from the wolf's eye. The narrator perhaps suggests that the caresses of the girl who has slept on his back will cure the wolf's insatiable appetite.

Mon Chaperon Rouge has an open ending, which consists, in fact, of the superposition of multiple endings. On the final double spread, the narrator asks pointedly if this is heaven or hell, but the question is not answered, leaving readers to decide where little girls who follow wolves are likely to end up, regardless of the color of their eyes. Ikhlef's initiatory story works in disturbingly shifting ways. The ambiguity is upheld in Gauthier's illustration of a serene Red Riding Hood, whose dual nature is suggested by a face half in darkness, half in light. She is still on the wolf, whose fur she caresses, but now he has been reduced to a wolfskin rug on the floor. His bright red tongue lolls lifelessly from his mouth. The images of hell and the fall from paradise certainly dominate the final illustration. The protagonist's braid again takes the form of a serpent whose fangs, like the gaze out of the corner of the girl's eye, are directed at the half-hidden figure of a grinning wolf-devil surrounded by infernal flames in the background. The wolf is presented here as "the devil in hell," reminding us that the wolf has been associated with the devil for centuries.[18]

The only answer to the question is the smile that Red Riding Hood offers the wolf-devil, a knowing, satisfied smile that seems to complement her rather seductive gaze. No doubt it is the knowing smile of the initiated. Red Riding Hood has completed the initiatory journey that she began on the front endpapers. The small figure in red who climbs the monumental staircase must pass between two enigmatic, stone wolf-sphinxes who guard the threshold of a huge temple. Alone in the darkness, Red Riding Hood makes her way toward some mysterious, nocturnal initiation ceremony. The new knowledge that Red Riding Hood has gained on her journey through the dark woods gives her the knowing, enigmatic look of a Sphinx on the final page of the tale.

Ikhlef and Gauthier's Red Riding Hood is a complex, multifaceted character cast in a variety of conflicting roles, effectively exploding the stereotypical image of the classic fairy-tale heroine. She becomes, in turn, an object manipulated by the wolf—a Red Riding Hood cello played by a Picasso-like wolf (plate 27), a courageous heroine who saves herself by impaling the wolf, a diabolical creature with devil's horns, a temptress in the form of a new Eve, and a mysterious girl-wolf. The heroine is alternately wolf tamer, wolf slayer, wolf companion, and wolf. The ambiguity with which Little Red Riding Hood and the wolf are portrayed in *Mon Chaperon Rouge* is announced in Gauthier's cover illustration, where the little girl in red and the wolf become extensions of each other. It is impossible to say where the wolf ends and Red Riding Hood begins. The retellings examined in the following section carry even further this blending of the two characters.

Riding Hood Wolves

Little Red Riding Hood and the Wolf have frequently been depicted as a kind of hybrid creature. Sometimes the author or illustrator deliberately creates an ambiguous situation in which readers or viewers cannot determine whether the girl is wearing a wolfskin or whether she is actually inside the wolf's jaws in the process of being swallowed. While child viewers of Pef's drawing of Little Red Riding Hood's face peering out of the open wolf's jaws on the title page of "Le conte du Petit Chaperon rouge" will probably assume that the wolf is eating the girl, adult viewers may wonder if she is not wearing a very real looking wolf's head. The wolf's upper jaw forms a kind of pointed bonnet that is not unlike the one the heroine wears in the illustration on the first page of the story, which reinforces this interpretation. The cover of *Akazukin wa nido umareru* (Little Red Riding Hood is born twice, 1999), Japanese author Mitsuse Yanase's psychological examination of the tale, depicts an androgynous-looking Little Red Riding Hood wearing a garment that is at once hood and wolfskin. The long red cape has claws, a tail, and a large hood topped with a wolf's head that rests on the little girl's head. The serene Japanese Riding Hood peers out at the viewer from the dark yawning hole of the wolf's open jaws, but at the same time the little girl appears to be disguised as the wolf. Increasing the ambiguity of the illustration, Red Riding Hood holds a large knife in her right hand immediately above their superposed hearts.

The title of this section was inspired by *Petits Chaperons Loups* (Little Riding Hood Wolves), yet another of Christian Bruel's provocative picture books that features the fairy-tale heroine. Like *Rouge bien rouge*, Nicole Claveloux, whose unique, irreverent style has great adult appeal, illustrated it. *Petits Chaperons Loups* was one of the first books published by Éditions Être, the publishing house Bruel created after the discontinuation of Le sourire qui mord. At the time of the book's publication in 1997, an interviewer asked Bruel about the ambivalent target audience of his sophisticated picture books. The author-publisher expressed his objection to the idea of books *for* children (livres pour enfants) and his belief in the importance of stories that are accessible to children, yet touch adults. His books may include references that can only be decoded by adults, but there is always a level for children. The author-publisher is concerned by the fact that many children's books ignore complete chunks of the reality children experience, including violence, a central theme in *Petits Chaperons Loups*.

The evocative, ambiguous title of *Petits Chaperons Loups* inextricably links Riding Hoods and Wolves. The innovative picture book, which folds out to reveal two books in one, suggests a fusing of the two characters, but a separate book within the book is devoted to each of the characters, and the covers of those books suggest an inversion of the binary roles in the tale. The illustration that serves as a cover to the Little Red Riding Hood book on the left depicts a chubby little girl donning a brand new wolf costume, apparently to play the role of the wolf (plate 28). The wolf doesn't seem to mind dressing up as the little girl, as he is already wearing a replica of Little Red Riding Hood's costume, complete with accessories (wooden clogs and basket). In the end, however, the little girl seems to prefer her own role, as the two small vignettes on the final pages depict a disdainful Little Red Riding Hood striding off in her underwear and clogs, with her reclaimed clothes in her arms, and the wolf running to hail a cab in his birthday suit, looking suddenly decidedly naked.

The versatile format of *Petits Chaperons Loups* invites multiple readings. Each double spread of the two books consists of a color illustration on one side and a small pen-and-ink drawing on the other, but they are reversed in the two books so that the color illustrations are side by side in the middle. The pages of the two books can be turned simultaneously or randomly so that the pictures can be mixed and matched to create a multitude of strange encounters and jarring situations. The reader can concentrate on the diptych formed by the color illustrations in the center or read each book separately. Or the reader can engage in a more complex reading that tries to integrate all four pictures. This is truly a picture book for all ages.

Readers are obliged to play an active role in creating the narrative. Except for the first illustrations of the disguises, which constitute inside covers for the two books, there is no clear relationship between the facing color illustrations in the two books. By mixing up the order, the reader can find combinations that seem more logical, for example, Little Red Riding Hood as a nurse with a needle behind her back and a bandaged wolf in a hospital bed, or Little Red Riding Hood holding out a pen and a document to be signed and the wolf holding a pencil and a file full of documents. The wolf grasping the old-fashioned lead pencil could also be paired with the picture of a determined Little Red Riding Hood lugging a cumbersome computer.

The relationship between the large color pictures and the small black-and-white vignettes of each individual book is often much more obvious, but young children are apt to ignore these tiny drawings. The wolf in the garb of a magician confidently waving his magic wand is juxtaposed with a small picture of a sheepish wolf holding his paws in front of his private parts, while the wand lies on the ground where he seems to have dropped it after accidentally making his clothes vanish. The small vignette of a handheld video game of the wolf chasing Little Red Riding Hood is placed opposite a wolf leaning coolly against a pinball game that displays a very sexy Betty Grable–like Riding Hood in a slinky red dress. The direction of the wolf's gaze strongly suggests, however, that this picture should be juxtaposed with the one of Little Red Riding Hood bending over her basket and revealing her underpants (plate 29). It is even possible that the sly little girl is deliberately offering the macho wolf a titillating glimpse beneath her red outfit. The sexual innuendo in these illustrations seems intended for adults.

Young children delight in the violent situations that confront Little Red Riding Hood and the wolf, but some of the more subtle allusions will escape them. The needle hidden nonchalantly behind Little Red Riding Hood's back in one of the color illustrations is obviously filled with the vaccine depicted in the opposite vignette (the lamb on the label suggests that it is intended to make the wolf as meek and mild as a lamb). This double spread brings new meaning to the juxtaposition of Nurse Riding Hood with the Frankenstein-like wolf on the corresponding page of the wolf's book: perhaps the docility potion had the reverse effect! The bandaged wolf in the hospital bed is also linked to the previous picture in the wolf's book that portrays him dressed in camouflage clothing and loaded down with heavy weapons. It seems that his plan may have backfired. Perhaps his bomb exploded before the clock in the vignette struck the Little Red Riding Hood that marks the hour. That might explain why the little girl is pointing at the wolf and laughing hysterically in the first illustration of her book. Like F'Murr's comic of the wolf plagued by Little Red Riding Hood pests, *Petits Chaperons Loups* presents a wolf who is harassed by the little girl in red.

Not only full-grown wolves are tormented by Riding Hoods. One very witty picture in the wolf's book portrays a wailing baby cub holding a Little Red Riding Hood soother in one paw and pointing with the other at the source of his anguish. The corresponding vignette depicts one of his toys, a building block decorated on one face with granny in bed and on another with Little Red Riding Hood walking in the woods, underscoring how the little girl in red haunts the baby wolf and "cubhood" culture in general. This double spread and its counterpart in Little Red Riding Hood's book are more obviously interrelated than any others, because the heroine takes advantage of the wolf's youth and the fact that he can't read to have him sign a document. The vignette in her book is a small paw print that has obviously been made by the baby wolf, whose paws are visibly inked since he can't write. With tongue-in-cheek humor, Claveloux portrays the huge, Frankenstein-like wolf in the previous illustration holding out one large paw that also appears to have been inked for the same purpose. The implication is that grown-up wolves are equally illiterate. This clever Red Riding Hood is quick to take advantage of the wolf's weaknesses. Sometimes she resorts to using his tricks, including that of disguise. A vignette of three chubby Riding Hoods waving triangular semaphore flags finds its echo in a later vignette of a triangular road sign depicting the three pigs. In the color illustration beside it, Little Red Riding Hood, wearing the long white gloves of a gendarme, is directing traffic, obviously guiding the wolf toward the three pigs and out of her path.

Although not all of Claveloux's illustrations of the Wolf necessarily portray him as the underdog, the subtle connections between the pictures generally suggest that the little girl in red gets the better of the wolf, even when he is portrayed as a Frankenstein-like monster or a GI Joe figure. Unlike Kiki Smith's sculpture *Daughter*, of a bewildered Little Red Riding Hood, this one deliberately transforms herself into a wolf by donning a disguise that will allow her to run with the wolves. The box from which she has unpacked her wolf costume is appropriately decorated with a running wolf motif. In the end, however, she seems to decide that it is more fun to run with the wolves dressed in her own Little Red Riding Hood outfit.

The Riding Hood Wolf presented in the French picture book *Mina, je t'aime* (Mina, I love you, 1991), by Patricia Joiret and Xavier Bruyère, is more disturbing and predatory than Bruel and Claveloux's mischievous, unruly child. The sensuality and sensuousness of this picture-book retelling is somewhat reminiscent of Annie Riis's tale. In both works, colors, sights, sounds, and smells appeal to all the senses. The surprising outcome of the story is also rather similar. Yet the protagonist of this picture book targeted at children is far more troubling than the heroine of Riis's story marketed for adults. The dark and intense colors of Bruyère's illustrations create a mysterious, rather troubling atmosphere that is initially inexplicable. Carmina, a dangerous seductress, is part wolf. Her family name is Wolf and everything in this enigmatic story suggests that her beloved grandmother is a real she-wolf. From the beginning, Mina is described in terms that evoke a wolf:

she has "carmine cheeks," "little pointed fangs," and "a tawny mane." Many of the subtle signs of Mina's wolfish nature, which are embedded in both the text and illustrations, may very well go unnoticed even by adult readers. Eventually, however, attentive readers will recognize Mina's Wolf identity. The story retains a great deal of ambiguity, and the heroine's nature remains equivocal: she is cast in a dual role, at once girl and wolf. Her full name, Carmina Wolf, turns her into a Red Wolf that combines the roles of Red Riding Hood and the Wolf.

Almost from the outset, the heroine of *Mina, je t'aime* is portrayed in a sensual and seductive manner that should alert readers to underlying, darker, animal instincts. Bruyère offers one particularly sensual portrait of this modern, red-haired Riding Hood with red nails, red tights, and a red sweatshirt/minidress (plate 30). Her long, loose hair flows erotically over her shoulders as she lounges on a divan staring seductively at the viewer in a scene inspired by Titian's *Venus of Urbino*. Mina's "dancing little behind" is described as she sets out on the path in her sexy minidress. On the way to her grandmother's three boys from the village follow her; they in turn throw her notes containing the same declaration of love: "Mina, I love you." Initially, Carmina appears to be the victim of the importunate advances of three young would-be wolves. The first boy leaps out of the shrubbery and asks "pretty Mina, darling Mina" where she is going, the classic question of the wolf-seducer. Rather than give the naive answer of her predecessor, however, Mina replies sharply that it is none of his business and tells him to get lost, which he obligingly does.

These would-be-seducers appear awkward, even ridiculous, in the company of the self-confident young protagonist. The innocence and naivety of the heroine of the classic tale is transferred to the three boys, who become the victims of a young seductress. Mina performs a partial striptease at a stream in the forest, undoubtedly aware that at least one of the boys is watching her. This little Riding Hood is a man-eater. Mina has lured them into the forest so that she can offer her beloved, carnivorous grandmother "three good fat boys for dessert!" Although readers only see the grandmother through the eyes of the three boys or as a dark shadow through the bed curtain where she lies among her lambskins, the surprising ending establishes that Mina's beloved grandmother is a she-wolf with enormous jaws.[19] This Riding Hood not only runs with the wolves, she also has real wolf blood.

In Tanith Lee's "Wolfland," the protagonist's "werewolvery" is, like Carmina's, hereditary, at least in a dormant state (127). In the new cloak of scarlet velvet that her grandmother, Anna the Matriarch, sends her, Lisel imagines herself as "a dangerous blood-red rose" (107), a metaphor that evokes the title of the collection, *Red as Blood: Or Tales from the Sisters Grimmer*. Lisel sets out against her will to her eccentric grandmother's château, which is situated in the wild forest on land that was called the Wolfland for centuries and that is still surrounded by wolves. As the sled leaves the city, however, the girl, "ablaze in her scarlet cloak," feels "exhilarated," as if she is coming into her element. Listening to the wolves' howling at the château, she feels "a bizarre exhilaration, an almost-pleasure in the awful sounds which made the hair lift on her scalp and gooseflesh creep along her arms" (119). Running with the wolves is in this young girl's blood.

Lisel's wolfish tendencies come to the surface during the journey. Her reaction to the wolves running alongside her carriage reveals a darker side, a "malicious streak" in her that makes her yearn for a pistol or a knife. Readers do not realize until later that the grinning wolf on the running board of the carriage staring at her with eyes "like two little portholes into hell" is, in fact, her werewolf grandmother. Lisel responds like a wolf, flinging herself at the wolf on the other side of the door "with a shrill howl": "Her eyes also blazed, her teeth also were bared, and her nails raised as if to claw." As the narrator puts it, she seemed ready "to attack the wolf in its own primeval mode" (112). Anna explains later that "wolf-magic" is hereditary and that is why "Wolfland accord[ed] her an escort, a pack of wolves running by [her] on the road." According to the old lady, Lisel would not have survived the journey if she had not been "one of their kind" (134). Unbeknownst to her, the young girl was undergoing an initiation that could have proven fatal. The pack and its leader were testing Lisel to see if she was worthy of running with them.

In spite of the many signs that the grandmother is a werewolf, neither the protagonist nor readers decode them immediately. Lisel notices, for example, that her grandmother's nails and teeth are very long and discolored, but she takes them for the proofs of old age in an eighty-one-year-old woman who otherwise looks no more than fifty. Other signs include her diet of raw meat, the liqueur made from yellow flowers that can only be monkshood or wolfsbane, and the strange behavior of the horses in her presence. In the firelight, Anna's eyes resemble those of the wolf at the carriage window. A prominent stained glass window in the château portrays men transforming into wolves. The handsome husband of this cruel and indomitable Matriarch, a "monster" given to "outbursts of perverse lust and savagery" (109), was mysteriously murdered on one of the forest paths, and Lisel imagines him being torn apart by long pointed teeth. The girl is irritated at the thought of "wolves running" while her grandmother insists on leaving the gateway to the château open and she visualizes "mad Anna throwing chunks of raw meat to the wolves as another woman would toss bread to swans" (114). When Lisel realizes the great pale wolf beneath her window had been in the château, she wonders if it is a household pet. Paradoxically, the girl refers to these idiosyncrasies as mad Anna's "wolfish foibles" (120), without realizing how extremely apt the term is. Lisel reacts with amused skepticism when Anna confesses that she is a werewolf. By eating the yellow flowers that grow in the Wolfland, Anna had received the gift from the "wolfwoman" (130) or "the wolf goddess of the north" (134). Lee subverts the conventional view of lycanthropy as a "curse" inflicted on men by the devil and turns it into a "gift" bestowed on women by a goddess.

Although Lisel is tricked into becoming a werewolf by her grandmother, who thus escapes being bound to the earth as a phantom "in wolf form" (135), the girl carried the mark from birth. Her grandmother points to her hair, her eyes, her beautiful teeth, her love of the night and the forest, and the thrill she feels at the sound of the wolf's howl. Lisel's initial anger fades as she hears a wolf "sing" in the forest. Lee's evocative description of the girl's reaction constitutes the epigraph to this chapter: "She suddenly knew frost and running and black stillness, and a platinum moon, red feasts and wild hymnings, lovers with quicksilver eyes and the race of the ice wind and stars smashed under the hard soles of her four feet" (135). Another howl of the wolf calls irresistibly to Lisel, who hurriedly follows her grandmother out into the Wolfland under the full moon.

Lee's memorable retelling suggests even more strongly than Ikhlef and Gauthier's picture book that Red Riding Hoods who run with the wolves will end up in hell. At least, that is where Lisel tells her grandmother she will go, and the girl is following in her footsteps, or rather in her wolf tracks. In this haunting reversion, both Red Riding Hood and her grandmother run with the wolves as werewolves or "women-wolves." This life in the company of wolves allows both young girl and older woman to be master of their own destiny and to elude a life of subservience and victimization at the hands of a handsome human brute. While some Riding Hoods become aggressive, predatory animals as a means of self-defense or revenge against the male sex, others seem only to seek a sadistic pleasure in defeating the wolf at his own game. Whatever the case, these predatory Riding Hoods are following their natural instincts.

Not all Riding Hoods who keep company with wolves have wolfish instincts, however. They may merely enjoy the companionship of wolves as mentors, accomplices, friends, or lovers. Quite a number of Riding Hoods are sexually attracted to the wolf. Some seek to tame or domesticate the wolf in order to turn him into a docile pet or a submissive husband. More often sensual Riding Hoods prefer the wild, free life of wolves, and they run with them in defiance of society's conventions and taboos. Such retellings affirm woman's sensual animal nature over a socially constructed femininity. A striking example is the protagonist of Carter's story "The Company of Wolves," who chooses to join her wolf-lover's pack as a woman-wolf. Many contemporary Riding Hoods who run with wolves carry a wolf within. Like Joiret's Carmina, they may always have been aware of their wolf side, or, like Smith's *Daughter*, they may make that discovery quite suddenly. While some Riding Hood Wolves are disturbed or frightened by their wolfishness, others embrace and cultivate their wolfish nature. *La loba* or the Wolf Woman, as Estés envisages her, is simply a woman who chooses to live "in her natural wild state." It is only after she encounters the wolf in the woods that the life of Estés's protagonist can truly begin. In the case of these Riding Hoods, running with the wolves is a means of being true to their inner selves. Although not all of the Riding Hoods examined in this chapter are wolf-women or wolf-girls, they all have occasion to run with the wolves.

In retelling the story of Little Red Riding Hood, the authors and illustrators discussed in this chapter, many of whom are women, foreground the complex and often ambiguous relationships between Riding Hoods and wolves. Their multilayered works often target adults or adolescents, although some also address children. However, even the picture-book retellings seem intended largely for an older audience. For the most part, they are challenging and demanding recastings that question the cultural construction of both Riding Hoods and wolves. From Norway and France to Argentina and the United States, contemporary authors and artists are presenting readers of all ages with stories of unconventional Riding Hoods running with the wolves.

Epilogue

. . . it could be a spy story, a horror story, a detective story, an adventure story, or even a fairy tale, couldn't it?

—CARLES CANO, *T'he agafat, Caputxeta!* (Gotcha Little Red Riding Hood)

This book has been devoted to international retellings of *Little Red Riding Hood* in the field of literature, but the tale has been recycled for all ages in all aspects of contemporary culture. Since initiating research on *Little Red Riding Hood* prior to the tercentenary of Perrault's first literary version in 1997, I have been constantly encountering the globe-trotting little girl in red in the most unlikely places. In a doctor's office, a Little Red Cap, wearing the traditional costume of the Schwalm area of Germany, adorned an article on the Brothers Grimm in the December 1999 issue of *National Geographic*.[1] In 2002, the fairy-tale heroine, as the Swedish illustrator Svend Otto imagined her, graced the menu of the closing banquet of the fiftieth anniversary congress of The International Board on Books for Young People (IBBY) in Basel. En route to Norway to give a paper on *Little Red Riding Hood* in 2003, the *SAS Flightshop* magazine for the Scandinavian airline featured a suitcase with finger puppets of Little Red Riding Hood, the wolf, and the grandmother, which were handmade in St. Petersburg by mothers of physically challenged children. The 2004 edition of the Salon du Livre et de la Presse Jeunesse (Children's Book and Magazine Fair) in Seine-Saint-Denis, France, which coincided with a conference I was attending in Paris, featured a large exhibition titled *Dans la gueule du loup* (In the wolf's mouth), devoted uniquely to *Little Red Riding Hood*. An unending assortment of Red Riding Hood manifestations seemed to have been arranged for my personal benefit. Of course, the truth is that the little girl in red has become a universal icon that is omnipresent in contemporary culture.

The enduring appeal of *Little Red Riding Hood* with audiences of all ages can be attributed in part to the tale's truly remarkable capacity to adapt to virtually any art form or medium, ranging from literature and fine art to comics and cartoons, from movies and advertisements to video games and the Internet. Authors and illustrators for all ages, as well as artists, comics artists, cartoonists, filmmakers, game designers, greeting card designers, and ad writers, among others, have drawn inspiration from *Little Red Riding Hood*. Even politicians and statesmen have tried their hand at retelling the tale, often using the popular fairy-tale heroine to make political statements about subjects that have no relationship whatsoever to her story. Vladimir Putin, for example, appropriated the well-known characters to refer to the failure of previous attempts at reform in Russia and the fact that they had been merely cosmetic: "The wolf remained a wolf even in Grandma's disguise and swallowed Little Red Riding Hood after all."[2] It seems that there is no topic that cannot be "ridinghoodized." The story of Little Red Riding Hood has been recycled for all ages to discuss initiation, independence, rebellion, family relationships, parental authority, seniors, political correctness, gender, puberty, sexuality, rape, child abuse, love, hate, heroism, cruelty, criminality, murder, death, rebirth, alcoholism, gluttony, cannibalism, materialism, industrialization, urbanization, technology, pollution, ecology, revolution, and war. The famous tale's versatility is truly remarkable.

Long before globalization and rampant consumerism made product tie-ins to bestselling stories extremely big business, *Little Red Riding Hood* was a commodity that sold quite well beyond the world of books. This exploitation is facilitated by the fact that the familiar icon raises no copyright issues, despite David Fisher's tongue-in-cheek claim to the contrary in *Legally Correct Fairy Tales*. The popular tale has inspired a variety of items that are not only for children, such as makeup kits, ceramic coin banks, cookie jars, garden statues, figurines, toys, and games. One of the favorite furry hand puppets in the popular Folktails series by Folkmanis Puppets, bought by adults and children alike, is a large, cuddly version of the wolf that is pictured on their Web site in the arms of a little girl in a red hood. A set of nesting dolls sold in England, in which Little Red Riding Hood is the largest doll and consequently gobbles up the wolf, appeals to collectors of all ages. The classic Red Riding Hood toy is the versatile three-in-one doll that incorporates all the main characters of the tale. When the little girl with braids, wearing a red hood and cape and carrying a basket, is turned upside down, the doll becomes a smiling granny with white hair and spectacles, until the old lady's bonnet is flipped over to reveal the wolf wearing her nightgown and bonnet. I first saw the doll as a child in Canada, but was given my own "Peek-a-boo" doll in Japan while doing research on *Little Red Riding Hood* several years ago at the International Institute for Children's Literature, Osaka. This beloved doll, available on both sides of the globe, illustrates the universality of the fairy-tale heroine in popular culture.

A number of Little Red Riding Hood toys are actually targeted more at adults than children, as they are also marketed as collectors' pieces. The Pullip Red Riding Hood Fashion Doll from Japan is a collectible doll that retails for about one hundred dollars. A number of Red Riding Hood toys have been reviewed in *Raving Toy Maniac*, which, as the subtitle *The Magazine for Your Inner Child* suggests, is an online magazine for mature consumers. In 2001, Mezco Toyz offered a new interpretation of the tale in its first series of *Scary Tales* action figures, which included *Red* and the *Wolf*. The rather scantily clad Riding Hood wears a low-cut, laced-up, miniskirt dress, long, black leather gloves, and knee-high boots, along with her red cape and hood. A *Scary Tales* exclusive of *Red* repainted with a Latin twist as *Rojo Pequeña* (Little Red) was even part of the membership package of ClubMez, Mezco's Collectors' Club. Reminding us that fairy tales were not written to be "happy stories for children" but were "frightening tales intended for adults," the Scary Tales line is meant to present these classic characters in a more "accurate" way.

While many of these figures claim to target the adult market, they also appeal to younger consumers, particularly gamers. A character in the fighting game *Darkstalkers*, Baby Bonnie Hood, also known as B. B. Hood or Bulleta in Japan, is a cute, innocent-looking bounty hunter and serial killer of wolves who carries an Uzi and an arsenal of other weapons hidden in her basket. She is available in a two-figure pack that includes another character, Jon Talbain the werewolf. In a similar vein is American McGee's Red, the "big red wolf destroyer" from the video game *Red*, part of a "nightmare trilogy" based on the world's best-known fairy tales. In 2005, *Raving Toy Maniac* announced the "twisted toys" that HyperChild Workshop would produce in conjunction with American McGee's game trilogy, featuring a series of PVC figurines bound to illustrated books. These products are intended to appeal to adults, as indicated in the following statement by the video game designer: "It's time we took the fairytales away from the children and made them our own once more."[3] Designers of toys and video games are reclaiming Little Red Riding Hood for adults, but such products naturally attract younger consumers as well.

Little Red Riding Hood is not only a commodity in her own right. She has been used to promote products, ranging from cakes and creams to clothes and cars, in magazines, on television, and online. Her icon has been associated with Pleyben cakes, Lanvin chocolate, Camembert cheese, Crispers, Elesca instant breakfast, Heinz salad cream, Pepsi, Johnny Walker, Waterford crystal, Renault,

Winstar, Toyota Celica, Hertz Rent A Car, Philips telephones, Fender musical instruments, Chanel No. 5 perfume, Max Factor lipstick, and Salvatore Ferragamo's designer fashions. Advertising is not a new sideline for Little Red Riding Hood. As early as 1894, the fairy-tale heroine was promoting a brand of butter in France.[4] Consumers of all ages are enticed to spend their money by the persuasive little girl in red.

The fairy-tale heroine has starred on both the big and small screens in versions for a mixed audience. *Little Red Riding Hood* was the seventh episode in Shelley Duvall's award-winning, star-studded, live-action family series *Faerie Tale Theatre*, which lured big Hollywood talent to cable and revolutionized cable programming in the 1980s. Considered suitable for viewing by all ages, the series was rereleased in 1996 to launch Cabin Fever Entertainment's new children's label, Razzmatazz. Márta Mészáros's *Bye Bye Red Riding Hood* was also part of an award-winning family series, Rock Demers's Tales for All, but it was produced for the big screen. With Anne Ikhlef's *La véritable histoire du Chaperon Rouge*, the fairy-tale heroine made it to the Cannes Film Festival in 1985. David Kaplan's short black-and-white film *Little Red Riding Hood* (1997), a black comedy version starring Christina Ricci, played at over fifty international film festivals. Little Red Riding Hood has a more minor but still important role in the film *The Brothers Grimm*, which was released in 2005 with a PG-13 rating. Mészáros's and Ikhlef's crossover films are the only two mentioned in this book because they subsequently inspired a novel and a picture book respectively, and so generated significant literary retellings of Little Red Riding Hood.

The popular tale has been retold in a number of other films, several of which fall into the thriller or horror genres. It should probably come as no surprise that the story of a little girl devoured by a wolf should be seen as suitable fare for a thriller. Matthew Bright's 1996 film *Freeway* cast a serial sex killer in the role of the wolf. Ironically, Bob Wolverton is a child psychologist, but he meets his match in Vanessa (Reese Witherspoon), a California teen in a red leather jacket who has run away from social services, armed with the gun belonging to her boyfriend, Chopper. Another provocative psychological thriller in a somewhat similar vein is *Hard Candy*, by British director David Slade. This modern remake released in the United States in 2006 has the tagline "Strangers shouldn't talk to little girls." When a mature fourteen-year-old girl meets a charming thirty-two-year-old fashion photographer on the Internet and suspects him of being a pedophile, she goes to his house with the intention of confronting him. The 2000 film *Promenons-nous dans les bois,* released in English as *Deep in the Woods,* was hailed as the first French slasher movie, and it also features a predatory serial killer. Five young actors, whose repertoire consists solely of *Le Petit Chaperon Rouge,* are invited to perform the play at the castle of an aristocratic millionaire, who turns out to be the serial killer behind the wolf's mask. The title, which is taken from the popular French song associated with the children's game "Loup y es-tu?" is full of childhood resonances for Francophone viewers. Restricted to those twelve years of age and above, the movie targets especially the teenage audience of slashers like *Scream,* but an adult audience has appreciated the deeper resonances of the film. In 2003, Italy also produced a slasher film based on the tale. The twelve-year-old heroine of *Cappuccetto Rosso* (*Red Riding Hood*) and her imaginary friend, George, who wears a big bad wolf mask, decide to do away with all those people they feel deserve punishment, including her grandma. Finally, *A Wicked Tale,* released in 2005, is an experimental thriller by the Singaporean filmmaker Tzang Merwyn Tong. The short, hallucinatory film explores the subtext of violence and sexual awakening in a dark recasting of the tale that is "suggested for mature audiences," although it also has a cult following of teens. In the hands of horror movie producers and screenwriters, the fairy tale has gone from grim to grisly and gory! These are definitely not recastings for the faint of heart.

Over the years, Little Red Riding Hood has also appeared in a variety of animated films. One of Walt Disney's very first animated films was a silent black-and-white cartoon of *Little Red Riding Hood* produced in 1922. The Silly Symphony *The Big Bad Wolf,* released in 1934, has already been mentioned in chapter 3. A 1998 Disney animated short film, *Redux Riding Hood,* was nominated for an Academy Award, but was never released in theaters. Walt Disney carefully geared his films to an audience of all ages and censorship was never a problem. That was not the case for Tex Avery's remakes of the tale, in which violence and sexuality are key ingredients, as is biting sarcasm. The slapstick and gags appeal to children, while the self-reflexivity and sexual innuendos are there for the adult audience. In addition to cameos in several other Avery cartoons, the fairy-tale heroine starred in three formal adaptations of the tale. *Little Red Walking Hood* was created for Disney's main rival, Warner Brothers Studio, in 1937, whereas Avery's most popular and provocative retelling, *Red Hot Riding Hood,* was produced for the less-restrictive MGM Studios in 1943, as was *Little Rural Riding Hood,* released in 1949. The first sexy cartoon character, the remodeled Red was initially banned from television. The red-hot nightclub singer with the Betty Grable figure became a pin-up for soldiers in the armed forces during World War II, without losing her appeal with a younger audience. In 1944, Red became an obnoxious, loud-mouthed bobby-soxer in Warner Brothers' Bugs Bunny cartoon, *Little Red Riding Rabbit*. The most famous fairy-tale character of all time did not even get a cameo, although the wolf did, in DreamWorks's 2001 blockbuster, *Shrek*, but this glaring oversight was corrected in the sequel, *Shrek 2*. Unlike many fairy tales, Disney has not cinematized *Little Red Riding Hood* as a full-length animated film. However, in 2006, it became the subject of the computer-animated, full-length feature film *Hoodwinked*, which had limited crossover success and will certainly not impact the cultural imagination in the manner of Disney adaptations.

The dark, powerful anime feature film *Jin-Roh: The Wolf Brigade* (1998) borrows heavily and overtly from the tale of Little Red Riding Hood, although many viewers, adults as well as children, do not discover the intertextual references until late in the movie, if at all. *Jin-Roh*, which translates as Man-Wolf, is a science-fiction fairy tale directed by Hiroyuki Okiura and scripted by the legendary anime director Mamoru Oshii, based on his manga *Kerberos Panzer Cops*. In a post–World War II alternate reality in Tokyo, Fuse Kazuki is a member of The Wolf Brigade, a rogue organization within a police antiterrorist unit, and Red Riding Hoods are young girls who act as terrorist couriers, delivering bombs in satchels. The popular tale is embedded throughout *Jin-Roh*, read by a narrator from the book that belonged to a dead Red Riding Hood. The embedded book bears the German title, *Rotkäppchen*, even though the hypotext is not the Grimms' tale, but an unusual version from the oral tradition that very few viewers would recognize.[5] The intertextual resonances and the interweaving of the tale throughout the anime are what interest most adult viewers of this film, which was rated ages sixteen and up.

Little Red Riding Hood did not just become a film star in Hollywood and on television; she has also played on stage around the world for audiences of all ages. She even starred in a *kyogen*, or traditional Japanese play, by Man-no-jo Nomura, which was produced at the National Noh Theatre in Tokyo by the Shinsei no kai troupe. Little Red Riding Hood has appeared in musicals from the United States to Japan. She was one of the traditional fairy-tale characters in Stephen Sondheim and James Lapine's Tony Award–winning musical *Into the Woods*, which opened on Broadway at the Martin Beck Theatre on November 5, 1987 and was successfully revived for a new generation of theatergoers in 2002. The Japanese musical *Akazukin-chan no mori no ohkami tachi no kurisumasu*, produced in

1993 by Minoru Betsuyaku, tells the story of "The Wolves' Christmas in the forest of Little Red Riding Hood." In addition to the songs from musicals, Little Red Riding Hood has also been the subject of other musical renditions. Perhaps the best known is Robert Blackwell's "Lil' Red Riding Hood," recorded by Sam the Sham and the Pharaohs. The 1966 hit was introduced to a younger generation when it was used as the background music for a 2001 Pepsi One television commercial that cast the sexy actress Kim Cattrall as a Red Riding Hood-Wolf.

The story of Little Red Riding Hood has inspired some very exciting and innovative aesthetic experimentations that appeal to both adults and children, many of which are in book form. The characters and settings are entirely made from origami in Yoshihide and Sumiko Momotani's *Akazukin-chan* (Little Red Riding Hood), which includes fourteen pages of detailed instructions so adults and/or children can create their own origami version of the tale. Among the many versatile, multimedia artworks that the German-born American multimedia artist Kiki Smith has devoted to the fairy tale is a book, titled *Companion* (2000), which consists of accordion-folded photolithographs depicting a frieze-like procession of Little Red Riding Hoods and wolves. The unique format of the book, which appeals to collectors and children alike, culminates in a pocket with a memento of the fairy-tale heroine, a red hood, folded up inside. The story of Little Red Riding Hood inspired an entirely new technique for the Swiss artist Warja Lavater, whose celebrated series of "imageries" or "object-books" was initiated with *Le Petit Chaperon Rouge,* published in Paris in 1965. Except for the legend, the accordion book is wordless, retelling the tale in an elementary code based on colors and forms, which depicts Little Red Riding Hood as a red dot and the wolf as a black dot. In 1975, Jean Ache used a similar visual code, which he termed "narrative abstraction," to illustrate Perrault's tale in *Le monde des ronds et des carrés* (The world of circles and squares), where Little Red Riding Hood is a little red circle (or dot) and the wolf is a black square. Lavater now claims that the pictorial language of her *imagerie* appeals to all ages, but she was initially astonished when, after the publication of the luxury edition sold in museums and art galleries, she learned that children liked and apparently understood the book. While Martine Barnaby's *Containers of Red* (1999), an interactive CD-ROM that allows the possibility of formulating an almost infinite number of variations of the tale, is not geared toward children, it naturally appeals to their advanced technological skills. Children often appropriate artists' reworkings of *Little Red Riding Hood* even though they were intended only for adult art lovers.

A number of illustrators appropriate the general style or specific works of well-known artists to retell the story of Little Red Riding Hood. As we have seen, Kelek transplants the tale into a Renaissance painting by Vittore Carpaccio. In a strikingly different mode, Jean Lecointre uses bright-colored, garish photomontages that evoke the pop art of the 1950s in the French picture book *Les dents du loup* (The Wolf's Teeth, 2002). In some cases, illustrators actually parody earlier visual renditions of the tale. For example, Beni Montresor imitates Gustave Doré's famous engravings in his *Little Red Riding Hood,* while Anthony Browne parodies a familiar illustration of the tale by Walter Crane in *The Tunnel.* These rather sophisticated allusions to high art or to celebrated illustrations are not accessible to young readers and are obviously present for the cultured adults capable of identifying them.

Jean Ache's geometric recasting in *Le monde des ronds et des carrés* was undoubtedly inspired by an abstract rendition of the tale that he had done two years earlier for the magazine *Pilote,* as part of a series devoted to "*Le Petit Chaperon Rouge* in the style of . . ." famous twentieth-century artists. These masterly recastings pastiching celebrated painters illustrate eloquently the remarkable versatility of the fairy tale. The prolific French BD artist single-handedly offers seven *Little Red Riding Hood* masterpieces. They are a brilliant blend of popular culture and high art. Ache not only adapts the fairy tale to the codes of the comics genre, but he also cleverly imitates the art of seven renowned and very different artists, Henri (Le douanier) Rousseau, Fernand Léger, Bernard Buffet, Pablo Picasso, Giorgio de Chirico, Joan Miró, and Piet Mondrian. These reworkings are done with striking fidelity to the style of each artist and "co-signed," tongue in cheek, by the pastiched artist and Jean Ache. Although young French readers may be able to recognize and appreciate the style of most of the parodied artists, only a highly cultured adult audience can appreciate the precise allusions to specific paintings.

Little Red Riding Hood continues to inspire a whole new generation of young artists and illustrators. The exhibition at the Salon du Livre et de la Presse Jeunesse in France in 2004 provided a foretaste of the Red Riding Hood images that the future holds in store for audiences around the world. In addition to the works of major illustrators from Gustave Doré to Roberto Innocenti, the exhibition featured the best works of the nearly two thousand young artists from every continent who participated in the unique biennial international illustration competition *Figures futur,* whose theme in 2004 was *Le Petit Chaperon Rouge.* The fact that there were twice as many participants as in the previous competition is undoubtedly due to the popularity and power of this particular story and not the more mundane reasons put forth by the organizers. Although the competition is organized by a center for the promotion of children's books, the jury seemed to have a crossover audience in mind, selecting works that "demonstrated that strong images can be understood by all."[6] The forty-one young artists whose works were chosen by the jury to be included in the exhibition rendered the tale in every medium and mixed media imaginable, including India ink, crayon, pen, pencil, charcoal, pastel, watercolor, acrylic on celluloid, oil, collage, montage, modeling, peelings, plants, dyed fabrics, yarn, embroidery, woodcut, engraving, monotype, silkscreen printing, photographs, Photoshop enhanced painting, digital print, computer graphics, and interactive media. The award-winning work was an acrylic painting by the French artist Maud Riemann (plate 31). It depicts an old-fashioned black sewing machine in the shape of a wolf, making a row of white zigzag stitches, which look distinctively like teeth, on a large piece of red cloth. The jury gave special mention to seven works, one of the most interesting being a digitally colored ink drawing by the German illustrator Eleanor Marston, in which several scenes of Perrault's tale are condensed into a single, multilayered illustration (plate 32). The exhibition catalogue is full of remarkable, unpublished visual interpretations of the tale, which will hopefully find their way into print one day. The works of these young artists from around the world illustrate once again the enduring, universal appeal of *Little Red Riding Hood*.

Today, Little Red Riding Hood's appeal to young and old alike obviously extends well beyond the literary domain to all areas of high and low culture, including all of the new media technologies that have reclaimed the fairy tale for our times. This is particularly well illustrated by the popular cyberspace version, "Cyber Kaperucita," a retelling in computer jargon that has been widely circulated on the Web in the Hispanic world.[7] The age-old tale, which has its origins in the oral tradition, possesses an amazing capacity to adapt to new social and cultural contexts. It can be transposed to any time and any place.

This epilogue was meant to provide an overview of the extraordinary range and diversity with which *Little Red Riding Hood* is being recycled for all ages in all aspects of contemporary culture. One cannot help but wonder what new paths Little Red Riding Hood will travel in the twenty-first century. All the signs are that she will continue to inspire new retellings that appeal to adults, adolescents, and children, in all the literary genres, mediums, and new technologies.

Notes

Introduction

1. "À Mademoiselle," in Charles Perrault, *Contes de ma mère l'Oye*, illustrated by Gustave Doré, Folio Junior Édition Spéciale (Paris: Gallimard, 1997), 19.

2. Zohar Shavit, *Poetics of Children's Literature* (Athens: University of Georgia Press, 1986), 9, 13, 15.

3. Letter from Jacob Grimm to Arnim, 28 January 1813; quoted in Shavit, *Poetics of Children's Literature*, 21.

4. Quoted in the preface of *Not Quite as Grimm: Told and Illustrated by Janosch for Today*, trans. Patricia Crampton (London: Abelard-Schuman, 1974), 7.

5. Jack Zipes feels that the revisions of the Grimms' tales that he discusses in *Sticks and Stones*, revisions published from the early 1970s to the late 1990s, demonstrate that "there can be no fixed lines drawn between children's and adult literature." See Jack Zipes, *Sticks and Stones: The Troublesome Success of Children's Literature from Slovenly Peter to Harry Potter* (New York: Routledge, 2001), 107.

6. For more on the appeal of *Little Red Riding Hood* as an intertext, see Sandra L. Beckett, *Recycling Red Riding Hood* (New York: Routledge, 2002), xvi–xviii.

7. The classic tale of Little Red Riding Hood has nonetheless been the object of censorship in the United States, not because of its sexual content but because of its alleged promotion of alcohol.

8. See, for example, Carole Hanks and D. T. Hanks Jr., "Perrault's 'Little Red Riding Hood': Victim of the Revisers," *Children's Literature* 7 (1978): 68.

9. Bruno Bettelheim, *The Uses of Enchantment: The Meaning and Importance of Fairy Tales* (New York: Random House, 1975), 169.

10. Page references for all primary sources will be indicated in parentheses in the text. If page numbers are not cited, it is because the book is not paginated. All translations of texts not originally published in English are mine unless otherwise indicated.

11. Lewis C. Seifert, "France," in *The Oxford Companion to Fairy Tales*, ed. Jack Zipes (Oxford: Oxford University Press, 2000), 186.

12. Manlio Argueta wrote this prize-winning, allegorical, political novel in exile during the civil war in El Salvador.

13. Cornelia Hoogland, "Real 'Wolves in Those Bushes': Readers Take Dangerous Journeys with *Little Red Riding Hood*," *Canadian Children's Literature* 73 (1994): 20.

14. Quoted in Olivier Pascal-Moussellard, "Le Petit Chaperon bouge," in *20ᵉ Salon du Livre et de la Presse Jeunesse: Le programme*, supplément à *Télérama* no. 2862, 17 November 2004, 5.

15. Unlike many European fairy tales, the tale of Little Red Riding Hood has no equivalent in Japanese folktales.

Chapter 1

1. Catherine Orenstein, *Little Red Riding Hood Uncloaked: Sex, Morality, and the Evolution of a Fairy Tale* (New York: Basic Books, 2002), 4.

2. In French, girls who are no longer virgins are said "to have seen the wolf" (*avoir vu le loup*).

3. Perrault, *Contes de ma mère l'Oye*, 19–20.

4. See Philippe Ariès's landmark book on the history of childhood, *Centuries of Childhood: A Social History of Family Life*, trans. Robert Baldick (New York: Knopf, 1962).

5. See Bettelheim, *The Uses of Enchantment*, 168.

6. Ibid., 169.

7. Jack Zipes, *The Trials and Tribulations of Little Red Riding Hood: Versions of the Tale in Sociocultural Context*, 2nd ed. (New York: Routledge, 1993), 355, 356.

8. Jack Zipes, "A Second Gaze at Little Red Riding Hood's Trials and Tribulations," *The Lion and the Unicorn* 7–8 (1983–84): 84.

9. Jacob and Wilhelm Grimm, *The Annotated Brothers Grimm*, ed. and trans. Maria Tatar (New York: Norton, 2004), 410.

10. See Wilhelm and Jacob Grimm, *Rotkäppchen* (in Arabic), illustrated by Jenny Williams (Beirut/Cairo: Dar Almashruk, A.H. 1423 [A.D. 1992]).

11. Letter from Yvan Pommaux, 28 February 2001.

12. See Paul Delarue, *Le conte populaire français*, vol. 1 (Paris: Éditions Érasme, 1957), 373–75, 376, no. 6.

13. Eric Berne, *What Do You Say after You Say Hello?* (New York: Grove Press, 1972), 45.

14. Alain Journaud, review of *Mina je t'aime*, by Patricia Joiret and Xavier Bruyère, *Lire au Collège* 45–46 (Spring 1997): 47.

15. The subtitle of the document is "Overgriperes rett til å arbeide med barn eller barns rett til beskyttelse?" (Abusers' Right to Work with Children or Children's Right to Protection?).

16. Quoted in Sylvia and Kenneth Marantz, *Artists of the Page: Interviews with Children's Book Illustrators* (Jefferson, NC: McFarland, 1992), 8.

17. For a detailed study of the references to art works in *John Chatterton détective*, see Sandra L. Beckett, "Parodic Play with Paintings in Picture Books," *Children's Literature* 29 (2001): 175–95.

18. Margaret Bates, "Introduction," *Selected Poems of Gabriela Mistral*, trans. and ed. Doris Dana (Baltimore: Published for the Library of Congress by the Johns Hopkins University Press, 1971), xviii.

19. Letter from Wim Hofman, 26 May 2000. Posters for children have a very long tradition in The Netherlands, but adults often buy them. Although the poster was never printed, the tales were published individually in *Mikmak* (Mishmash), a children's magazine, beginning with "Roodkapje" in October 1993.

20. Quoted in Aukje Holtrop, "'Things Never Work Out for Snow White': Wim Hofman's Fairy Tales," an interview with Wim Hofman, *Vrij Nederland*, 17 May 1997.

21. E-mail from Wim Hofman, 13 December 2002.

22. Quoted in Holtrop, "Things Never Work Out for Snow White." The menace of evil even pervades Hofman's short poem, "Roodkapje" (1986), which isolates and develops a single, tranquil moment of the tale, the flower-picking scene.

23. Susan Brownmiller, *Against Our Will: Men, Women, and Rape* (New York: Fawcett Columbine, 1975), 310.

24. Quoted in Jeffrey Garrett, "'With Murderous Ending, Shocking, Menacing . . .': Sarah Moon's *Little Red Riding Hood* 10 Years After," *Bookbird* 31, no. 3 (1993): 9.

25. The vehicle takes on a further layer of menace when one realizes that it is meant to represent the Peugeots driven by Nazi officials in France.

26. This illustration is a preliminary work from 1988, which has previously been pub-

lished only in *Figures futur 2004: Young and New Illustrators of Tomorrow* (Seine-Saint-Denis: Centre de Promotion du Livre de Jeunesse, 2004), 20–21.

27. Qtd. in Garrett, "With Murderous Ending, Shocking, Menacing . . ." 9.

28. Letter from Isabelle Forestier, 5 October 2003. All subsequent comments attributed to Forestier are taken from this letter.

29. It was banned in a number of libraries in the United States. See Garrett, "With Murderous Ending, Shocking, Menacing . . ." 8.

30. Jack Zipes, *Fairy Tale as Myth/Myth as Fairy Tale* (Lexington: University Press of Kentucky, 1994), 148.

31. Zipes, "A Second Gaze," 230.

Chapter 2

1. Orenstein, *Little Red Riding Hood Uncloaked*, 194.

2. See Review of *Little Red Riding Hood* by Beni Montresor, *Horn Book Magazine*, 1992.

3. Lennart Hellsing, "Perrault's Rödluva," in *Böcker Ska Blänka som solar: En bok till Vivi Edström*, ed. Boel Westin (Stockholm: Rabén and Sjögren, 1988), 74.

4. Erich Fromm, *The Forgotten Language: An Introduction to the Understanding of Dreams, Fairy Tales, and Myths* (New York: Holt, Rinehart and Winston, 1951), 240.

5. Bettelheim, *The Uses of Enchantment*, 173.

6. Hellsing, "Perrault's Rödluva," 76.

7. Orenstein, *Little Red Riding Hood Uncloaked*, 36.

8. *Oxford English Dictionary*, 1864, s.v. "chaperon." In his "Le petit chaperon rouge" ("Little Red Riding Hood") for adults, Jacques Ferron makes the meaning quite clear when he refers to the grandmother as "an old lady who had been much chaperoned in her youth." He blames this chaperoning for the fact that the grandmother had married "a

domineering man who, mercifully, had left her a widow." Since her husband's death, the old lady has been living out her days "unattended, free and happy" in a little bungalow in l'Abord-à-Plouffe in Quebec (30).

9. Paul Delarue, ed., "The Story of Grandmother," in *The Borzoi Book of French Folk Tales* (New York: Knopf, 1956), 230n2.

10. See Yvonne Verdier, "Grand-mères, si vous saviez . . . : Le Petit Chaperon Rouge dans la tradition orale," *Cahiers de Littérature Orale* 4 (1978): 25–26.

11. Orenstein, *Little Red Riding Hood Uncloaked*, 81.

12. See Delarue, *Le conte populaire français*, vol. 1, 381, no. 35, iv.

13. Charlotte Otten, *A Lycanthropy Reader* (New York: Dorset Press, 1986), 8.

14. The term is borrowed from Cornelia Hoogland, "Galloway's Grim Tales," review of *Truly Grim Tales*, by Priscilla Galloway, *Canadian Children's Literature* 82 (1996): 86.

15. Kertzer refers, in particular, to the thirty-eight versions included in the second edition of Zipes's anthology. See Adrienne Kertzer, "Reclaiming Her Maternal Pre-Text: Little Red Riding Hood's Mother and Three Young Adult Novels," *Children's Literature Association Quarterly* 21, no. 1 (1996): 20.

16. Ibid.

17. A more detailed analysis of this novel can be found in my *Recycling Red Riding Hood* (308–31).

18. Carmen Martín Gaite, "Entrevistamos a . . . Carmen Martín Gaite," interview by *Peonza, Peonza* 24 (March 1993): 26–28.

19. See Carmen Martín Gaite, *El cuento de nunca acabar* (Madrid: Trieste, 1983), 158–60.

20. Ibid., 23, 158.

21. Gerald Peary, "Little Red Riding-hood," *Sight and Sound* 57 (Summer 1988): 150.

22. The use of black-and-white clips from the film to illustrate the novel heightens the realism.

23. In the English-language edition, the first name of the mother is also that of the actress who played the part, Pamela Collyer, but in the French-language edition her name is Louise. The name Pamela has been retained in this study.

24. Unfortunately, the English-language edition translates the word *sorcières* as "magicians" (7).

25. Like Ferron, Julien breaks with the common pattern identified by the same critic, in which the young person takes the "failure" of his or her elders as the point of departure for a renewed quest. Maximilien Laroche, "Nouvelles notes sur 'le Petit Chaperon rouge' de Jacques Ferron," *Voix et Images du Pays* 6 (1973): 105.

26. Peary, "Little Red Ridinghood," 150. The Polish actor Jan Nowicki is Márta Mészáros's third husband, and he has appeared in all her films.

27. See Lena Kareland, "'Il y a un trou dans la réalité': Le conte dans le roman suédois du XXe siècle: une perspective féminine," in *Tricentenaire Charles Perrault: Les grands contes du XVIIe siècle et leur fortune littéraire,* ed. Jean Perrot (Paris: In Press, 1998), 359.

28. Letter from Anne Bertier, 31 July 2003. Unless otherwise indicated, all subsequent comments attributed to Bertier are taken from this letter.

29. The werewolf theme recurs in Miwa Ueda's *Tsukiyo no Akazukin* (Little Red Riding Hood on a moonlit night), which appeared in the Kodansya Comics series. It is a love story in which a high school girl goes alone to a house where a doctor is rumored to be studying werewolves. The title of these comics is often misleading, as they generally have little to do with the story of Little Red Riding Hood, but merely capitalize on the fairy-tale heroine's popularity.

30. Bettelheim, *The Uses of Enchantment,* 173.

31. See Caroline Rives, "Tomi Ungerer: Un diable en paradis?" *La Revue des Livres pour Enfants* 171 (September 1996): 95–97; and R. A. Siegel, "The Little Boy Who Drops His Pants in a Crowd: Tomi Ungerer's Art of the Comic Grotesque," *The Lion and the Unicorn* 1, no. 1 (1977): 30–31.

32. "Little Red Riding Hood," *Alibi* 11, no. 6, 7–13 February 2002.

33. This story is found in *Tomi Ungerer's Erzählungen für Erwachsene*. See Caroline Rives, "Tomi Ungerer: Un diable en paradis?" *La Revue des Livres pour Enfants* 171 (September 1996): 96.

Chapter 3

1. In the title of the retelling by Deonísio da Silva, a Brazilian author who writes for both children and adults, Caperucita is designated as *A melhor amiga do lobo* (The wolf's best friend, 1990).

2. F'Murr, signed with anywhere from one to eight *r*'s, is the pseudonym of Richard Pezaret.

3. The poem was available on the Internet site of Acción Democrática Cubana (Cuban Democratic Action) prior to its publication.

4. The quotations from Gwen Strauss are all taken from the Introduction to *Trail of Stones.*

5. Orenstein, *Little Red Riding Hood Uncloaked,* 148.

6. The BD first appeared in Gotlib's groundbreaking *Rubrique-à-brac*, which were later published by Dargaud in five volumes.

7. *Playboy* (November 1979): 270.

8. E-mail from Geoffroy de Pennart, 11 June 2001.

9. Quoted in Gabriel d'Aubarède, "Écrire pour les enfants," *Les Nouvelles Littéraires,* 22 March 1956, 4.

10. Marc Soriano, *Guide de littérature pour la jeunesse* (Paris: Flammarion, 1976), 67.

11. The *Burlington Free Press*, 25 March 1980, 13A; reproduced in Wolfgang Mieder, "Survival Forms of 'Little Red Riding Hood' in Modern Society," *International Folklore Review* 2 (1982): 26.

12. The quotations from "Le loup" are taken from this edition, published in 1979, and the translations are mine.

13. Sophie Quentin, "De la tradition orale aux adaptations modernes: 'Le Petit Chaperon rouge' ou le carrefour des écritures . . . ," in *Écriture féminine et littérature de jeunesse*, ed. Jean Perrot and Véronique Hadengue (Paris: La Nacelle/Institut Charles Perrault, 1995), 208.

14. Pierre Gripari, *Pierre Gripari et ses contes pour enfants*, interviews with Jean-Luc Peyroutet (Mérignac, France: Girandoles, 1994), 13, 8. The author has suggested that certain chapters of *Patrouille du conte* could be read to youngsters, and the year in which the novel appeared for adults, the chapter "Le loup" was appropriated for children and published under the title "Le loup et la grand-mère" in the collection *Le grand méchant loup, j'adore*.

15. See, for example, Janet and Allan Ahlberg's *Jeremiah and the Dark Woods* (1977) and *The Jolly Postman: Or Other People's Letters* (1986).

16. Claire-Lise Malarte, "The French Fairy-Tale Conspiracy," *The Lion and the Unicorn* 12, no. 2 (1988): 118.

Chapter 4

1. The genre of young adult fiction is a prime example of crossover fiction, as it appeals to both teens and adults.

2. Letter from Paul Biegel, 28 December 2002. Unless otherwise indicated, all subsequent quotations from Biegel are taken from an interview he granted me on 5 April 2000.

3. See Bettelheim, *The Uses of Enchantment*, 8.

4. A more literal translation of the preface title would be "Are you it yourself?" This reflects the book's Dutch title, which would literally be translated as "Who You Dream About Is You."

5. Bettelheim, *The Uses of Enchantment*, 94.

6. Joyce Thomas, "Woods and Castles, Towers and Huts: Aspects of Setting in the Fairy Tale." *Children's Literature in Education* 17, no. 2 (1986): 126–34.

7. *Encyclopedia of Magic and Superstition* (London: Octopus Books, 1974), 60.

8. Biegel wrote a story titled *The Curse of the Werewolf* (1981) a few years after the publication of *Wie je droomt ben je zelf*.

9. Bettelheim, *The Uses of Enchantment*, 172.

10. Biegel gives a classic example of this helplessness on page 7 of his preface.

11. "Report of the Jury Awarding the State Prize for Children's and Young People's Literature for 1973," translated by Patricia Crampton, in *Junior Bookshelf* 39, no. 1 (February 1975): 9.

12. Mello is convinced that if an adult doesn't like a story, a child probably won't like it either. E-mail from Roger Mello, 26 September 2003. Unless otherwise indicated, all subsequent quotations from the illustrator are taken from this e-mail.

13. In *Being and Nothingness*, Sartre makes the distinction between the unproblematic being of the world of things, which exist in themselves (*en-soi*) and that of human beings, who exist for themselves (*pour-soi*) because of their consciousness.

14. Gloria Pondé, "Les relectures des *Contes* de Perrault au Brésil: *Fita verde no cabelo*, de Guimarães Rosa," in *Tricentenaire Charles Perrault: Les grands contes du XVIIᵉ siècle et leur fortune littéraire*, ed. Jean Perrot (Paris: In Press, 1998), 332.

15. Ibid., 335.

16. See ibid., 336.

17. Mello admits his own predilection for the game when he was a child.

18. E-mail from Roger Mello, 17 October 2003.

19. Pondé, "Les relectures des *Contes* de Perrault au Brésil," 332.

Chapter 5

1. See Delarue, *Le conte populaire français*, vol. 1, 375, IV; 376–80, no. 6, 13, 28, 29, 31.

2. Sarah Greenleaf, "The Beast Within," *Children's Literature in Education* 23, no. 1 (1992): 56.

3. The Wolf would bring the action to a halt with the same lines in *Red Hot Riding Hood* (1943).

4. Roderick McGillis, "'Ages All': Readers, Texts, and Intertexts in *The Stinky Cheese Man and Other Fairly Stupid Tales*, in *Transcending Boundaries: Writing for a Dual Audience of Children and Adults*, ed. Sandra L. Beckett (New York: Garland, 1999), 116.

5. A third story, titled "Le Noël politiquement correct du petit Chaperon rouge" (Little Red Riding Hood's politically correct Christmas) constitutes a "flash-back" to the infancy of "la Chaperonne rouge," and belongs, as the author writes in a tongue-in-cheek footnote, to the Little Red Riding Hood cycle, as well as to the Santa Claus cycle (57).

6. When mothers are deceived by the book's cover and want to buy it for their children, the author firmly dissuades them. E-mail from Pierrette Fleutiaux, 7 November 2005.

7. Marc Soriano, *Les Contes de Perrault: Culture savante et traditions populaires*, rev. ed. (Paris: Gallimard, 1977), 13.

8. E-mail from Pierrette Fleutiaux, 1 September 2003. All subsequent comments attributed to Fleutiaux are taken from this e-mail unless otherwise indicated.

9. Quoted in Terri Windling's introductory notes to Fleutiaux's "The Ogre's Wife" (488).

10. E-mail from Pierrette Fleutiaux, 7 November 2005.

11. Letter from Annie Riis, 4 March 2001. All subsequent comments attributed to Riis are taken from this letter unless otherwise indicated.

12. See Delarue, *Le conte populaire français*, vol. 1, 376–80, no. 3 (Nivernais-Morvan), no. 6 (Morvan), no. 10 (Vallée de la Nièvre), no. 21 (Forez), no. 22 (Haute-Loire), no. 24 (Haute-Loire), no. 25 (Loire), no. 29 (Hautes-Alpes).

13. See ibid., 379–80, no. 24, 25, and 28.

14. Quoted in Kerryn Goldsworthy, "Angela Carter," *Meanjin* 44, no. 1 (1985): 10.

15. This is in keeping with the version from the Haute-Loire.

16. Cristina Bacchilega, *Postmodern Fairy Tales: Gender and Narrative Strategies* (Philadelphia: University of Pennsylvania Press, 1997): 159n15.

17. Marina Warner, *From the Beast to the Blonde: On Fairy Tales and Their Tellers* (London: Chatto and Windus, 1994), 181.

18. See T. H. White, ed., *The Book of Beasts*, being a translation from a Latin bestiary of the twelfth century (London: Cape, 1954), 59.

19. For a more detailed analysis of *Mina, je t'aime*, see Beckett, *Recycling Red Riding Hood*, 130–44.

Epilogue

1. Thomas O'Neill, "Guardians of the Fairy Tale: The Brothers Grimm," photographs by Gerd Ludwig, *National Geographic* 196, no. 6 (1999): 112–13.

2. Susan J. Cavan, "Hey There Little Red Riding Hood . . ." *The NIS Observed: An Analytical Review* 8, no. 13 (2003).

3. *Raving Toy Maniac: The Magazine for Your Inner Child*, 15 January 2006, www.toymania.com/news/messages/6884.shtml.

4. Beurre d'Isigny, Bretel Frères, Valognes (France), anonymous poster, 1894, Collection Bibliothèque Forney.

5. In this particular version, the little girl is given an outfit made entirely of metal, as in an oral version from the Haute-Loire. See Delarue, *Le conte populaire français*, vol. 1, 379, no. 24.

6. Florence Haguenauer, "Images of the Future around a Timeless Fairy Tale," in *Figures futur 2004*, 12.

7. "Cyber Kaperucita: Un cuento de hadas . . . en el cyberespacio!" Terra, 27 December 2003, www.terra.es/personal/gmalpart/chorrada/esp/cyber.htm.

Bibliography

Primary Sources

Abayo et al. *Érase veintiuna veces Caperucita Roja.* Translated by Kiyoko Sakai and Herrín Hidalgo. Libros para niños. Valencia: Media Vaca, 2006.

Ache, Jean [Jean Huet]. *Le Petit Chaperon rouge* à la manière de Buffet, Chirico, Léger, Miró, Mondrian, Picasso et Rousseau. *Pilote* 692 (1973): 7 p. Reprinted in *Pilote: Annuel* (1974): 7 p.

———. *Le monde des ronds et des carrés.* Adapted and translated by Christine Huet. Tokyo: Librairie Çà et Là, 1975.

Ahlberg, Janet, and Allan Ahlberg. *Jeremiah in the Dark Woods.* Harmondsworth: Kestrel Books, 1977.

———. *The Jolly Postman: Or Other People's Letters.* London: Heinemann, 1986.

Ali, Agha Shahid. "The Wolf's Postscript to 'Little Red Riding Hood.'" In *A Walk through the Yellow Pages.* Tucson: SUN/Gemini Press, 1987.

Argueta, Manlio. *Caperucita en la zona roja.* Havana: Casa de las Américas, 1977. Translated by Edward Waters Hood under the title *Little Red Riding Hood in the Red Light District.* Willimantic, CT: Curbstone Press, 1998.

Avery, Tex. *Little Red Walking Hood.* Warner Brothers, 1937.

———. *Red Hot Riding Hood.* MGM, 1943.

———. *Little Rural Riding Hood.* MGM, 1949.

Aymé, Marcel. *Les contes du chat perché.* Illustrated by Nathan Altman. Paris: Gallimard, 1934.

———. *The Wonderful Farm.* Illustrated by Maurice Sendak. Translated by Norman Denny. New York: Harper and Row, 1951.

———. *The Magic Pictures: More about the Wonderful Farm.* Illustrated by Maurice Sendak. New York: Harper, 1954.

———. "Le loup." In *Les contes bleus du chat perché,* 8–28. Folio Junior. Paris: Gallimard, 1987.

Bertier, Anne. *Mon Loup.* Orange: Grandir, 1995.

Betsuyaku, Minoru. *Akazukin-chan no mori no ohkami tachi no kurisumasu.* Musical. Music by Akihito Komori. Tokyo: Shinsuisha, 1993.

Biegel, Paul. *Wie je droomt ben je zelf.* Illustrated by Carl Hollander. Haarlem: CPNB (Commissie voor de Collectieve Propaganda van het Nederlandse boek or Committee for the Collective Promotion of Dutch Books); Uitg. Mij I Holland Uitgeversmaatschappij Holland (now Uitgeverij Holland), 1977.

Blackwell, Ronald. "Lil' Red Riding Hood." Sung by Sam the Sham and the Pharaohs. Los Angeles: Metro-Goldwyn-Mayer, 1966.

Block, Francesca Lia. "Wolf." In *The Rose and the Beast: Fairy Tales Retold*, 99–129. New York: Joanna Cotler Books/HarperCollins, 2000.

Borneman, Elsa I. *El lobo rojo y Caperucita feroz*. Buenos Aires: El Ateneo, 1991.

The Brothers Grimm: Little Red Riding Hood. Directed by Chris Doyle. New York: Goodtimes, 2004.

Browne, Anthony. *The Tunnel*. New York: Knopf, 1989.

Bruel, Christian. *Petits Chaperons Loups*. Illustrated by Nicole Claveloux. Paris: Éditions Être, 1997.

———. *Vous oubliez votre cheval*. Illustrated by Pierre Wachs. Paris: Le sourire qui mord, 1986.

Bruel, Christian, and Didier Jouault. *Rouge, bien rouge*. Illustrated by Nicole Claveloux. Paris: Le sourire qui mord, 1986.

Byatt, A. S. *Possession: A Romance*. London: Chatto and Windus, 1990.

Cano, Carles. *T'he agafat, Caputxeta!* Illustrated by Gusti. Valencia: Bruño, 1995.

Cappuccetto Rosso. Directed by Giacomo Cimini. Koa Films Entertainment, Rome, 2003.

Carter, Angela. *The Bloody Chamber*. New York: Penguin, 1979.

Chocano, José Santos. "El lobo enamorado." In *Poemas del amor doliente*, 63–64. Santiago, Chile: Nascimiento, 1937.

Clément, Claude. *Un petit chaperon rouge*. Illustrated by Isabelle Forestier. Paris: Grasset and Fasquelle, 2000.

Craipeau, Jean-Loup. *Le Petit Chaperon bouge*. Illustrated by Clément Oubrerie. Paris: Hachette Jeunesse, 1997.

Cross, Gillian. *Wolf*. London: Oxford University Press, 1990; London: Puffin, 1992.

Dahl, Roald. "Little Red Riding Hood and the Wolf." In *Revolting Rhymes*, 30–33. Illustrated by Quentin Blake. New York: Knopf, 1982.

Delarue, Paul. "Le conte populaire français." Vol. 1. Paris: Éditions Érasme, 1957.

Delarue, Paul, ed. "The Story of Grandmother." In *The Borzoi Book of French Folk Tales*, 230–32. Translated by Austin E. Fife. Illustrated by Warren Chappell. New York: Knopf, 1956.

Disney, Walt. *Little Red Riding Hood*. 16-millimeter Laugh-o-Gram silent short animated film. 1922.

Dumas, Philippe, and Boris Moissard. "Le Petit Chaperon Bleu Marine." In *Contes à l'envers*, 15–26. Illustrated by Philippe Dumas. Paris: L'École des Loisirs, 1977.

Ekman, Fam. *Rødhatten og Ulven*. Oslo: Cappelen, 1985.

Estés, Clarissa Pinkola. "The Wolf's Eyelash." In *Rowing Songs for the Night Sea Journey, Contemporary Chants*, 1970. Reprinted in *Women Who Run With the Wolves: Myths and Stories of the Wild Woman Archetype*. New York: Ballantine Books, 1992.

Ferron, Jacques. "Le petit chaperon rouge." In *Contes*, 162–65. Montreal: HMH, 1968. Translated by Betty Bednarski under the title *Tales from the Uncertain Country*, 39–43. Toronto: Anasi, 1972.

Fetscher, Iring. "Rotschöpfchen und der Wolf." In *Wer hat Dornröschen wachgeküßt? Das Märchen-Verwirrbuch*. Hamburg: Classen, 1972.

Fisher, David. "USA v. Wolf, Deposition of Mr. Wolf," and "Little Red Riding Hood v. Regal Pictures, Inc." In *Legally Correct Fairy Tales*, 33–44, 89–97. New York: Warner Books, 1996.

Fleutiaux, Pierrette. "Petit Pantalon Rouge, Barbe-Bleue et Notules." In *Métamorphoses de la reine*, 103–38. Paris: Gallimard, 1984.

———. "Préface." In *Métamorphoses de la reine*, 9–12. Paris: Gallimard, 1984.

———. "The Ogre's Wife." In *The Year's Best Fantasy and Horror: Fifth Annual Collection*, 488–505. Edited by Ellen Datlow and Terri Windling. New York: St. Martin's Press, 1992.

F'Murr [Richard Pezaret]. *Au loup!* Paris: Minoustchine, 1974; reprint, Paris: Dargaud, 1993.

Freeway. Directed by Matthew Bright. August Entertainment, 1996.

Galloway, Priscilla. "The Good Mother." In *Truly Grim Tales*, 74–96. Toronto: Lester, 1995.

García Sánchez, José Luis, and Miguel Ángel Pacheco. *El ùltimo lobo y Caperucita*. Illustrated by Miguel Ángel Pacheco. Barcelona: Labor, 1975.

Garner, James Finn. "Little Red Riding Hood." In *Politically Correct Bedtime Stories: Modern Tales for Our Life and Times*, 1–4. New York: Macmillan, 1994.

Gearhart, Sally Miller. "Roja and Leopold." In *And a Deer's Ear, Eagle's Song, and Bear's Grace: Animals and Women*. Edited by Theresa Corrigan and Stephanie Hoppe. Pittsburgh: Cleis Press, 1990.

Gotlib [Marcel Gotlieb]. "Une ordonnance maladroite." In *Rubrique-à-brac*, 111–18. Paris: Dargaud, 1970; reprint, Paris: Pocket BD, 1989.

Grimm, Wilhelm, and Jacob Grimm. *Complete Fairy Tales of the Brothers Grimm*. Translated by Jack Zipes. 2 vols. New York: Bantam Books, 1988.

———. *Rotkäppchen* (in Arabic). Illustrated by Jenny Williams. Beirut and Cairo: Dar Almashruk, A.H. 1423 [A.D. 1992].

———. *Rotkäppchen*. Illustrated by Susanne Janssen. Munich: Carl Hanser Verlag, 2001.

———. *The Annotated Brothers Grimm*. Edited and translated by Maria Tatar. New York: Norton, 2004.

Gripari, Pierre. *Patrouille du conte*. Lausanne: L'Âge d'Homme, 1983.

———. "Le loup" and "Le petit chaperon malin." In *Marelles*, 13–14, 33–34. Illustrated by Chica. Paris: Grasset Jeunesse, 1996.

Guimarães Rosa, João. *Grande sertão: Veredas*. Translated by James L. Taylor and Harriet de Onis under the title *The Devil to Pay in the Backlands*. New York: Knopf, 1963.

———. "Fita verde no cabelo." In *Ave, palavra*. Rio de Janeiro: José Olympio, 1970.

———. *Fita verde no cabelo: Nova velha estória*. Illustrated by Roger Mello. Rio de Janeiro: Nova Fronteira, 1992.

Hamada, Shoko. "Akazukin wa ookami otoko no yume wo miru." Hakusensha Lady's Comics. Tokyo: Hakusensha, 1993.

Hard Candy. Directed by David Slade. Seattle: Vulcan Productions, 2005.

Harte, Bret. "What the Wolf Really Said to Little Red Riding-Hood." In *Complete Poetical Works*, 248. New York: Houghton Mifflin, 1899.

Hendriks, Maria. *Makwelane and the Crocodile*. Illustrated by Piet Grobler. Cape Town: Human and Rousseau, 2004.

Hofman, Wim. "Roodkapje." *Mikmak* 1 (October 1993): 10–11.

Hoodwinked. Directed by Cory Edwards. Screenplay by Cory and Todd Edwards and Tony Leech, 2006.

Hopkinson, Nalo. "Riding the Red." In *Black Swan, White Raven*, 56–60. Edited by Ellen Datlow and Terri Windling. New York: Avon Books, 1997.

Ikhlef, Anne. *La véritable histoire du Chaperon Rouge*. Performed by Justine Bayard and Didier Sandre, France, 1985.

———. *Mon Chaperon Rouge*. Illustrations by Alain Gauthier. Paris: Seuil Jeunesse, 1998.

Into the Woods. Music and lyrics by Stephen Sondheim. Directed by James Lapine. 1987.

Ishinomori, Shotaro. "Akazukin-chan." In a volume offered by the magazine *Girl's Club* 40, no. 3 (1962). Tokyo: Kodansya, 1962.

Jacintho, Roque. *O Lobo Mau Reencarnado*. Illustrated by Joel Linck. Rio de Janeiro: Federação Espírita Brasileira, 1974. Translated by Evelyn R. Morales and S. J. Haddad under the title *The Big Bad Wolf Reincarnate*. Illustrated by Joel Linck. Rio de Janeiro: Federação Espírita Brasileira, 1981.

Janosch [Horst Eckert]. "Das elektrische Rotkäppchen." In *Janosch erzählt Grimms' Märchen und zeichnet für Kinder von heute: 50 ausgewählte Märchen*, 102–7. Weinheim, Germany: Beltz and Gelberg, 1972. Translated by Patricia Crampton under the title *Not Quite as Grimm: Told and illustrated by Janosch for today*. London: Abelard-Schuman, 1974.

Jin-Roh: The Wolf Brigade. Written by Mamoru Oshii. Directed by Hiroyuki Okiura. Tokyo: Bandai Visual, 1998.

Joiret, Patricia. *Mina, je t'aime*. Illustrated by Xavier Bruyère [Xavier Van Buylaere]. Paris: L'École des Loisirs, 1991.

Julien, Viviane. *Bye Bye Chaperon Rouge*. Montreal: Québec/Amérique, 1989. Translated by Frances Hanna under the title *Bye Bye Red Riding Hood*. Montreal: Montréal Press, 1990.

Lamblin, Simone, ed. *Le grand méchant Loup, j'adore*. Illustrated by Françoise Boudignon. Paris: Le Livre de Poche, 1983.

Lanigan, Carol. "All the Better to See You." In *Rapunzel's Revenge*, 27–29. Illustrated by Siobhan Condon and Wendy Shea. Fairytales for Feminists. Dublin: Attic Press, 1985.

La Salle, Bruno de. *Le Petit Chaperon Rouge*. Illustrated by Laurence Batigne. Paris: Casterman, 1986.

———. "La petite fille qui savait voler." In *La pêche de vigne et autres contes*, 55–81. Illustrated by Catherine Roubeyrol. Paris: L'École des Loisirs, 1996.

Lavater, Warja. *Le Petit Chaperon Rouge: Une imagerie d'après un conte de Perrault*. Paris: Adrien Maeght, 1965.

Lavater, Warja, after Charles Perrault. *Imageries*. Six animated films. Paris: Cinquième Agence, 1995.

Lecointre, Jean. *Les dents du loup*. Paris: Thierry Magnier, 2002.

Lee, Tanith. "Wolfland." In *Red as Blood: Or Tales from the Sisters Grimmer*, 106–36. New York: DAW Books, 1983.

Léon, Pierre. *Le mariage politiquement correct du petit Chaperon rouge et autres histoires plus ou moins politiquement correctes avec notices explicatives pour servir à la morale de notre temps*. Toronto: Éditions du GREF, 1996.

Little Red Riding Hood, Faerie Tale Theatre. Produced by Shelley Duvall. Directed by Roger Vadim. Performed by Malcolm McDowell and Mary Steenburgen. For the cable television network Showtime, 10 November 1983.

Little Red Riding Rabbit. Directed by Friz Freleng. Warner Brothers, 1944.

Martín Gaite, Carmen. *El cuento de nunca acabar*. Madrid: Trieste, 1983.

———. *Caperucita en Manhattan*. Madrid: Siruela, 1990.

Merseyside Fairy Story Collective (Audrey Ackroyd, Marge Ben-Tovim, Catherine Meredith, and Anne Neville). *Red Riding Hood*. Liverpool: Fairy Story Collective, 1972.

Mészáros, Márta. *Bye Bye Red Riding Hood*. Produced by Rock Demers and Gabor Hanak. Written by Márta Mészáros and Éva Pataki. Coproduced by Les Productions La Fête Inc. (Canada), with the participation of Téléfilm Canada, Super Écran (Premier Choix TVEC Inc.) and Hungarofilm-Mokeep (Hungary), 1989.

Mieder, Wolfgang, ed. *Disenchantments: An Anthology of Modern Fairy Tale Poetry*. Hanover, NH: University Press of New England, 1985.

Mistral, Gabriela. "Caperucita Roja." In *Ternura*, 136–37. Madrid: Saturnino Calleja, 1924.

Momotani, Yoshihide, and Sumiko Momotani. *Akazukin-chan*. Tokyo: Seibundou-Shinkousha, 1996.

Montresor, Beni. *Little Red Riding Hood*. New York: Doubleday, 1991.

Pef [Pierre Ferrier]. "Le conte du Petit Chaperon rouge." In *Contes comme la lune*. Vol. 14, 391–93. Paris: Messidor/La Farandole, 1991.

Pennart, Geoffroy de. *Le loup est revenu!* Paris: Kaléidoscope, 1994.

———. *Je suis revenu!* Paris: Kaléidoscope, 2000.

Perrault, Charles. *Les contes de Perrault*. Illustrated by Gustave Doré. Paris: Pierre-Jules Hetzel, 1861.

———. *Perrault's Complete Fairy Tales*. Illustrated by W. Heath Robinson. Translated by A. E. Johnson and others. New York: Dodd, Mead, 1961.

———. *The Fairy Tales of Charles Perrault*. Translated and with a foreword by Angela Carter. Illustrated by Martin Ware. London: Victor Gollancz, 1977.

————. *Le Petit Chaperon Rouge*. Illustrated by Sarah Moon. Mankato, MN: Creative Education, 1983.

————. *Contes de Charles Perrault*. Illustrated by Kelek. Paris: Hatier, 1986.

————. "Le Petit Chaperon rouge." In *Contes*, 5–14. Le Livre de Poche Jeunesse. Illustrated by Gustave Doré. Paris: Hachette Jeunesse, 1989.

————. *Contes de ma mère l'Oye*. Illustrated by Gustave Doré. Folio Junior Édition Spéciale. Paris: Gallimard, 1997.

————. *Le Petit Chaperon Rouge*. Illustrated by Éric Battut. Paris and Zurich: Bilboquet-Valbert/Bohem Press, 1998.

Pommaux, Yvan. *John Chatterton détective*. Paris: L'École des Loisirs, 1993.

Promenons-nous dans les bois. Directed by Lionel Delplanque. Paris: Fidélité Films, 2000.

Riis, Annie. "Ulven og Rødhette." In *Kom inn i min natt, kom inn i min drøm*, 25–31. Edited by Solveig Bøhle. Illustrated by Fam Ekman. Oslo: Gyldendal, 1986.

Riley, James Whitcomb. "Red-Riding Hood." In *The Complete Works of James Whitcomb Riley*. Vol. 1, 66. Edited by Edmund Henry Eitel. Indianapolis: Bobbs-Merrill, 1913.

Rivero, Raúl. "Version libre" and "Version libre . . . 2." In *Corazón sin furia*. Logroño, Spain: AMG Editor, 2005.

Scieszka, Jon. "Little Red Running Shorts." In *The Stinky Cheese Man and Other Fairly Stupid Tales*. Illustrated by Lane Smith. New York: Viking, 1992.

Sexton, Anne. "Red Riding Hood." In *Transformations*, 72–79. Boston: Houghton Mifflin, 1971.

Sharpe, Anne. "Not So Little Red Riding Hood." In *Rapunzel's Ravenge: Fairytales for Feminists*, 47–49. Illustrated by Siobhan Condon and Wendy Shea. Dublin: Attic Press, 1985.

Shrek. Directed by Andrew Adamson and Vicky Jenson. DreamWorks, 2001.

Shrek 2. Directed by Andrew Adamson, Kelly Asbury, and Conrad Vernon. Dream-Works, 2004.

Silva, Deonísio da. *A melhor amiga do lobo*. Illustrated by Lucia Hiratsuka. Rio de Janeiro: FTD, 1990.

Sondheim, Stephen, and James Lapine. *Into the Woods*. New York: Theatre Communications Group, 1987.

Strauss, Gwen. "The Waiting Wolf." In *Trail of Stones*, 14–17. Illustrated by Anthony Browne. London: Julia MacRae Books, 1990.

Thurber, James. "The Little Girl and the Wolf." In *Fables for Our Times and Famous Poems Illustrated*, 5. New York: Harper and Row, 1940.

Tikkanen, Märta. *Rödluvan*. Stockholm: Trevi, 1986.

Tsutsui, Keisuke [Konishi Masao]. *Mouhitori no Akazukin-chan*. Illustrated by Masaya Kaburaki. Tokyo: Nihon Hoso Shuppan Kyokai, 1975.

Ueda, Miwa. *Tsukiyo no Akazukin*. Kodansya Comics. Tokyo: Kodansya, 1989.

Ungerer, Tomi. "Little Red Riding Hood." In *A Story Book from Tomi Ungerer*, 84–91. New York: Franklin Watts, 1974. Published in German under the title "Rotkäppchen." In *Märchenbuch*, 85–93. Zurich: Diogenes, 1975.

————. Poster for the exhibition *Le Petit Chaperon Rouge dans tous ses états*, Les Plateaux-Scène Nationale Angoulême, 1992.

————. *Poster.* Zurich: Diogenes Verlag, 1994, 108.

Valenzuela, Luisa. "Si esto es la vida, yo soy Caperucita Roja." In *Simetrías*, 111–25. Buenos Aires: Editorial Sudamericana, 1993. Translated by Margaret Jull Costa under the title "If this is life, I'm Red Riding Hood." In *Symmetries*. London: High Risk Books/Serpent's Tail, 1993.

Vendel, Edward van de. *Rood Rood Roodkapje.* Illustrated by Isabelle Vandenabeele. Wielsbeke, Belgium: Uitgeverij De Eenhoorn, 2003.

Villaespesa, Francisco. "Caperucita." In *Poesías completas.* Compiled by Frederico de Mendizabal. 2 vols., 1:557; 2:1479. Madrid: Aguilar, S.A. de Ediciones, 1954.

Walt Disney Studios. *The Big Bad Wolf.* A Silly Symphony. Directed by Bert Gillett. 1934.

————. *Redux Riding Hood.* Directed by Steve Moore. Story by Dan O'Shannon. 1998.

Wegman, William. *Little Red Riding Hood.* New York: Hyperion, 1993.

Wiemer, Rudolf Otto. "Der Alte Wolf." In *Neues vom Rumpelstilzchen und andere Märchen von 43 Autoren*, 73. Edited by Hans-Joachim Gelberg. Illustrated by Willi Glasauer. Weinheim, Germany: Beltz and Gelberg, 1976.

Young, Ed. *Lon Po Po: A Red Riding Hood Story from China.* New York: Philomel Books, 1989.

Zupan, Vitomil. "A Fairy Tale." *Literary Review* 14 (1971): 298.

Secondary Sources

Ariès, Philippe. *Centuries of Childhood: A Social History of Family Life.* Translated by Robert Baldick. New York: Knopf, 1962.

Bacchilega, Cristina. *Postmodern Fairy Tales: Gender and Narrative Strategies.* Philadelphia: University of Pennsylvania Press, 1997.

Bang, Molly. *Picture This: Perception and Composition.* Boston: Little, Brown, 1991.

Bates, Margaret. "Introduction." In *Selected Poems of Gabriela Mistral*, xv–xxvi. Translated and edited by Doris Dana. Baltimore: Johns Hopkins University Press, 1971.

Beckett, Sandra L. "Le Petit Chaperon rouge globe-trotter." In *Tricentenaire Charles Perrault: Les grands contes du XVIIᵉ siècle et leur fortune littéraire*, 365–75. Edited by Jean Perrot. Paris: In Press, 1998.

————. "Parodic Play with Paintings in Picture Books." *Children's Literature* 29 (2001): 175–95.

————. *Recycling Red Riding Hood.* New York: Routledge, 2002.

————. "Retelling *Little Red Riding Hood* in Contemporary Canadian Children's Literature." In *Windows and Words: A Look at Canadian Children's Literature in English*, 61–76. Edited by Aïda Hudson and Susan-Ann Cooper. Ottawa: University of Ottawa Press, 2003.

Berne, Eric. *What Do You Say after You Say Hello?* New York: Grove Press, 1972.

Bettelheim, Bruno. *The Uses of Enchantment: The Meaning and Importance of Fairy Tales.* New York: Random House, 1975.

Brownmiller, Susan. *Against Our Will: Men, Women, and Rape.* New York: Fawcett Columbine, 1975.

Cavan, Susan J. "Hey There Little Red Riding Hood . . ." *The NIS Observed: An Analytical Review* 8, no. 13, 22 August 2003.

Chalou, Barbara Smith. *A Postmodern Analysis of the Little Red Riding Hood Tale.* Lewiston, NY: Edwin Mellen Press, 2002.

Darnton, Robert. *The Great Cat Massacre and Other Episodes in French Cultural History.* New York: Basic Books, 1984.

Dundes, Alan, ed. *Little Red Riding Hood: A Casebook.* Madison: University of Wisconsin Press, 1989.

Encyclopedia of Magic and Superstition. London: Octopus Books, 1974.

L'Équipe de *Livres Jeunes Aujourd'hui.* "Un auteur de livres illustrés: Philippe Dumas." *Livres Jeunes Aujourd'hui* 2 (February 1982): 59–64.

Estés, Clarissa Pinkola. *Women Who Run With the Wolves: Myths and Stories of the Wild Woman Archetype.* New York: Ballantine Books, 1992.

Figuresfutur 2004: Young and New Illustrators of Tomorrow. Seine-Saint-Denis: Centre de Promotion du Livre de Jeunesse, 2004.

Fromm, Erich. *The Forgotten Language: An Introduction to the Understanding of Dreams, Fairy Tales, and Myths.* New York: Holt, Rinehart and Winston, 1951.

Garrett, Jeffrey. "'With Murderous Ending, Shocking, Menacing . . .': Sarah Moon's *Little Red Riding Hood* 10 Years After." *Bookbird* 31, no. 3 (1993): 8–9.

Genardière, Claude de la. *Encore un conte?: Le Petit Chaperon Rouge à l'usage des adultes.* Nancy, France: Press Universitaire de Nancy, 1993.

Genette, Gérard. *Palimpsestes: La littérature au second degré.* Paris: Seuil, 1982. Translated by Channa Newman and Claude Doubinsky under the title *Palimpsests: Literature in the Second Degree.* Lincoln: University of Nebraska Press, 1997.

Goldsworthy, Kerryn. "Angela Carter." *Meanjin* 44, no. 1 (1985): 110.

Greenleaf, Sarah. "The Beast Within." *Children's Literature in Education* 23, no. 1 (1992): 49–57.

Gripari, Pierre. *Pierre Gripari et ses contes pour enfants.* Interviews with Jean-Luc Peyroutet. Mérignac, France: Girandoles, 1994.

Haase, Donald. "Motifs, Making Fairy Tales Our Own: Yours, Mine, or Ours? Perrault, the Brothers Grimm, and the Ownership of Fairy Tales." In *Once Upon a Folktale: Capturing the Folklore Process with Children,* 63–71. Edited by Gloria Blatt. New York and London: Teachers College Press, 1993.

Haase, Donald, ed. *Fairy Tales and Feminism: New Approaches.* Detroit: Wayne State University Press, 2004.

Haguenauer, Florence. "Images of the Future around a Timeless Fairy Tale." In *Figures futur 2004: Young and New Illustrators of Tomorrow,* 10–12. Seine-Saint-Denis: Centre de Promotion du Livre de Jeunesse, 2004.

Hanks, Carole, and D. T. Hanks Jr. "Perrault's 'Little Red Riding Hood': Victim of the Revisers." *Children's Literature* 7 (1978): 68–77.

Hellsing, Lennart. "Perrault's Rödluva." In *Böcker ska blänka som solar: En bok till Vivi Edström*, 74–78. Edited by Boel Westin. Stockholm: Rabén and Sjögren, 1988.

Hollindale, Peter. "Why the Wolves Are Running." *The Lion and the Unicorn* 23, no. 1 (1999): 97–115.

Holtrop, Aukje. "'Things Never Work Out for Snow White': Wim Hofman's Fairy Tales." An interview with Wim Hofman. *Vrij Nederland*, 17 May 1997.

Hoogland, Cornelia. "Real 'Wolves in Those Bushes': Readers Take Dangerous Journeys with *Little Red Riding Hood*." *Canadian Children's Literature* 73 (1994): 7–21.

―――. "Galloway's Grim Tales." Review of *Truly Grim Tales*, by Priscilla Galloway. *Canadian Children's Literature* 82 (1996): 85–87.

Kareland, Lena. "'Il y a un trou dans la réalité': Le conte dans le roman suédois du XXᵉ siècle: une perspective féminine." In *Tricentenaire Charles Perrault: Les grands contes du XVIIᵉ siècle et leur fortune littéraire*, 355–64. Edited by Jean Perrot. Paris: In Press, 1998.

Kertzer, Adrienne. "Reclaiming Her Maternal Pre-Text: Little Red Riding Hood's Mother and Three Young Adult Novels." *Children's Literature Association Quarterly* 21, no. 1 (1996): 20–27.

Kühleborn, Heinrich E. *Rotkäppchen und die Wölfe: Von Märchenfälschern und Landschaftszerstörern*. Frankfurt: Fischer Taschenbuch Verlag, 1982.

Laroche, Maximilien. "Nouvelles notes sur 'le Petit Chaperon rouge' de Jacques Ferron." *Voix et Images du Pays* 6 (1973): 103–10.

Levorato, Alessandra. *Language and Gender in the Fairy Tale Tradition: A Linguistic Analysis of Old and New Story Telling*. New York: Palgrave Macmillan, 2003.

Malarte-Feldman, Claire-Lise. "Les Couleurs du Petit Chaperon . . ." *Merveilles et Contes* 1, no. 2 (1987): 88–96.

―――. "The French Fairy-Tale Conspiracy." *The Lion and the Unicorn* 12, no. 2 (1988): 112–20.

―――. "La Nouvelle Tyrannie des fées, ou la réécriture des contes de fées classiques." *French Review* 63, no. 5 (1990): 827–37.

―――. "Du conte de fées littéraire au conte pour enfant ou *Des Histoires ou contes du temps passé avec des moralités* aux *Contes de Perrault*." *Merveilles et Contes* 5, no. 2 (1991): 235–45.

Martin, Serge. *Les contes à l'école: Le(s) Petit(s) Chaperon(s) Rouge(s)*. Paris: Bertrand-Lacoste, 1997.

Martín Gaite, Carmen. "Entrevistamos a . . . Carmen Martín Gaite." Interview by Peonza. *Peonza* 24 (March 1993): 26–28.

McGillis, Roderick. "'Ages All': Readers, Texts, and Intertexts in *The Stinky Cheese Man and Other Fairly Stupid Tales*." In *Transcending Boundaries: Writing for a Dual Audience of Children and Adults*, 111–26. Edited by Sandra L. Beckett. New York: Garland, 1999.

Mieder, Wolfgang. "Survival Forms of 'Little Red Riding Hood' in Modern Society." *International Folklore Review* 2 (1982): 23–40.

———. "Grim Variations from Fairy Tales to Modern Anti-Fairy Tales." *Germanic Review* 62, no. 2 (1987): 90–102.

Nikolajeva, Maria. *Children's Literature Comes of Age: Toward a New Aesthetic*. New York: Garland, 1996.

Nikolajeva, Maria, and Carole Scott. *How Picturebooks Work*. New York: Garland, 2001.

Norwegian Commission for Children, Commission for the Rights of Children. "When Little Red Riding Hood Meets the Wolf." Norway, 1994.

Ohira, Ken. *Shinryo-shitsu ni Kita Akazukin*. Tokyo: Hayakawa-Shobo, 1994.

O'Neill, Thomas. "Guardians of the Fairy Tale: The Brothers Grimm." Photographs by Gerd Ludwig. *National Geographic* 196, no. 6 (1999): 102–29.

Orenstein, Catherine. *Little Red Riding Hood Uncloaked: Sex, Morality, and the Evolution of a Fairy Tale*. New York: Basic Books, 1992.

Otten, Charlotte. *A Lycanthropy Reader*. New York: Dorset Press, 1986.

Pascal-Moussellard, Olivier. "Le Petit Chaperon bouge." In *20ᵉ Salon du Livre et de la Presse Jeunesse: Le programme*. Supplément à *Télérama*, no. 2862, 17 November 2004, 5.

Peary, Gerald. "Little Red Ridinghood." *Sight and Sound* 57 (Summer 1988): 150.

Perrot, Jean. *Art baroque, art d'enfance*. Nancy, France: Presses Universitaires de Nancy, 1991.

Perrot, Jean, ed. *Tricentenaire Charles Perrault: Les grands contes du XVIIᵉ siècle et leur fortune littéraire*. Paris: In Press, 1998.

Pesch, Otto Hermann. *What Big Ears You Have! The Theologians' Red Riding Hood*. Translated by Grant Kaplan and Linda M. Maloney. Collegeville MN: Liturgical Press, 2000.

Pondé, Gloria. "Les relectures des *Contes* de Perrault au Brésil: *Fita verde no cabelo*, de Guimarães Rosa." In *Tricentenaire Charles Perrault: Les grands contes du XVIIᵉ siècle et leur fortune littéraire*, 331–37. Edited by Jean Perrot. Paris: In Press, 1998.

Puentes de Oyenard, Sylvia. "Una aproximación a Caperucita Roja desde Perrault a nuestros días." In *El cuento: Mensaje universal*, 71–93. Montevideo: Ediciones A.U.L.I./Asociación Uruguaya de Literatura Infantil-Juvenil, 1994.

Quentin, Sophie. "De la tradition orale aux adaptations modernes: 'Le Petit Chaperon rouge' ou le carrefour des écritures . . ." In *Écriture féminine et littérature de jeunesse*, 203–17. Edited by Jean Perrot and Véronique Hadengue. Paris: La Nacelle/Institut Charles Perrault, 1995.

"Report of the Jury Awarding the State Prize for Children's and Young People's Literature for 1973." Translated by Patricia Crampton. *Junior Bookshelf* 39, no. 1 (1975): 9–11.

Review of *Little Red Riding Hood* by Beni Montresor. *Horn Book Magazine*, 1992.

Ritz, Hans. *Die Geschichte vom Rotkäppchen: Ursprünge, Analysen, Parodien eines Märchens*. Göttingen: Muriverlag, 1997.

———. *Hans Ritz gibt heraus: Bilder vom Rotkäppchen*. Kassel: Muriverlag, 2007.

Rives, Caroline. "Tomi Ungerer: Un diable en paradis?" *La Revue des Livres pour Enfants* 171 (September 1996): 88–101.

Russell, David, L. "Young Adult Fairy Tales for the New Age: Francesca Lia Block's *The Rose and the Beast.*" *Children's Literature in Education* 33, no. 2 (2002): 107–15.

Shavit, Zohar. *Poetics of Children's Literature.* Athens: University of Georgia Press, 1986.

Siegel, R. A. "The Little Boy Who Drops His Pants in a Crowd: Tomi Ungerer's Art of the Comic Grotesque." *The Lion and the Unicorn* 1, no. 1 (1977): 26–32.

Skjønsberg, Kari. "*Le Chaperon Rouge* en Norvège." In *Tricentenaire Charles Perrault: Les grands contes du XVIIe siècle et leur fortune littéraire,* 349–54. Edited by Jean Perrot. Paris: In Press, 1998.

Soriano, Marc. *Guide de littérature pour la jeunesse.* Paris: Flammarion, 1976.

———. *Les Contes de Perrault: Culture savante et traditions populaires.* Rev. ed. Paris: Gallimard, 1977.

Tatar, Maria. *The Hard Facts of the Grimms' Fairy Tales.* Princeton, NJ: Princeton University Press, 1987.

———. *Off with Their Heads! Fairy Tales and the Culture of Childhood.* Princeton, NJ: Princeton University Press, 1992.

Thomas, Joyce. "Woods and Castles, Towers and Huts: Aspects of Setting in the Fairy Tale." *Children's Literature in Education* 17, no. 2 (1986): 126–34.

Ungerer, Tomi [Jean Thomas]. *Affiches.* Paris: L'École des Loisirs, 1994.

Uther, Hans-Jörg. *The Types of International Folktales: A Classification and Bibliography.* Parts 1–3. Helsinki: Suomalainen Tiedeakatemia (Academia Scientiarum Fennica), 2004.

Verdier, Yvonne. "Grand-mères, si vous saviez . . . : Le Petit Chaperon Rouge dans la tradition orale." *Cahiers de Littérature Orale* 4 (1978): 17–55.

Warner, Marina. *From the Beast to the Blonde: On Fairy Tales and Their Tellers.* London: Chatto and Windus, 1994.

White, T. H., ed. and trans. *The Book of Beasts,* being a translation from a Latin bestiary of the twelfth century. London: Cape, 1954.

Yanase, Mitsuse. *Akazukin wa nido umareru.* Tokyo: Gentosha, 1999.

Zipes, Jack. *Fairy Tales and the Art of Subversion: The Classical Genre for Children and the Process of Civilization.* New York: Wildman, 1983.

———. "A Second Gaze at Little Red Riding Hood's Trials and Tribulations." *The Lion and the Unicorn* 7–8 (1983–84): 78–109.

———. *The Trials and Tribulations of Little Red Riding Hood: Versions of the Tale in Sociocultural Context.* 2nd ed. New York: Routledge, 1993.

———. *Fairy Tale as Myth/Myth as Fairy Tale.* Lexington: University Press of Kentucky, 1994.

———, ed. *The Oxford Companion to Fairy Tales.* Oxford: Oxford University Press, 2000.

———. *Sticks and Stones: The Troublesome Success of Children's Literature from Slovenly Peter to Harry Potter.* New York: Routledge, 2001.

Index

Note: Italic locators reference illustrations in the text. Locators containing "cp" indicate an illustration in the color plate section and are numbered 1–32.